The Art of the Song Recital

The Art of the Song Recital

Shirlee Emmons
Stanley Sonntag

SCHIRMER BOOKS
A Division of Macmillan Publishing Co., Inc.
NEW YORK

Collier Macmillan Publishers
LONDON

Schirmer Books
A Division of Macmillan Publishing Co., Inc.
866 Third Avenue, New York, N. Y. 10022

Collier Macmillan Canada, Ltd.

Library of Congress Catalog Card Number: 78-66978

Printed in the United States of America

printing number

10

Library of Congress Cataloging in Publication Data

Emmons, Shirlee.
    The art of the song recital.

    Bibliography: p.
    1. Singing--Instruction and study. 2. Singing--
Interpretation (Phrasing, dynamics, etc.) 3. Musical
accompaniment. I. Sonntag, Stanley, joint author.
II. Title.
MT892.E54   784.9'34   78-66978
ISBN 0-02-870530-0

With gratitude to
Douglas Moore
who, by taking the time to give us his list of the ten best
American songs, pointed out the path which led to this
work.

If less is more, one great song is worth ten merely adroit symphonies. To say "you can have it for a song" is to sell the form cheap.

NED ROREM

Contents

Preface

Our purpose in writing this book is not only to share with others our genuine love for the song recital but also to give extensive, thoroughgoing, and definitive insights into the attributes that can render it at once a great art and a magnificient entertainment.

With our own students and those we meet in our travels we are constantly reminded of their need for information on the subject. Their teachers are, of course, well-informed, but struggling against time restrictions that do not permit individual and extended guidance. A lack of comprehensive literature on the subject of song recital is evident. We intend in this book to give the singer clear, methodical, and serviceable information on every facet of the recital art. We have spent twenty years in the performance of song recitals and we have done these programs together. We have written this book committed to the idea that the singer-accompanist *team* is by far best qualified to construct such a book, particularly the discussion of the universally esteemed but rarely encountered art—program building. One cannot deny that boredom, induced by bad, repetitious, and unimaginative programming has dampened some public enthusiasm. This book sets out to instruct its readers in the very techniques that will avoid boredom and kindle audience excitement.

We believe that the American singer is eminently qualified to raise the art of the recital to a new height. In spite of the fact that a virtual handful of European artists seems to dominate the recital field, why should American singers, with their special gifts, humbly abandon the field to others? Foreign recitalists offer to the art of the recital, with rare exceptions, either evenings composed entirely of German Lieder (occasionally French) or evenings composed of arias sung by operatic artists who are the "biggest" names in the profession but who are seldom the best recitalists. We agree with Gunther Schuller, who said in a *New York Times* interview in 1977:

> Until now, we've been celebrating every European import—whether it's a tenor, or a composer, or a bassoon player—it's assumed he's better than our own homegrown product. My ambition, for the rest of my life, is to try to stamp out this damned inferiority complex we have.

Perhaps the twentieth century, with its cataclysmic changes cutting across life and customs, calls for an expansion or refurbishing of the song recital concept. This book will offer many innovative ideas along this line that will challenge the energies and excite the imagination of present and future recitalists. We will also treat such contributory factors as the artist's social responsibilities before and after the recital, so important in building future audiences.

Most of what you will read in this book has not been dealt with in other publications. We have earnestly set about to cover all aspects of the song recital as thoroughly as possible. Most voice teachers are skilled at teaching much more than vocal technique. But such nonvocal skills can be taught by others—or certainly with the help of this book. Our aim is to present the bulk of these peripheral materials so as to save the voice teacher's most valuable commodity—time.

Wishing this to be essentially a practical book—informative and utilitarian above all—we have tried to delete esthetics and reminiscences, for there are many excellent books on such subjects available at any book store. This book is concerned with the practicalities of performance. It can be divided into some rough groupings.

After the first chapter on the history of the song recital, you will find three chapters that discuss program building—possibly the most important subject matter this book has to offer. Surprisingly little of a comprehensive nature has been written elsewhere on this theme. We begin in Chapter 2 with a discussion of the existing types of recital programs and a very practical "how-to" outline of our personal method for constructing a program. Following in Chapter 3 are five of our own nontraditional programs, each with a step-by-step explanation of all decisions taken, meticulously following the order of the master-outline and illustrating its principles. Conclusions are drawn as to the final success or failure of each program. Chapter 4 includes fourteen programs, traditional as well as specialized, for varying forces, unaccompanied by explanations.

Because we expect young singers to make maximum use of this book, Chapter 5 is geared to them and their problems, concluding with several programs for beginning recitalists and two debut programs with a scenario describing each of the two young artists.

Chapters 6 through 10 are firmly related to technical subjects. We place extraordinary emphasis upon the need to upgrade one's acting skills in recital. Therefore, Chapter 6 (The Singing Actor) is perhaps the most important chapter in the book, next to the chapters on program-building. Chapter 7 (The Accompanist) gives much practical help, as well as discussions of psychological relationships between the coach-accompanist and his singers. Because there are so many fragmentary and peripheral skills that a singer/accompanist team needs to know, Chapter 8 is devoted entirely to questions on these subjects, with appropriate answers. In this group is a small but provocative chapter about musical and literary research and a lengthy, critical discussion of study and memorizing methods.

The next rough grouping includes four chapters (11–14) about several special types of vocal music—twentieth-century New Music, Ensemble Music, The Song Cycle, and Folk and Popular Music. Each chapter begins with a short history of that particular type of song material, considers for what type of singer it is well-suited, and finally discusses its programming uses. The New Music chapter offers three tables containing information about twentieth-century composers and styles with the purpose of orienting the singer to this literature.

The last chapter spells out some hopes for a renaissance of the recital, some remedies for present ills, some suggestions for a new look, and a challenge to the young recitalist.

It is expected that voice teachers, whether in their own private studios or in institutions, whether teachers of private or class lessons, will find the entire book of interest and help in their work, as will coaches and accompanists. Undergraduate or beginning recitalists, we believe, will find in this book virtually everything they need to learn the art of the recital. Professional singers will probably find pertinent information of most value in the program-building chapters (2, 3, 4), the acting and research chapters, (6, 9) and the musical resource chapters (11, 12, 13, 14). Teachers of accompanying or vocal literature classes will find undeniably useful information in the chapters related to their subject matter. Furthermore, we believe that master courses in program-building or the art of the recital could be taught with these materials as text. The three tables of information about New Music and the appendices containing repertoire lists should prove vastly interesting and time-saving for all performing musicians and their teachers. Drama coaches will find that Chapter 5 and 6 relate especially well to their subject, and young composers of vocal music may find Chapter 10 of value in their work.

At the end of the chapters, where applicable, Guidelines for Practice in acquiring skills have been added. Teachers will find it possible, by assigning these specific exercises outside of class or lessons, to save their own time while assuring that the student acquire the requisite knowledge. Students who read this book without the guidance of a teacher will find the Guidelines contributory to their self-study programs.

Possibly our most important reason for writing this book was the deep love we hold for the song recital itself. We feel impelled to contribute to the profession what we know of the beauty, the excitement, and the personal and artistic gratification with which the recital repays those who master its provocative form. Skillful practitioners of the art will surely be recompensed by what Leslie Howard once called "the sublime satisfaction which is the immediate reward of a perfect communion between both sides of the [proscenium arch]."

Acknowledgments

We wish to thank, first and foremost, Donald Wigal, who, while special projects editor at Delacourt, gave us our first encouragement and tangible support in this project. The membership of the New York Singing Teachers' Association and the National Association of Teachers of Singing—in particular Ingrid Sobolewska, Daniel Ferro, Cesare Longo, Donald Read, Mari Taniguchi, Gladys Mathew, Sofia Steffan, Emmy Hauser, Lola Hayes, Chloe Owen, Rosemary Leeder, David Garvey, Beatrice Krebs, Carol Knell, and Marjorie Gerson—were unfailingly supportive, giving professional advice as well as their time. The students of Princeton University and Manhattanville College, in the midst of their active schedules, took time to answer questionnaires, giving us their ideas about the book's contents. From their ranks we wish to single out for thanks Ann Monoyios, Bill Clark, Michael Steinberg, and Paul Genecin, who read parts of the manuscript of this book and contributed from their own knowledge to its improvement, and Katherine Rohrer and Marie-Louise Rodén for their selfless and willing assistance in countless ways not limited to scholarliness.

We are grateful to all the publishers of works listed in our repertoire lists for their cooperation, but especially to Almarie Dieckow of Magnamusic-Baton, Inc., and Ruth Elliott of Schott & Co., Inc. We acknowledge with gratitude the very apt suggestions of Elaine Bonazzi and her husband, Jerome Carrington. In our efforts to include as many vocal works by black composers as possible, Dorothy Rudd Moore and Kermit Moore were of great help, as was Dr. Willis Patterson, compiler of "Anthology of Art Songs by Black American Composers." With regard to the repertoire lists, we were determined also to catalogue many vocal works by women. Nancy Van de Vate and the League of Women Composers, Adrienne Fried Block and Carol Neuls-Bates working on a bibliography of women in American music, and the staff of the American Music Center in New York were all sympathetic to our aims and generous with their knowledge and assistance, as were the employees of Joseph Patelson's Music House, most especially Diana Herman.

We are also deeply appreciative of the specialized and, typically, generous assistance given by our friend, the respected composer and teacher Jack Beeson.

A final recognition of the many contributions by friends and associates to the substance of this book: thanks to Howard Shanet, Evelyn Hertzmann, Kenneth Smith, Larry Wasserman, Sylvia Paz, David Kotick, Dr. David Podell, Ruth Ihrig, David Garvey, John Wustman, Rollin Baldwin, Philip Hallie, Maury Lorey, Mark Berger, Carol Emmons, and Gloria Stern.

We acknowledge the debt we owe to two magnificent volumes—the *Dictionary of Contemporary Music*, edited by John Vinton, and *Twentieth Century Music*, by Peter Yates—for the vast information contained therein, as well as the part their musical philosophies played in expanding our attitudes toward contemporary music.

We have been most fortunate in this work to have the expert assistance of our editors, Ken Stuart and Abbie Meyer, whose unfailing good humor and charm accompanied all their advice.

1 The Song Recital

EVOLUTION

Before the nineteenth century, musical perform-
ances were limited to churches or to palaces of the nobility and musical
works were tailor-made for a particular audience. Palestrina's great religious works were intended for the prelates and congregations of the Italian church. Bach's cantatas were specifically attuned to the congregation
of St. Thomas' Church in Leipzig. Domenico Scarlatti's compositions
were heard for years only by the Spanish court, just as performances of
Haydn's works were attended mainly by the Esterházy nobility. In Germany, around the turn of the century, collections of secular songs were
intended for performance in the parlors of specific social groups.

Late in the nineteenth century, when solo music went "on the road,"
the new and foreign audiences before whom it was performed did not entirely understand the performers' intentions. Fashionable Italian opera,
which had started its world touring at a much earlier date, had already
been favorably received by the public. Audiences, accepting its more obvious attributes, were accustomed to listen for the aria, often paying little attention to the rest of the opera and conversing to the sound of the
recitatives.[1] Only as the twentieth century drew near did the enlarging
mass audience become conscientious and attentive.

---

1. These cases of audience and individual naiveté may be cited: (a) in Vienna, audiences for
a time preferred Rossini to Beethoven; (b) popular audiences thought Spohr equal if not
superior to Beethoven; (c) Stendahl considered Mozart's music too Germanic and studied in comparison to Pergolesi's music; (d) George Bernard Shaw tried valiantly to exert
his influence to make Beethoven as popular as Mendelssohn and Spohr.

Personal appearances being professionally and financially valuable, nineteenth-century star singers made great efforts to schedule concert appearances whenever their operatic schedule permitted. Traveling performers like Nellie Melba and Jennie Lind charmed the general public with those operatic arias, resplendent with pyrotechnics, that their devoted public expected to hear. Simple tunes, if included at all, were a pleasant but unimportant part of the evening's entertainment. On some occasions assisting artists were contracted to appear in duets with the star singer. When feasible, orchestras were hired. In the absence of an orchestra, the dubious duties were performed by an accompanist, who was cautioned to appear not too conspicuous.[2]

Since those days the psychological attitudes of audiences have gone through many changes. As the twentieth-century mass audience grew up, it began to look upon music as it did upon horse-racing, betting, and other professional sports—as a pastime in which they did not take part. This audience tended to become resistant to all unknown music, old or new. The period after World War II added another immense upheaval in audience psychology. A new musical acclimatization, similar to the change from polyphony to harmony in the seventeenth century, was taking place (and has yet to be completed). The erasure of boundaries between consonance and dissonance that some composers had attempted at the turn of the century and the confusing array of new compositional techniques—mixed media, aleatory, electronic, computer, neoclassical, total serialism—all have left much of the mass audience at sea.

The modern audience, formed by the pressures of past events, can be said to be comprised of three types of individuals: (1) the enthusiast, whose musical appreciation and understanding is superior, who therefore has an incentive to investigate and enjoy any new music, whether contemporary or from the past; (2) the connoisseur of good music who hastens to admire chic music, which is in vogue and pleases the prevailing taste; (3) the remaining individual, typical of the majority, who accepts his standards and convictions second-hand.

For a brief period in America the recital flourished in the persons of such greats as Lehmann, Tourel, and Frijsch. For the past several decades the solo recital, instrumental as well as vocal, has been in decline. Today, the number of solo song recitals given each season falls far below that of other types of concerts. Entire seasons may pass with no more than one or two exciting recitals. However highly regarded as an art form when well done, the ingredients and techniques of the song recital are poorly understood by the general public.

2. Even as late as the 1930s the art of accompanying was not always understood. Gerald Moore tells us in his book, *Am I Too Loud?*, that some of his fellow professionals regarded the accompanist's work with a jaundiced eye. Moore, Gerald, *Am I Too Loud?* Macmillan, 1962, p. 180.

The decline of the solo song recital is attributable to many factors. In recent years, the music profession has not lived up to what audiences have expected. Too frequently, recitals are musically skilled and sophisticated, but dramatically haphazard and amateurish. Lacking entertainment value, such recitals do not compete successfully with other twentieth-century forces and trends. Either the song recital must carve out a contemporary niche for itself, or it runs the risk of either disappearing from the professional concert stage, or at best mutating into total elitism practiced only by European specialists. Its rebirth is long overdue. It should no longer be viewed as a "snob" occasion or a "status" evening but, in the words of the English novelist Henry Green, as "a long intimacy between strangers."

Filling the large halls of the increasing number of new performing arts centers scattered about the United States has depended largely on the drawing power of charismatic (formerly known as glamorous) artists. Indeed, one publicity director epitomized the situation by declaring, "It helps to have an artist who has cut off his ear."

Whatever one is impelled to say about that old star system during the heyday of the solo recital in the 1940s and 1950s, it did help to draw the audience into the hall, where presumably they liked what they heard and saw, since they returned often. Before a recital Lily Pons would arrive at a city in her own railroad car. Maria Jeritza wrote a newspaper column about beauty hints. Many serious singers made movies, beginning with Geraldine Farrar. It was not unusual to see a concert artist arrive with her entourage, among which were a maid, a PR man, two Borzoi dogs, and a suspiciously unattached young male. Following this glamorous epoch, the ordinary girl next door was suddenly in vogue. Concert stars were photographed cooking their own recipes for goulash in their very own simple Connecticut kitchens. It did not take long before reverse chic and total understatement took over. Having, with the power of their 1960s movement, reduced everyone to a moral statement of blue jeans or their equivalent, the rock stars then proceeded to dress and behave in outlandishly glamorous fashion. The field was theirs. (It is hard to compete with a sequined jumpsuit.) Losing its glamor, the song recital lost a great deal. The audience must be coaxed into the hall before a recital can be presented. There are many methods; glamor is not an inconsiderable one.

Although not crucial in itself, the results of this policy have wreaked havoc upon the weakened stature of the solo recital precisely when the onslaughts of television and the long-playing record were strongest.

Simple boredom is one of the strongest reasons for the decline of the song recital. Rigid preservation of familiar repertoire by local concert organizations (instigated and promoted by big concert bureaus) has contributed to this situation. The tight control over these programs is totally in the hands of artists' managers. It was they who approved the content of each program, often overriding the vociferous protests of singers, who were anxious to program music written before Bach and after Stravinsky. As one result, many localities bowed out of community concert series because they felt that the artists were "singing down to them," depriving them of the chance to become au courant with musical happenings. It is a very dangerous ploy to consistently underestimate the capacities of the musical mass audience.

Eventually, managerial representatives who pandered to the local committee chairman's desire for "the *very* best works by the *very* best performers" fostered programs restricted to practically a handful of European artists. These artists, who often were not good recitalists, contributed their share to the weakening of the song recital. Americans are easily persuaded by hyperbolic publicity to regard only European superstars as worth hearing. Moderately successful American artists have a hard time surviving. But great art is nourished by the middle levels of competent craftsmen in the arts who should not be made to feel that they are failures when they do not command international adulation.

All too familiar to musicians are the old rebuttals to the "give 'em what they want" philosophy. Filling the hall *is* a proper and valid concern. Nevertheless, the hall has often *not* been filled as a result of giving them what they supposedly wanted. Was something wrong with the theory? Was the hall simply too large for recital? Was the repertoire repetitive ad nauseum and the acting too often next to nonexistent? One might have expected dullness to be attacked by the critics. In effect, critics have the power to dictate programming according to their personal taste. Yet, actual complaints of "too much variety" have revealed that the critics often had standards which related too little to the normal audience's appetite for variety.

Television, the foremost communications revolution of the second half of the twentieth century, has given the mass audience a taste for larger musical forces—Baroque ensembles, duet and joint recitals, chamber music aggregations of all kinds, and every imaginable type of avant-garde multimedia performances. One lone unamplified singer and one accompanist performing a repertoire that is all but unknown to those who grew up with television find it hard to command attention.

Television, in addition to addressing itself to the famed twelve-year-old mentality, has lowered the common denominator of the musical level at which we are bombarded. It has also shortened our attention span, decreased our willingness to listen carefully, and has eroded our capacity for listening quietly to entertainment in a group. (When were you last treated at the movie theater to the *alta voce* comments of the stranger sitting next to you who presumably thinks he is watching television in his own living room?) Public television has stimulated grass roots interest in things theatrical, benefiting opera and the theater, but it has not managed the same impact on the song recital. Our recital programming has not kept pace; our recital acting has not improved. Only a few especially talented recitalists have attempted to revitalize the drama of recital. Why should a music lover take the trouble to attend a recital unless the fare competes, nominally at least, with an evening of commercial television?

Publicly supported musical events can scarcely compete with free commercial television. Something must be charged for the ticket, whether or not it actually defrays the cost. The film industry managed to survive the competition from the television industry during the sixties. We must do the same. We must put together a better product by improving our programming and our skills. Commercial recordings, a magnificent but mixed blessing, have had a profound effect on music appreciation, but they have also made us justifiably lazy. Unless one has tasted the excitement of live performance with all of its attendant risks, what compelling reasons can be found for leaving the cozy hi-fi room at home, where no one will challenge the favorite artist's interpretation? Why venture forth to hear music that is not recorded? After all, how good can it be if it is not on a disc? Such attitudes are surprisingly prevalent today especially among the young, many of whom have never heard a live, unamplified performance of any kind, let alone a song recital. On the other hand, the repertoire which they play to test their elaborate equipment has converted some hi-fi addicts (previously immune to the delights of serious music) into fans of Beethoven and Bach. Let us be grateful that the long playing records have enlarged the potential musical audience but let us not elevate recordings to a position as sole measurement of a definitive reading.

In summation, let us use the succinct statement of Paul Hartman, formerly of the Lake George Opera Company, now manager of the Regina Symphony Orchestra, Saskatchewan, Canada: "We must break down the stereotype of the recital as a dull affair geared only to the elite." Of course there is absolutely no reason why this refined art must put people off by its elegance or why it must be boring because of its refinement. We can erase boredom and we can substitute entertainment with no lowering of standards. It is up to the music profession to show mass audiences that a song recital is, above all, enjoyable.

Indisputably, interest in the song recital has temporarily waned. Why *not* let it die? Why *not* look back with nostalgia once a year to Tourel's triumphant debut recital, sipping champagne to the memory? The answer is simple. We would forever deny ourselves access to the only medium for live performances of our tremendous heritage of song literature—the song recital. Recordings scarcely suffice. They offer one frozen, locked-in interpretation. Recitals offer personal expressivity, the stylistic projection of the whole performer, and an experience that is always real and stimulating.

CONTEMPORARY PROGRAMMING

In its purest form, the song recital is truly a product of the twentieth century. The practice of arranging songs in chronological order was pioneered by Marcella Sembrich. Fine artists like Elisabeth Schumann, Aksel Schiotz, Lotte Lehmann, Elena Gerhardt, and Alexander Kipnis preferred to sing the great songs of Schubert, Schumann, and Brahms in place of arias. American artists Mack Harrell and Marian Anderson and the Danish-born singer Polva Frijsch continued the practice. Recitalists of the forties, fifties, and sixties Jennie Tourel, Elisabeth Schwarzkopf, Dietrich Fischer-Dieskau, Peter Pears, Kathleen Ferrier, Gerard Souzay, Judith Raskin, Janet Baker, Donald Gramm, Shirley Verett, and Hermann Prey limited their recitals almost exclusively to song literature.

From the repertoires of these singers we have chosen six representative programs. Schwarzkopf, Raskin, and Souzay are principally German or French song recital specialists. Tourel, Verrett, and Gramm (despite his American program) display in their programs a broad repertoire. We also present six other programs devised by fine recitalists and fine programmakers whose names are not household words, although they deserve to be.

Jennie Tourel
MEZZO-SOPRANO

I. From Rosie Bow'rs   Henry Purcell

II. Six Songs from the *Spanisches Liederbuch*   Hugo Wolf
    Nun wandre Maria
    Die ihr schwebet
    Bedeckt mich mit Blumen
    Ach, im Maien war's
    Geh! Geliebter, geh' jetzt!
    Bitt' ihn O Mutter

III. Die Junge Magd, Opus 23 No. 2 (Trakl)   Paul Hindemith
    voice, flute, clarinet, string quartet

INTERMISSION

IV. L'Absence (Gautier)   Hector Berlioz
    Le Temps des Lilas   Ernest Chausson
    Violon   Francis Poulenc
    Vilanelle des petits canards   Emmanuel Chabrier

V. Under the Mask (Lermontov)   M. A. Balakirev
    So Soon Forgotten (Apuchtin)   P. I. Tchaikovsky
    The Snowdrop   A. T. Gretchaninov
    Eternal Love (Pushkin)   A. T. Gretchaninov

Gerard Souzay
BARITONE

I. Chanson Louis XIII   Anonymous
    Ma bergère, non légère   Gabriel Bataille
    Cachez, beaux yeux   Antoine Boisset
    Amants, aimez vos chaînes   Jean Baptiste Lully

II. Quatre romances   Charles Gounod
        Au rossignol
        Chanson de printemps
        L'Absence
        Viens! les gazons sont verts

III. Chansons madécasses   Marice Ravel
        Nahandove!
        Aoua!
        Repos

INTERMISSION

IV. L'Espace du dedans   Henri Sauguet
        Repos dans le malheur
        La jeune fille de Budapest
        Dans la nuit

V. L'Adolescence Clémentine   Jean Françaix
        De Jan-Jan
        Mon coeur est tout endormy
        D'une vieille dame fort pâle et d'un vieil gentilhomme
        Complainte
        Avant naissance

Elisabeth Schwarzkopf
SOPRANO

I.	Bist du bei mir	J. S. Bach
	Einem Bach der fliesst	Christoph Gluck
	Wonne der Wehmut	Ludwig van Beethoven
	Warnung .	W. A. Mozart
II.	An Sylvia (Shakespeare)	Franz Schubert
	Die Liebe hat gelogen	
	Die Voegel	
	Der Einsame	
	Ungeduld	
III.	Der Nussbaum	Robert Schumann
	Auftraege	Robert Schumann
	Da unten im Tale	Johannes Brahms
	Och Moder	Johannes Brahms

INTERMISSION

IV.	Die Sproede	Hugo Wolf
	Die Bekehrte	
	Als ich auf dem Euphrat schiffte	
	Kennst du das Land	
V.	Du denkst mit einem Faedchen	Hugo Wolf
	Wir haben beide	
	Nein, junger Herr	
	In dem Schatten meiner Locken	
	Die Zigeunerin	
VI.	Wiegenlied	Richard Strauss
	Schlechtes Wetter	
	Hat's gesagt, bleibt's nicht dabei	

Donald Gramm
BASS-BARITONE

I. Three Poems by William Blake   Virgil Thomson
              The Divine Image
              Tiger! Tiger!
              "And did those feet . . . ?"

II. Three Poems by E. A. Robinson   John Duke
              Richard Cory
              Luke Havergal
              Miniver Cheevy

III. Blue Mountain Ballads (Tennessee Williams)   Paul Bowles
              Cabin
              Lonesome Man
              Sugar in the Cane
              Heavenly Grass
     Four Poems by Walt Whitman   Ned Rorem
              As Adam early in the morning
              To You
              Look down, fair moon
              Oh, you, whom I often and silently come
     Two Songs   Richard Cumming
              Go Lovely Rose (Edmund Waller)
              A Ballad of the Good Lord Nelson (Lawrence Durrell)
                     INTERMISSION

IV. Songs by Charles Ives
              General William Booth Enters into Heaven (Lindsay)
              Side Show (Ives)
              The Things Our Fathers Loved (Ives)
              The Greatest Man (Anne Collins)
              The Circus Band (Ives)

V. Favorite American Concert Songs Selected from the Works of:
              Carpenter, Speaks, Nevin, Cadman, Watts, Wolfe,
              MacDowell, Beach

Judith Raskin
SOPRANO

I. An Chloe (Jacobi)   W. A. Mozart
    Als Luise (Baumberg)
    Warnung (Anon.)

II. Erlafsee (Mayrhofer)   Franz Schubert
    Auf dem Wasser zu singen (Stolberg)
    Die Vögel (Schlegel)
    Frühlingstraum (Müller)
    Seligkeit (Hölty)

III. Das Mädchen spricht (Gruppe)   Johannes Brahms
     Immer leiser wird mein Schlummer (Lingg)
     Geheimnis (Candidus)
     Botschaft (Daumer)

INTERMISSION

IV. Sieben frühe Lieder   Alban Berg
            Nacht (Hauptmann)
            Schilflied (Lenau)
            Die Nachtigall (Storm)
            Traumgekrönt (Rilke)
            Im Zimmer (Schlaf)
            Liebesode (Hartleben)
            Sommertage (Hohenberg)

V. Four Songs   Gustav Mahler
            Rheinlegendchen (*Des Knaben Wunderhorn*)
            Ich atmet' einen linden Duft (Rückert)
            Wo die schönen Trompeten blasen
               (*Des Knaben Wunderhorn*)
            Wer hat dies Liedlein erdacht?
               (*Des Knaben Wunderhorn*)

Cesare Valletti
TENOR

I.	Nel puro ardor (from "Euridice")	Jacopo Peri
	A porfiria vecchiarella (from "Orazio")	Alessandro Stradella
	Cara e dolce	Alessandro Scarlatti
	Ne men con l'ombre	G. F. Handel
	Che vuole innamorarsi	Alessandro Scarlatti
II.	Auflösung	Franz Schubert
	Der Jüngling an der Quelle	Franz Schubert
	Nacht und Träume	Franz Schubert
	Der Musensohn	Franz Schubert

INTERMISSION

III.	I Pastori	Ildebrando Pizzetti
	San Basilio	Ildebrando Pizzetti
	Serenata (from "Sette Canzoni")	G. Francesco Malipiero
IV.	Marcello's Aria (from "Il Duca d'Alba")	Gaetano Donizetti
V.	There is a Lady Sweet and Kind	Norman dello Joio
	How Do I Love Thee	Norman dello Joio
	Feast of Lanterns (from the Chinese)	Granville Bantock

Shirley Verrett
MEZZO-SOPRANO

I.	Confusa, smarrita (*Catone in Utica*)	Giovanni Pergolesi
	D'amor l'arcano ascoso (*Flaminio*)	
	Serbi l'intatta fede	
II.	Nicht wiedersehen!	Gustav Mahler
	(*Des Knaben Wunderhorn*)	
	Rheinlegendchen	
	(*Des Knaben Wunderhorn*)	
	Wiegenlied (Dehmel)	Richard Strauss
	Für fünfzehn Pfennige	
	(*Des Knaben Wunderhorn*)	
	Befreit (Dehmel)	

INTERMISSION

III.	Three Spirituals (Titles to be announced)	
IV.	À sa Guitare (Ronsard)	Francis Poulenc
	Adeline à la Promenade (Garcia Lorca)	
	C'est ainsi que tu es (Vilmorin)	
	Vous n'écrivez plus? (Jacob)	
	Sanglots (Apollinaire)	
	Air vif (Moréas)	
V.	Una voce poco fa (*Barber of Seville*)	Gioacchino Rossini

Sofia Steffan
MEZZO-SOPRANO

I. An die Hoffnung (from Tiedge's   Ludwig van Beethoven
       Urania), Opus 94
    Two songs from "Egmont," Opus 84
           Die Trommel gerühret
           Freudvoll und Leidvoll

II. Sechs Deutsche Lieder, Opus 103   Ludwig Spohr
           Sei still mein Herz
           Zwiegesang
           Sehnsucht
           Wiegenlied
           Das heimliche Lied
           Wach auf
               mezzo-soprano, clarinet, and piano

III. Parto, ma tu, ben mio (*La Clemenza di Tito*)   W. A. Mozart
               mezzo-soprano, clarinet, and piano
                    INTERMISSION

IV. From the Diary of Virginia Woolf   Dominick Argento
           The Diary
           Anxiety
           Fancy
           Hardy's Funeral
           Rome
           War
           Parents
           Last Entry

Carol Knell
MEZZO-SOPRANO

I.	O nube! che lieve per l'aria ti aggiri (from *Maria Stuarda*)	Gaetano Donizetti

II.	Maria Stuart Lieder, Opus 135
	Abschied von Frankreich
	Nach der Geburt ihres Sohnes
	An die Königin Elisabeth
	Abschied von der Welt
	Gebet

Robert Schumann

III.	Cinq Chansons (Mary Stuart)
	Pour lui j'ay méprisé
	Car c'est le seul désir
	Sans cesse mon coeur sent
	Vous m'estimez légère
	O Domine Deus

Jean Berger

voice, viola, cello, flute

INTERMISSION

IV. Music from the courts where Mary Stuart
resided or was imprisoned

The Court of Henry II

J'ay cause de moy contenter	Matthieu Sohier
Vous perdez temps	Claudin de Sermisy
Le chant des oiseaux	Clément Janequin

The Court of Mary Stuart

In a garden so green	16th cent. Scottish (Anon.)
Richt soir opprest	
O lusty May	

The Court of Henry VIII

O My Hart	Henry VIII
Canary	Caroso/Praetorius
A Robyn, Gentil Robyn	William Cornish
It Was a Lover and His Lass	William Byrd
Now o Now I Needs Must Part	John Dowland

voice, old instrument ensemble, dancers

Paul Sperry
TENOR

I.	Histoires Naturelles (Renard)	Maurice Ravel
	Le Paon	
	Le Grillon	
	Le Cygne	
	Le Martin-Pêcheur	
	La Pintade	
II.	La Grenouillière (Apollinaire)	Francis Poulenc
	Paul et Virginie (Radiguet)	
	Dernière poème (Desnos)	
	Reine des mouettes (Vilmorin)	
	Montparnasse (Apollinaire)	
III.	La statue de bronze (Fargue)	Eric Satie
	Daphênéo (God)	
	Le Chapelier (Chalpult)	

INTERMISSION

IV.	Noch (Night; Polonski)	P. I. Tchaikovsky
	Za oknom (Behind the window; Polonski)	
	Ne ver, moi drug (Don't believe, my friend; Tolstoy)	
	Sred schumnovo bala (At the Ball; Tolstoy)	
V.	Auf der Bruck (Schulze)	Franz Schubert
	Am See (Bruchmann)	
	Die Liebe hat gelogen (Platen)	
	Der Einsame (Lappe)	
	Nacht und Träume (Collin)	
	Der Musensohn (Goethe)	

Chloe Owen
SOPRANO

I. Contemplazioni di Michelangelo   Nicholas Flagello
            Come può esser
            Ben doverrieno
            Ben fu
            Di più cose

II. Chansons de Ronsard   Darius Milhaud
            A une fontaine
            A cupidon
            Tais-toi, Babillarde
            Dieu vous garde!

INTERMISSION

III. Sieben Frühe Lieder   Alban Berg
            Nacht (Hauptmann)
            Schilflied (Lenau)
            Die Nachtigall (Storm)
            Traumgekrönt (Rilke)
            Im Zimmer (Schlag)
            Liebesode (Hartleben)
            Sommertage (Hohenberg)

IV. Flamenco Meditations   Carlos Surinach
        (Elizabeth Barrett Browning)
            How do I love Thee?
            Yet, love, mere love, is beautiful indeed
            When our two souls stand up erect and strong
            The face of all the world is changed
            If thou must love me let it be for naught

Jeanne Beauvais
SOPRANO

I.	Un jeune coeur (*Les Aveux Indiscrets*) L'art surpasse ici la nature (*La Belle Arsène*) L'orage (*La Belle Arsène*) Ariette de la Vieille (*Rose et Colas*)	Pierre Monsigny
II.	Paysage triste Les Papillons Narcisse à la Fontaine Crépuscule Phidylé	Reynaldo Hahn Ernest Chausson Jules Massenet Jules Massenet Henri Duparc

III.	Poèmes pour la Paix sur la Poésie du Passé
	    Sonnet (Olivier de Magny)
	    Sonnet (Jean Daurat)
	    L'Hymne de la Paix (Jean Antoine de Baif)
		Ned Rorem

INTERMISSION

IV.	Mélodies Passagères (Rilke)
	    Puisque tout passe
	    Un cygne
	    Tombeau dans un parc
	    Le clocher chante
	    Départ
		Samuel Barber

V.	Cocardes (Cocteau)
	    Miel de Narbonne
	    Bonne d'enfant
	    Enfant de Troupe
		Francis Poulenc

Helen Vanni
MEZZO-SOPRANO

I. Air de Clytemnestra: Armez-vous d'un
noble courage (*Iphigénie en Aulide*)   Christoph Gluck
Air de Larissa (*Il Trionfo di Clelia*)   Christoph Gluck
Per pietà, bell'idol mio   Vincenzo Bellini
Qual farfalletta amante   Alessandro Scarlatti

II. Und steht ihr früh am Morgen auf   Hugo Wolf
Du denkst mit einem Fädchen
Wohin mit der Freud
Frage nicht
Die Kleine

III. Ch'io mi scordi di te (K. 505)   W. A. Mozart

INTERMISSION

IV. Chansons de Bilitis   Claude Debussy
La Flûte de Pan
La Chevelure
Le Tombeau des Naïades

V. Meinem Kinde   Richard Strauss
Ruhe meine Seele
Einerlei
Wie sollten wir geheim sie halten

THE RECITALIST

Presented with such examples of excellent recital programming, we must confront the song recital as a uniquely difficult and demanding art form. Singers who wish to succeed in it must understand fully the techniques involved. They must have ample time to perfect themselves in the skills required. Above all, they must truly wish to do so. (They cannot carelessly toss off a recital at Alice Tully Hall between two operatic appearances.)

Rewards and Satisfactions

True, the recital does not earn great financial returns. If the art were flourishing, it would undoubtedly pay well. In lieu of monetary return, singers who study recital will gain vocal stamina, will determine and improve their musical capacities, acquire self-confidence, forge a personal style of communication, and attain the versatility that a nonspecializing American singer must have. Finally, even if they never sing recitals professionally, or even if their talents prove to be better suited to opera than to recital, they will nevertheless improve their operatic skills from a study of recital. (See Chapter 5.)

Singing recitals is much more difficult to do well than singing opera or oratorio. Judith Raskin, the brilliant American soprano, was asked which of the two, opera or recital, she loved more. She replied, "Opera is my true love, I expect, but recital has taught me so much! In a recital I know my voice completely and what I am capable of. I use this knowledge in my opera roles."

Personal gratification is one of the most satisfying rewards one recieves from performing a successful recital. To be able to hold an audience in the palm of one's hand for some two hours so that one's performance becomes a total musical experience will not only accelerate one's growth as an artist but will effect a great sense of confidence and pride in one's individual talent. Continued practice in recitals rewards the singer with a distinct personal style of performance—a very valuable asset. It must be remembered, however, that imagination and personality cannot flourish without the bedrock of vocal and musical security, skills that are best developed in recital.

Skills

Having read a description of the intoxicating rewards of the song recital, you may well feel compelled to ask: "How can I become a good recitalist?" You will need every one—a small assortment will not do—of the following skills:

1. a well-trained and reasonably beautiful voice
2. advanced musicianship
3. an attractive and vital personality
4. the ability to project and communicate
5. the ability to think and perform on many levels
6. the ability to go beyond what can be taught
7. versatility of styles (for the American singer)
8. musical and literary insight
9. musical and literary imagination
10. good health and the determination to keep it.

Building a career as a Lieder singer obviously calls for a number of different skills. Acting ability, for example, is an important talent for any singer. The song singer par excellence, while bestowing loving attention upon the song's details, must understand the need to retain the scope of its larger pattern. Building a fine song recital also demands of singers some degree of scholarship. Not only is it their responsibility, but it is perhaps the best device for extending the boundaries of their artistic imaginations. They need to experience the thrill of research and the triumph of discovering the unusal or the unique.

It is our opinion, however, that contrary to an unfortunate and widely circulated myth, only a quality voice can do justice to the many demands that song literature presents and that only a quality voice can reflect adequately the beauty, color, and emotional nuances of both music and text. A voice too far past its prime cannot meet these special demands. A quality voice, by our definition, is one of pleasing timbre, with a personal sound characteristic.

As to the less beautiful, or time-worn, voice, let us in fairness determine how the myth originated. Certainly the veteran of a successful operatic career has developed a high level of maturity, wisdom, vocal awareness, audience expertise, and musical knowledge. There is no question that he has advantages, but are these not the very same qualities that the younger singer needs to attain? And how better can he do it than in the one medium which calls for a high level of them all?

The "Entertainer"

It is imperative to recognize that the song recital, however aesthetic and refined it may be, is meant to be enjoyed. The prime purpose of a recital cannot be educational, although its educational value is an inherent factor. Every recital, indeed every group of songs, should have a scenario as interesting and absorbing as is possible to concoct artistically.

A musician cannot be unaware of the horror with which some people regard the word "entertainment" when applied to a song recital. It immediately conjures up spectors of lowered standards, worthless musical values, a lack of serious textual message, inferior poetry, "show-biz" acting, lack of finesse, even crass vocal or musical tricks! We do not believe that to entertain is contemptible. We believe that entertainment connotes excitement, as well as higher musical and vocal standards, better music, a challenging repertoire that includes twentieth-century compositions, total communication through fine acting, an attractive physical appearance, elegant execution, and subtle and discriminating taste in programming.

The material requirements of a song recital are very simple—a singer, an accompanist, and a place of performance, but the skills required of a song recitalist are myriad. Nevertheless, for intelligent singers recital singing is the most satisfying way to keep in touch with their craft: the rewards are numberless.

2 Program Building

THE TRADITIONAL RECITAL PROGRAM

Before considering the so-called "specialized" type of recital, let us discuss the structure of a traditional American recital program. It might commence with music from seventeenth- and eighteenth-century Italian composers, or with music of the German Baroque, or possibly with works by English composers such as Purcell. During the first half of the program there would surely be German Lieder and perhaps some French romantic songs. The second half would certainly include something more modern, possibly in a more unusual language, and the recital would probably finish with a group of songs in English, with an emphasis on American composers. You will observe that such an arrangement automatically provides a chronological order and the sine qua non of the nonspecialist's recital—variety within unity. In a sense, our traditional recital might be viewed as an "international excursion, a tour of national character and nature."[1]

Consider for a moment the psychological effect of such a program upon a popular audience, "popular" as opposed to more worldly, or more comprehending, listeners. Members of such an audience are divisi-

1. We are indebted to Professor Jackson Hill of the Bucknell University music department for this description.

ble into several groups: (1) those who have been attracted by the program because the music is most important to them; (2) those who are supporters of the singer—fans, relatives, students; (3) those who are, at best, curious to hear and assess the singer's skills; (4) those who have been brought to the concert by someone else, perhaps even against their will; and (5) those who are basically inimical, with a "show-me" state of mind. Regardless of the disparate attitudes of the audience members, all have this in common: during the first group none of them is ready to join in an emotionally gripping kind of music. It is simply too early. The audience is at this moment still separate, still individual, and still partially concerned with private thoughts and worries brought into the hall. Although music of any period will serve, Renaissance, Classical, and Baroque music are ideal for the opening moments of a traditional recital. During these moments the singer effaces personality to a high degree. He asks little more than attention from his audience, fully intending that his artistry elicit more than this later on. He presents his qualifications. His psychological calling-card states: this is what I look like; this is what my voice sounds like; this is how I sing; this is what kind of a musician I am. Minimal involvement is required from the audience during this first group.[2]

As the program proceeds, the chronological order of musical styles ensures that the audience involve itself more willingly as the communication between artist and audience becomes progressively more personal. Assuming that the artist does his or her job well, by the end of the program a rapport has been established that has literally broken down the natural barriers that were present at the beginning of the recital. The formality with which the recital so suitably began has been eroded by subtle degrees until, at the end, a relationship so familiar has been forged between artist and audience that encores inevitably become informal moments between friends. A so-called traditional recital program, then, implying a basic historical order of styles, makes it simple to follow the psychological dictates of the recital as a social occasion.

It has been fashionable lately, in an effort to assign blame for the lowered appeal of the song recital, to point an accusing finger at this traditional type of program. But we must bear in mind that the traditional program, although seemingly stilted and old-fashioned, does offer cer-

2. We believe that this issue is rendered superfluous by the following three comparisons. One natural law is provided by drama itself. Good dramaturgy dictates that the play, although it contains many risings and fallings of the emotional thermometer, seldom, if ever, *begins* with a soul-stirring climax. A second logical example is furnished by any social gathering. During the first moments participants shake hands and voice remarks which are almost exclusively social formulas, such as, "How do you do?" "Isn't the weather grand?" The hostess's duty is to ease the transition from formality to informality by supplying a few details about each person's background, "Mr. X is in stocks and

tain advantages. The variety of styles, languages, and dramatic means ensured by the traditional format serves young singers especially well. (If one regards a sampling of debut programs, these musical and dramatic contrasts would also appear to be consistent with the demands of a young artist's debut concert; see Chapter 5.) Even if a gifted young singer were to be a crackajack musician, intellectually superior, and possessing the effortless vocal techniques of a natural singer, it is unlikely that he or she would be able to sustain a specialized program. The musically sophisticated audience simply does not trust a specialized program in the hands of a youthful singer, whom they might even consider presumptuous. Young singers properly spend their early years training their voices. They do not have the time, nor frequently the desire, to do the research required to build an advanced program. Indeed the traditional format appears to be disadvantageous only to the advanced singer because of its relative lack of sophistication due to its predictability and the fact that it is, in consequence, sometimes judged to reflect badly upon the singer's artistic maturity.

In refining the parameters of a true song recital we must accept at the outset that it is to be made up of song materials. An operatic aria is complete in the context of the opera scene for which it has been created. The story, the stage setting, the chorus, the orchestra, and other elements make the aria a thrilling experience in opera. These elements are missing on the concert platform. The tenor in tails who sings Pagliaccio's lament with piano accompaniment sets himself at an automatic disadvantage. With the tremendous wealth of great song material available, no song recitalists need to subject themselves to any such disadvantage. Use of early or obscure opera arias, of course, is a different matter, the audience not being accustomed to the full panoply of its operatic performance.

It is practical to bear in mind that what we call a traditional recital is only traditional in America, possibly also in England. A traditional recital in Germany consists primarily of Lieder, in France, of mélodies. Certainly an evening of German Lieder by an accomplished German singer may well be a beautiful experience, but such a recital should, in our opinion, be considered as a specialist's offering, and not as the one and only definition of a recital's proper content. Nor should nationalism limit a cosmopolitan viewpoint in programming. Specialization always will be welcome. Fine as it may be, however, the scope of the recital form is limited in the minds of the song-loving public when little or no other song literature is offered in contrast.

bonds." But seldom, if ever, do you find people who have just been introduced discussing the intimate and emotional details of their lives until they are much better acquainted. And third, why is it that the spot reserved for the "headliner" in a vaudeville show is next to closing?

THE SPECIALIZED PROGRAM

Some possible departures from the traditional recital format are suggested below.

1. A program of songs in one language

   as: all-English (American and British composers)

   or: all-Spanish (Spanish, Cuban, South American composers)

2. A program of songs from one period

   as: all-Romantic

   or: all-Baroque

3. A program of songs from one country

   as: all composed by French composers

4. A program from the compositions of a single composer

   as: Die schöne Müllerin

   or: all individual compositions by Schubert

5. A program of music by only two composers, or from only two periods, or in only two languages

   as: one half all Haydn, one half all Liszt for solo pianist and singer plus accompanist, each artist performing works by both composers

   or: first half Baroque, second half contemporary compositions, performed by singer plus accompanist only

6. A program of song cycles

7. A program given by two artists

   as: all duets

   or: part solos and part duets

   or: alternating solos by two artists[3]

8. A program in which the singer is joined by a chamber group

   as: partly singer as soloist, partly singer plus chamber group

9. A program based on a special theme

   as: Cathy Berberian's program of *fin de siècle* music in a Victorian setting

   or: Evelyn Lear's program of her 'favorite' music

---

3. For example, Wolf's *Italienisches Liederbuch* has been sung by a mezzo-soprano and a baritone alternating songs from two pianos, with two accompanists.

or: works by American composers who were influenced by French poets or musicians

10. A program using the work of one poet set by various composers

   as: Shakespeare, Verlaine, Rilke, or Baudelaire

11. A program of ethnic inspiration written by composers *not* of that background

   as: music derived from the Spanish style by non-Spanish composers such as Bizet, Chabrier, Castelnuovo-Tedesco, Moussorgsky, and numerous American composers

It bears repeating that such programs require expertise.

BUILDING VOCAL RECITAL PROGRAMS

In Chapter 3, five different types of vocal recital programs from the above list are discussed in detail as to when and why the choices were made. These programs were constructed according to the tenets of the following outline, the authors' personal method for program building. As such it is not everyone's cup of tea. No doubt it will appear at first glance excessively simplistic. Our response must also be simplistic: it works well! As promised in the introduction, we offer it as the most practical help we have to give. When elaboration upon any outline point is called for, it will be indicated by a boldface superscript and found at the end of this chapter in the form of explanatory notes.

A Method Outline

I. Deciding on the overall theme.

   A. The survey session.

   1. Allow time for an open-ended, far-ranging session![1]

   2. Consider the following factors in looking for the overall idea:

      a. The singer's previous programs in this locality.[2]

      b. Any special interests of the audience.[3]

      c. The skills of the artist.[4]

      d. The present point of the singer's career.[5]

  e. Any possibility for programming music of a topical or local interest.[6]

  f. Special musical or literary interests of either artist.[7]

  g. Any moral commitments to a specific type of music held by either artist.[8]

  h. The size of the hall.[9]

3. Weigh the value of your choice as to whether its musical worthiness (apart from the critically important matter of its vocal suitability)[19] equates to its enjoyment value.[10]

4. Pick and choose from the array of composers.

  a. Variety within unity is an absolute necessity![11]

    (1) Variety of styles.[12]

    (2) Variety of historical periods.[12]

    (3) Variety of language.[12]

    (4) Variety within the oeuvre of one composer.[12]

    (5) Variety between familiar and unfamiliar repertoire.[12]

    (6) Variety of tempos and keys.[13]

  b. Articulate several possible plans for program order.

    (1) Remember that variety is still a prime requirement.

    (2) Some scheme for where climaxes should occur must be found.[14]

    (3) Rough out a provisionary length for the program.[15]

B. Research.

1. Delegate the research duties.[16]

  a. Research the historical period for composers and their repertoire.

  b. Assemble the maximum available repertoire of songs from chosen composers.

    (1) From music already known to the two artists and their teachers.

    (2) From the library.

      (a) Reference books listing complete works of composers.

        (i) *Groves Dictionary of Music and Musicians*
        (ii) *Dictionary of Contemporary Music* (Vinton)

      (b) Actual music on library shelves.

      (c) Music and recordings available at branch libraries.

    (3) From publishers' lists and music store shelves.

2. Several sessions will be necessary, in the studio and outside it.

II. Exploration before decision.

  A. The screening meeting.

1. Be fair to the composer; have this meeting at a time when both artists are in good physical form and in high spirits.

2. Leave an open-ended period of time for the meeting.[1]

3. Play though all assembled materials. Sight-read. Do not attempt finished performances. Listen and react from the heart rather than the head. Mark all pieces that appeal emotionally (*not* intellectually yet) to both artists within some twenty bars or less. Ruthlessly abandon the others.[17]

B. The meeting for final choices.

1. With both artists prepared for a more analytical session, this meeting, also open-ended,[1] must be devoted to an evaluation of the songs marked at the previous meeting.

   a. Confining yourselves to one composer at a time, play completely through each song.[18]

   b. Make a comparative rating of each song's appeal, remarking the very best ones, judged on vocal or pianistic suitability. [19, 21]

2. From all the newly marked, very best songs, evaluate them as to type.[20]

3. After deciding the optimum number of songs to be included in each group,[15] narrow down the preferred songs list to the correct size, choosing cannily for maximum effect and variety, with special attention to tempos and keys, making certain that each song maintains the purpose of the group in the master design.[21]

4. Having followed this procedure for each group, reevaluate the juxtaposition of the groups to each other. Readjust composers or groups as needed to build the climax successfully.[14, 22]

5. When various provisional group placements seem to offer just about equal advantages, consider the look of the program page, which also exerts an influence upon the audience.[22]

Explanatory Notes

1. Now, not later, is the time to discuss all contributory elements of program construction. Don't take shortcuts at this meeting. Take time *now* to think thoroughly about your decisions, to use your imagination, and to mull over all possibilities. If you do not, at a later time all progress will inevitably be halted for reassessment of problems which should have been solved previously.
2. Several questions concerning previous programs in the same locality ought to be raised. How many previous appearances were there and what kind of a program was presented each time? Ought the type of program be changed this time in the interests of variety? Were the previous programs well-received? Were there any criticisms? Were there any requests from the community related to programming, concert attire, etc.?
3. Many examples of special audience interests come to mind. The audience members could be especially sympathetic to twentieth-century repertoire. They might be members of a society devoted to French culture. They might live in a town with a large ethnic popula-

tion, such as Czechoslovak. The concert subscribers might be a popular mass audience, an elite and highly sophisticated Lieder-loving group, or a university audience. Each type would dictate a slightly different response.

4. The maturity and/or state of artistic development of both singer and accompanist must be assessed when contemplating the type of program. (Can or should a young mezzo sing *Frauenliebe und -leben* at the age of nineteen?) The chosen program must of course be well within the capabilities of both artists. If the singer is famous for a certain skill, then an example should be programmed lest the audience feel cheated. Perhaps the advance publicity has led the community to expect a display of a certain repertoire. It would be wise not to disappoint them. (See Publicity Bio, Chapter 8.) Perhaps an important critic is scheduled to be present at the concert. The singer must have the wisdom to evaluate and display his or her (pre-tested and) assured skills.

5. With reference to the chronological point of the singer's career, here are a few examples of some typical concerns. Is he breaking new ground with his recital performance? Was he formerly known for opera? Would he look inexperienced if he did a traditional recital program? Would she appear audacious or impertinent if her program were all Lieder? Did she recently finish doing a special Stravinsky program in New York City? Could she, or should she, capitalize on the attendant publicity by repeating it here in toto or in part?

6. Consideration of topical or local interests might lead the singer to program Christmas music in December, American music on an American holiday, Charles Ives's compositions in July around his birthday, Mahler's music during the year of his centennial anniversary, Philadelphia-born composers' works in Philadelphia, or music by Scandinavian composers in the state of Wisconsin.

7. The following list is comprised of several not-so-imaginary scenarios describing background details that might well give birth to special and compelling musical or literary interests on the part of the singer or accompanist.

   a. The accompanist has a passion for French music of all kinds acquired as a youth, because of his family's business and consequent travels in France.

   b. The singer has enjoyed a close relationship with Heitor Villa-Lobos in Brazil and New York, which has resulted in authoritative interpretations and a desire to program not-so-well-known works of this composer.

   c. The accompanist's conviction (acquired during her reading about the period) that the concert-going public would find a program of music about and from the Victorian era unusual and interesting persuades her to research and plan such a program.

   d. Undergraduate years of academic absorption with the writings of James Joyce leads to the desire to program some of the many musical works incorporating his poetry and prose.

   e. An unintentional but provocative exposure to the strange life and intriguing poems of Léon-Paul Fargue inspires the singer's wish to proselytize on behalf of his genius by programming composers who set Fargue's poetry.

8. Frequently, a mere musical interest becomes so compelling that it is transformed into a moral crusade, even dictating career directions. A determination to show the world that American music is every bit as good as European music, or that performances of New Music are crucial to our musical life, or that so-and-so, although unknown, is a fine composer destined for fame and deserving a hearing, or that the world, erroneously envisaging Andalusian music as the prototypical "Spanish" music, must be instructed in the output from other regions of Spain—these are illustrations of musical rationales that can properly give direction to much programming done by those artists so galvanized to constructive action.

9. Most conspicuous is the need to match repertoire with the size of the hall. Artists should consider whether songs usually requiring a closer proximity between audience and stage are suitable in a larger hall, and whether, having programmed such intimate songs, it will be necessary to sing with different dynamic levels than those with which this repertoire is usually performed. Good acoustics in a very large hall such as New York's Carnegie Hall, permit more flexibility than in large halls lacking in proper sound-carrying potential. Program building must be moderated accordingly.

10. The recital must be enjoyable. It is an entertainment, however lowbrow that word may appear to some. "Worthy" as an adjective applied to music need not translate to "boring"! As a matter of fact, there will indeed be a demise of the song recital form if newer audiences are not soon convinced that it is, or can be, intellectually, vocally, dramatically, and musically, entertaining. Not every single composition on the program must be the greatest piece ever written. If by so doing the enjoyment of the audience is heightened, matters other than musical worth may take the lead, even as Shakespeare took care to include in his tragedies characters who could provide comic relief. The audience will be grateful to discover that the recital not only enriches them culturally but is an enjoyable and entertaining experience.

11. The dual criteria of an imaginative and successful recital are unity and variety. There is a constant interplay between the two. Like twins, they complement each other and bask in each other's reflection. Still, many pedantic persons wrongly persist in interpreting program variety as a *lack* of unity. "What is important [in a program] is contrast. Always contrast."(Vladimir Horowitz)* Indeed, an artist whose skills are inspired and highly advanced might be able to sustain a musical evening in spite of some lack of programming variety. In short, the more a recital stays within a unified and limited scope, the more skilled a singer must be.

   For the average singer, however, such a procedure presents a real risk. When the group (or program) has automatic variety, it is prudent to search for unity. When the group (or program) has unity, then the concern must be for variety. One at the expense of the other equals boredom, and boredom is the ultimate crime, punishable by a graduating disinterest in song recital. A group of songs by two or more composers can be considered to have variety, but unless care is taken to provide a common focus of interest, it may well lack unity. A "traditional" program has both variety and unity built in. An entire group of Schubert songs has unity, but when badly chosen, may not have variety. The same may be said for a program unified by the exclusive use of, for instance, the poetry of Verlaine.

12. Unless the singer is an expert and the program is meant to be a totally specialized one, he or she will find it expedient to employ a variety of styles (i.e., not all Impressionistic songs), a variety of historical periods (i.e., not all from the Baroque), a variety of languages (i.e., not all in English), a variety within the oeuvre of one composer (i.e., not all frothy Schubert songs about brooks, unless under one opus number), or a variety between familiar and unfamiliar repertoire (i.e., not all "old favorites" by Schumann).

13. Closely related to the subject of song programming is the matter of key colors and key relationships from song to song.

   On the issue of key color there are two philosophical camps among singers. The first theory discredits any consideration of key color as relatively unimportant, its followers believing that much of the subject lies within the realm of personal aesthetics. A concern for the vocally comfortable key and well-defined interpretation are considered more important for the executant, as well may be. A second thesis holds that each song composer, though he or she may differ considerably from other composers in his or her concepts of key color, has nevertheless conceived his or her songs in a special and particular key at the original writing, whether or not this fact has been actually articulated.† Followers of this philosophy are uncompromising in retaining the original key. They choose their songs accordingly and transpose only if absolutely necessary.

   There are two parallel schools of thought in the matter of key relationships between songs. Protagonists of the first recognize the obvious laws of key contrast (i.e., one should not sing four consecutive songs in C major), but they do not involve themselves further in the issue. Vocal comfort and interpretation are their predominant con-

---

* Helen Epstein, "The Grand Eccentric of the Concert Hall," *The New York Times Magazine*, Jan. 8, 1978, p. 15.
† Rimsky-Korsakov interpreted the major keys of C, D, A, F, and F-sharp as white, yellow, rosy, green, and grey-green, respectively, while Scriabin thought of the same keys as red, yellow, green, red, and bright blue. Willi Apel, ed., *Harvard Dictionary of Music* (Cambridge: Belknap Press, 1959).

cerns. Supporters of the second school postulate that in arranging a group of songs for performance one should lay particular stress upon the psychological differences between the keys of each song. They bolster their argument by pointing to the fact that composers have chosen unalterable sequences of keys for certain effects when writing cyclically. Supporters of this view say that key relationships may be remote or close. Close keys of a given tonality are a perfect fifth or fourth, a major or minor third or sixth, or a parallel key (e.g., C major and C minor). All other keys are remotely related (e.g., C major and F-sharp major). Theories like this reasonably assert that choice of keys by composers is not haphazard. Though the subject of key color is largely subjective, key relationship—closeness or remoteness in particular—can act as a valuable guide in an arrangement of songs within a group. If a sharp or abrupt contrast is needed, moving to a remote key in the next song would prove advisable. If a smooth transition or linking quality, such as we find between certain cycle songs, is needed, close keys are in order.

14. The traditional recital has a pre-set, more or less chronological order. Even as a church service bound by a strict liturgy need not rely upon the dramatic instincts of its minister or priest (as opposed to a service unfettered by liturgical order that leaves everything to be determined by the cleric), so does the traditional program possess a tried-and-true format. However, as does the nonliturgal church service, so does the nontraditional or specialized program have a definite possibility for failure, due to the total freedom afforded the program builder.

    The order of an advanced program being absolutely open to discussion, the most efficient organizing factor is the construction of the program's climax. As a play builds, so must a recital build towards a climax. Where and how should the climax occur? Should there be one or two? Shall it be a climax by virtue of being the most exciting, or the must unusual, or the most difficult music? Shall it be placed before or after the intermission? All choices must make the best dramatic sense. The order of the group placement makes or breaks the climactic shape of the program itself. Similarly, each single song must support the intended design of the group.

15. Generally speaking, it is far better that a recital be too short than too long. A good rule of thumb is thirty minutes of actual music in each half, allowing three minutes between groups, one-half to one minute between songs, and a fifteen-minute intermission. This will total one and one-half hours in the hall. However, if by keeping to the traditional time limit you deny logic to the overall idea for your recital or in any way harm its effectiveness, then it is foolish to be so limited. Here is an example: In order to keep within the one hour limit it is not worth omitting the entire twentieth century from a program whose purpose is a chronological survey of music from a given country. On the other hand, the less experienced a singer is, the more care must be taken not to let it run on too long.

    The attention span of today's audience is unfortunately not what it was in the past. Assorted villains, such as television, share the blame. The modern audience is persuaded to enjoy a recital when excessive length is not a characteristic. The artist will be truly gratified to hear after the concert: "I could have listened for another hour!"

16. The amount of research to be done depends upon how well both artists know the repertoire. Suppose that the concert is to take place in Racine, Wisconsin, and that the community has asked to hear some Danish compositions, a field in which neither artist is knowledgeable. In such a case, painstaking research is more of a necessity.

17. Why is it so important to react nonintellectually at this point? To begin with, you have already judged the composer's musical worthiness previously. Now is the time to judge its personal appeal to you. Since you have so much repertoire from which to choose, why perform songs you do not like? Do not allow anyone or anything to persuade you to program a song because you feel you must. The reason is purely selfish—you will never perform really well a song you do not like. And why add this extra burden to your performance concerns? Later on in the program-building procedure you will once again judge intellectually, this time as to whether a song is musically, dramatically, and vocally effective within the group.

18. To be sure, one hopes that the talented and industrious recitalist will perform many recitals. The fortuitous discovery of good song repertoire, even if impractical for one

specific recital, should be noted in the memory, or better, recorded by the artist on a special list kept for future use. In assembling songs for the recital at hand, be aware of other compositions you come across that may be appropriate for future performances.

19. Some points about the song's vocal suitability you may wish to consider are: whether the tessitura and the range are right for you; whether there are any lengthy phrases or dynamic requirements beyond your present control; whether it is better for a male or female voice; whether the pianistic requirements are easily met by the accompanist; and whether the ensemble demands are within your capabilities as a team.

20. Song types include:

    a. The *narrative* song, which tells a story

    b. The *lyric* song, which deals with emotions, atmosphere, sometimes personal responses (revery, contemplation) to aspects of nature

    c. The *character* song, which delineates through the text one or more of the following characteristics of the protagonist: gender, name, personality traits, physical attributes

    d. The *fun* song, which is concerned with humor, frivolity, or nonsense

    e. The *pyrotechnic* song, which primarily reveals the vocal skills of the singer and which may be, but is not necessarily, of musical worth.

Evaluation of the various types of songs is helpful; perhaps you would not wish to program three passionate love songs or three funny songs by the same composer.

21. In most cases it is advisable to form a group of songs from the oeuvre of one composer only. In this way the audience is allowed to settle into the genre of that composer and feel some fuller experience with his or her representative work. Occasionally, however, a composite group has value, provided the idea is not used too often. Countries producing prolific songwriters have all given birth to both major and minor composers. If we dismiss as minor *all* songs by Reynaldo Hahn, we deprive ourselves forever of "Le Rossignol des Lilas." If we dismiss *all* the songs of Georges Bizet, we deprive ourselves forever of "Chanson d'Avril." If we ignore *all* the songs of Ildebrando Pizzetti, we deprive ourselves of "I Pastori," one of the great art songs of the twentieth century. It seems criminal to disdain minor composers who may have produced one or two real "jewels." Their combined output of songs, frequently very beautiful, furnishes a vast repository for programming. Combining a group of songs written by such composers is a perfect method for serving the public a tasty vocal antipasto.

22. All other things being equal, a tie-breaker in the decision-making process can be the actual look of the program. When the program *appears* to be long, unremitting, and therefore taxing or boring, the audience might well believe that it *is* going to tax or bore them. The following two diagrams point up the psychological effect communicated by a program's appearance.

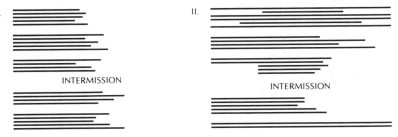

Program I strongly conveys at first glance the idea of a lengthy, wearying list, however interesting the groups may prove during performance.

Were the diagrams filled out with the missing information, the effect would be substantially the same. Program I lacks visual appeal, which may dampen audience enthusiasm at the outset. Under these conditions, you cannot feel confident of their attention; you must, rather, struggle to gain it. The layout of Program II, on the other hand, attracts their eye and piques their interest.

You have gone to great lengths to construct a program which embodies the maximum musical quality and dramatic contrast. The printed program is your calling card. Even before the audience sees *you*, it sees your program. Why put yourself at a disadvantage when you could so easily seize this opportunity to whet their interest by making your musically attractive program *visibly* interesting. You have nothing to lose and everything to gain!

GUIDELINES FOR PRACTICE

1. Put together a program for voice(s) and two pianos. As a headstart we have provided you with eight composers who have written for this combination:

Ned Rorem	Dieter Schönbach
Charles Ives	Frederick Jacobi
Aldo Clementi	René Leibowitz
Donald Lybbert	Giancarlo Malipiero

2. Arrange the plan of a program for a baritone voice with this theme: "One Entire Day from Sunrise to Sunset." Then do the same for your own voice.

3. Devise a program that will include two elements of visual interest.

4. Formulate a program for contralto with the theme of Easter. Then do the same for your own voice.

5. Plan a program of sonnets for a tenor voice. You will find definitions and descriptions for all types of sonnets in *Webster's New International Dictionary*. Here are the names of eight composers who have written songs to sonnets:

Mario Castelnuovo-Tedesco	Douglas Moore
Benjamin Britten	Miriam Gideon
Paul Hindemith	Ildebrando Pizzetti
Henri Sauguet	Ludmilla Ulehla

Now do the same for your own voice category.

6. Put together a program of folk music for a young bass-baritone. Then do the same for your voice.

7. Construct a program for voice with piano and voice with instruments on the theme of spring.

8. Block out a joint program of all-Italian music for two voices with instruments.

9. To illustrate the point that no musical combination is too unlikely or bizarre not to have been adopted by inventive composers, put to-

gether a program for soprano with one (or two) bass viols. It can be done.

10. Build a program of Baroque music for two sopranos with and without accompanying instruments in addition to keyboard.

11. Devise a program using works by women composers, including at least one work for voice and instrument(s). You may draw from the list of contemporary composers in Chapter 11 (Programming). Here is a list of women composers from other eras:

Marion Bauer	Augusta Holmes
Mrs. H. H. A. Beach	Alma Mahler
Antonia Bembo	Fanny Mendelssohn
Carrie Jacobs Bond	Merle Montgomery
Lili Boulanger	Maria Teresa von Paradis
Francesca Caccini	Irene Poldowski
Cécile Chaminade	Margaret Ruthven
Fanny Dillon	Mary Turner Salter
Clara Edwards	Clara Schumann
Elisabeth de la Guerre	Barbara Strozzi

Constructing
3 Sample
Programs

This chapter is based on five representative programs performed by the authors in various cities and countries. To conform to the practical guidelines set forth in the introduction, the discussion of each program is presented as briefly as possible, in a "notes-only" style. These notes accord strictly with the order of the master-outline in Chapter 2. Follow closely the letters and numbers of the outline that give the decisions and choices made for each program discussed. The final decisions made at important stages of the process are highlighted for emphasis. If any of the decisions seem unclear, you may wish to review the explanatory notes following the master outline in Chapter 2 (gray pages).

How the Spanish Program Was Constructed

I. Deciding on the overall theme.

    A. The survey session.

    2. a. This was to be a first appearance in this Spanish-speaking country.

       b. Hispanic composers, Hispanic poets, also local poets and composers.

       c. No limitations—repertoire and language present no problem.

       d. This judged to be ideal time to take advantage of both local preference for Spanish music and the previously assembled Spanish repertoire of both artists.

       e. Must make special effort to search out local contemporary composers in order to cement good relations; also very interesting for both artists to find new works.

AN ALL-SPANISH PROGRAM

I. Songs from the Middle Ages and the Renaissance

Mariam Matrem	Anonymous
Ay trista vida corporal	Anonymous
Puse mis amores	Anonymous
Ardé, corazón, ardé	Luís de Narváez
Pase el agua, Julieta	Anonymous

voice and string quintet   ·

II. Arias from Tonadillas Escenicas

Confiado Jilguerillo (anon.)   Antonio Literes (arr. Nín)
(*Acis y Galatea*)

Alma sintamos (anon.)   Pablo Esteve (arr. Nin)
(*El luto de Garrido por la muerte de la Caramba*)

El jilguerito con pico de oro   Blas de Laserna (arr. Nín)
(anon.) (*Los Amantes Chasqueados*)

III. Zarzuela Arias

Seguidillas del oficial cortejante (anon)   Ventura Galván
(*Vagamundos y ciegos fingidos*)

Canción de cuna   Anonymous
(*El Gurrumino*)

Canción contra las madamitas   Antonio Rosales
gorgoriteadoras (anon.) (*El Recitado*)

voice and string quintet, two flutes

INTERMISSION

IV. Trois Mélodies (Gautier)   Manuel de Falla

Les Colombes
Chinoiserie
Seguidille

Psyché   Manuel de Falla

voice and violin, viola, flute, cello, harp

V. Andalusian Songs

Rima (Bécquer)	Joaquín Turina
Cantares (Campoamor)	
Las Locas por Amor (Campoamor)	

VI. The Twentieth Century

Neu	Frederic Mompou
De Ronda	Joaquín Rodrigo
Una palomita blanca	Joaquín Rodrigo
La Presumida	Amadeo Vives
Canto negro	Xavier Montsalvatge

f. The singer for the entire previous year has been pursuing a reading program on the history of Spanish music, having been made aware of the attractions of this music by one of her associates; she has during this time assembled a large Spanish language repertoire.

g. As a result of the above reading, the singer feels a crusading desire to demonstrate the breadth of Spanish music styles from periods previous to the well-known composers such as Falla and Obradors.

h. Large stage and small auditorium.

Both artists are stimulated by the idea of doing an entire program of Hispanic music. Decision is made to do a comprehensive program of Spanish music, all factors clearly supporting this decision.

3. From a historical point of view, there can be no question as to the worthiness; from a musical point of view, judgments must be made to keep musical level at a high caliber. Because of the colorful and earthy quality of much Spanish music, the enjoyment value is built in.

Since no obstacles suggest themselves, the choice of an all-Spanish program remains intact.

4. a. Because modern Spanish music is based on dance rhythms, urban street music, strong gypsy *cante hondo* materials, recognizable flamenco themes, it is rather exotic-sounding to American ears; by same token Hispanic music from modern period tends to sound "typically Spanish" to us, whereas we easily recognize music with sound of Andalusian region only; therefore, search for variety is central to desire to display all kinds of Spanish music; unity guaranteed in theme idea.

(1) It should be simple to find variety of styles, given the historical scope of the program, but styles other than the familiar Andalusian regional one must be sought.

Search will center upon finding examples of medieval pilgrim's songs, cantares de gesta, various types of secular villancicos from the Renaissance, arias from early mythical-legendary zarzuelas as well as popular zarzuelas, songs from tonadillas escenicas, arias from the modern zarzuela, examples of Italianate writing by Spanish-born composers, displaced Spanish composers, and Hispanic composers from Cuba, Mexico, South and Central America.

(2) The goal is to try to find music from as many periods as possible, especially earlier than modern era.

Composers from medieval and Renaissance periods who might be productive are Del Encina, Escobar, de Bibera, de la Torre, Vasquez, Milán, Valderrábano, Fuenllana, Hidalgo; from the seventeenth and eighteenth centuries, Blas de Castro, Navarro, Marín, Durón, Literes, Esteve, Guerrero, Galván, Blas de Laserna, Rosales; from the modern period, usual names would be Barbieri, Vives, Valverde, Martin y Soler, Breton, Chapí, Albéniz, Pahissa, Mompou, Esplá, Halffter (Rodolfo and Ernesto), Rodrigo, Chavez, Montsalvatge, Surinach, Toldra, Cristobal Halffter.

(3) Nature of program necessitates using only music by Hispanic composers, whether living in Spain or elsewhere.

Decision is made to limit works to those by Hispanic composers but to hope to find works by Spanish composers written in other languages—most likely in French.

(4) Plan is to make a large effort in this category—most especially Falla, Rodrigo, Obradors, Turina.

(5) Relatively few Spanish songs are actually familiar to general audiences, but Andalusian style presents a sense of familiarity; therefore artists plan to program an entire group of songs with strong Andalusian flavor.

(6) Many groups in this program will necessitate care with keys and tempos.

b. Very clear that the order must be chronological so as to best serve the idea.

(2) Program's climax is indigenous to the historical/chronological order of the program: that is, it will come at the very end of the program, preceded by slow build-up.

(3) Program may be longer than average; acceptable within reason in view of need for survey.

B. Research.

1. a. Vast research for composers has already been made by singer.

b. (1) Singer and accompanist have in personal libraries much repertoire from modern Spanish period, sufficient from which to choose one group.

Turina, Obradors, Falla, Granados, Rodrigo, Monsalvatge already in artists' libraries; early music from previously mentioned associate available also, including Narváez, Encina, Vasquez, de la Torre.

(2) Found considerable amount at the library.

The fine Nín arrangements of early zarzuela arias, Bal y Gay and José Subirá's editions of tonadilla arias, songs by Mompou, Vives, Rodrigo; and by Falla: a set of songs written in French and "Psyché," also written in French.

(3) Some early music was ordered from Barcelona; other early materials photostated from music owned by associate; still other early pieces discovered on records by Victoria de los Angeles and tracked down from publishers; Cuban and South American music found on shelves.

II. Exploration.

A. Since all Spanish music previous to the modern period was more or less unknown, much time was spent playing through and listening to earlier repertoire with a special effort toward finding works other than those in the familiar Andalusian style.

B. From the early historical periods, artists try to find the best examples of medieval and Renaissance compositions that ought to include samples of Mozarabic influence and some secular villancicos of different types. From later periods, the search is for the best and most varied examples of representaciones, vocal pieces, arias from all kinds of zarzuelas and tonadillas escenicas, also representative pieces showing the efforts of Spanish composers to write Italian opera. Both artists want to use "Psyché" if at all possible because it uses the French language and instruments other than the piano. Also, they search for the most effective examples of Andalusian music with flamenco, gypsy, and dance elements, having decided to include a short group of these. From contemporary period, artists are searching for Hispanic composers inside and outside of Spain.

3. Group 1:   At the outset, decision is to place the songs in strict chronological order, to the degree that it is possible. "Mariam Matrem" is the earliest song for which music is available. Therefore it must be included. "Ay Trista Vida" is very famous and deserves to be included; also it offers possibility for unaccompanied chant with melismatic passages. Being limited at this time (in terms of what is printed and what photostated copies of music are in their possession) to Renaissance villancicos, the last three songs are chosen for variety. A large group of five songs are chosen in order to try to cover both the medieval and Renaissance eras. Keys and tempos as well as content are taken into consideration when looking for most variety. "Puse mis amores" is fast and humorous and is an example of a villancico picaresco. "Ardé, corazón" is slow, short, very romantic, and a fine example of one setting of many of same poetry (called a "diferencias"). "Pase el agua" is a typical Renaissance danceform with which to end the group. Unity, although threatened by use of two eras in one group, is good due to title of group and careful chronology.

Special research has to be done in order to learn proper pronunciation of the Portuguese-Galician and Catalan languages in which the songs were written and/or pronounced. Artists would like to use old instruments but they are not available. Consequently, since "Psyché" requires strings, flute and harp, it is decided to arrange the songs of Groups 1 and 3 for a combination of these instruments.

Group 2:   Three of the best and most varied arias (in terms of content, tempo and keys) from the Spanish Baroque lyric-drama forms are chosen from Nín's set of arrangements. The group is held to three, since Group 1 is so long. "Alma sintamos," being the only slow and intense aria, naturally falls into the center slot, keys coming out well rather by accident. Unity is in the title.

Group 3:   From an edition of tonadilla arias three of the best are chosen, with due regard to variety of keys and tempos. The lullaby is placed between the two more colorful pieces. Since the instruments are available, they are used here also. Unity is in the title.

Group 4:   "Psyché" is not long enough to stand alone. Since the language is French and Falla's excellent three French songs are unknown to the general public, it is decided to program them as one group. It is fitting that Falla, being the most famous and the most brilliant composer coming from Spain, have a group to himself. Originally, we had in mind to add Falla's "Soneto a Córdoba," a taxing piece for soprano and harp. However, considering the fact that the following group was also vocally taxing and that the concentration span of the audience at this point would be automatically lower, it was decided to finish the group with "Psyché."

Group 5:   This slot was deemed a good place for the typical Andalusian group, which, all being very colorful, made a good contrast with Group 4. Wishing to end with the fastest one, the artists placed "Las Locas por Amor" at the end. The grand passion and rhapsodic quality of "Rima" is a little too similar to "Las Locas por Amor." Therefore, the extended melisma and fioratura—another typical feature of Andalusian music—of "Cantares" is best in the center position. Unity is afforded by one composer and one region of Spain.

Group 6:   Two reasons prompt the use of five songs, a longish group: three of the songs are very short indeed; artists wish to display the work of as many composers as possible. They feel that unity is provided by the use of the title. Wishing to start final group with an extended effect of quiet and gentleness as contrast to the preceding Andalusian group, "De Ronda," "Una Palomita Blanca" and "Neu" should be placed near beginning. "De Ronda" being quiet and childlike, "Palomita" quiet and gently sad, "Neu" quiet and tragic, they choose to use the most intensely quiet song, "Neu," to open the group. "De Ronda" then provides a relief from the tragedy of "Neu" before returning to sadness again in "Palomita." "Canto Negro" with its Cuban rhythms provides the most scintillating and brilliant quality, which will end the group strongly. Therefore, "La Presumida," a character song of great charm, is placed before "Canto Negro."

4. Confined somewhat by the decision to follow chronological order, Group 1 must be medieval and Renaissance; Part II is clearly defined,

and the only decision concerns Groups 2 and 3. Since either can be first, variety is served by placing the piano/voice group between the two instrumentally accompanied groups.

5. Titles provide enough visual interest to mitigate the onus of a rather thick program.

Responses and Results: Did It Work?

This program was altogether a delight to the audience. They enjoyed the colorful, though unfamiliar, material, the new forms, the variety of instruments, the many regional and historical styles, and the familiar, highly charged Andalusian songs. The program notes were accepted with lively interest by the audience and were actually read, in spite of their daring length.

The artists felt at the conclusion that the concert had been too long, but audience members did not concur. They did feel that the time required for changing chairs, stands, and personnel for the various groups had been excessive, but that the organization of the program was good enough to withstand this drawback.

The gown was designed to suggest a classic Spanish look without being a travesty of a Spanish costume. Over a slender, red crepe, sleeveless sheath floated black lace, short and close to the body in front, cape-like and voluminous behind. Thus the colors were "Spanish" while the style was not. A black lace fan was used, sparingly, during the group of tonadilla arias only.

How the Romantic Program Was Constructed

I. Deciding on the overall theme.

  A. The survey session.

   2. a. This program is to be the first recital in new locality.

    b. Local audience surfeited with twentieth-century and pre-Bach music.

    c. No limitations; furthermore, special talents for Romantic repertoire.

    d. At present point in singer's career it seems inadvisable to do a traditional program in this locality where repertoire strengths should be shown.

    e. No possibility for programming music of topical or local interest.

    f. Accompanist has deep interest in Romantic era.

    g. Accompanist feels moral commitment because he believes Romantic era unfairly neglected, especially in this locality.

AN EVENING OF ROMANTIC SONG

I.   Five Songs for Voice and Guitar   Carl Maria von Weber
        Maienblümlein (Eckschläger)
        Heimlicher liebe Pein (Volkslied)
        Lass mich schlummern (Kotzebue)
        Die Zeit (Stoll)
        Mein Schätzerl ist hübsch (Volkslied)

II. Meine Rose (Lenau)   Robert Schumann
     Singet nicht in Trauertönen (Goethe)   Robert Schumann
     Melancholie (traditional Spanish,   Robert Schumann
        trans. Geibel)
     Schneeglöckchen (anon.)   Robert Schumann
     Alte Laute (Kerner)   Robert Schumann

III. Chanson d'Avril (Bouilhet)   Georges Bizet
     Absence (Gautier)   Georges Bizet
     Prends garde! (Barbier)   Charles Gounod
     Boléro (Barbier)   Charles Gounod
                    INTERMISSION

IV. Stornello   Giuseppe Verdi
     Brindisi   Giuseppe Verdi
     Lo Spazzacamin   Giuseppe Verdi

V.   Cigánské Melodie   Opus 55 (Heyduk)   Antonin Dvořák
        Má Píseň Zas
        Kterak Trojhranec Muj Přerozkošně Zvoní
        A Les Je Tichy Kolem Kol
        Když Mne Stará Matka
        Struna Naladěna
        Široké Rukavy A Široké Gaté
        Detje Klec Jestřábu

h. Available recital hall is perfect size for an essentially intimate program.

Choice is made to construct an all-Romantic program. In this case, accompanist's personal interest is the catalyst for the decision.

3. Artists believe Romantic music to be worthy; they wish, in a sense, to crusade for its worthiness. Romantic music represents a welcome change to this audience, hence it will give them enjoyment.

Choice of an all-Romantic music program remains, since its musical worthiness does equate to its enjoyment value.

4. a. A primary problem surfaces; all music is from one era—the Romantic era; variety will be a problem, but unity is guaranteed in choice of theme.

   (1) In order to preserve variety, composers must be chosen from countries other than Germany.

Italy: will be difficult to find composers of Italian songs of Romantic era; Verdi virtually alone.

France: Fauré, Chausson, Duparc, Bizet, Massenet, Gounod are possibilities; decision is made to choose from neglected rather than well-known—Bizet and Gounod.

Germany: possibilities are Wolf, Brahms, Mendelssohn, Schumann, Mahler, Strauss; Schubert is discarded for vocal reasons; Mendelssohn and Wolf are discarded because they have been done recently; Schumann emerges as choice because vocally suitable, beloved by both artists.

   (2) Impossible to have variety of periods.
   (3) Taken care of by (1).
   (4) This considered at II–B–3.
   (5) Restriction to Romantic music only facilitates finding familiar music and necessitates searching out unfamiliar.
   (6) Certain transpositions work favorably for key relationships when decided upon at II–B–3.

Bizet and Gounod basically unfamiliar; Schumann offers both. Verdi is unfamiliar as song composer. What is needed are songs in a nonstandard language. Dvořák's *Gypsy Songs* come as an inspiration. Further benefit is one very familiar song within the cycle: *Songs My Mother Taught Me.*

b. (1) Yes, should be more or less chronological.

Since program will be all-Romantic music, group one must demand less involvement from audience than most Romantic music; therefore earlier music is better. Weber is earliest.

(2) Scheme is fait accompli after Group 1 and the Dvořák is found.

(3) Smaller Verdi group provides balance in full program as well as second half.

B. Research.

1. **a.** Taken care of by knowledge of both artists.

    b. Volumes of music from all composers except von Weber are available.

      (1) Bizet, Verdi, Dvořák already in personal libraries.

      (2) Much Gounod is found in library.

        (a) Found in *Grove's Dictionary* that Weber had written simple songs for voice and guitar.

        (b) Weber guitar songs not on library shelves.

Musical value of songs is trusted in advance. Also, use of an instrument enhances its value as perfect solution to Group 1. (Six-month search for these guitar songs—at the time unpublished—led to Europe, research libraries, second-hand music stores, and friends.

      (3) Much Gounod is found in music stores.

II. Exploration.

  A. Screening.

  B. Final choices.

3. **Group 1:** Solution to group order is one in which maximum variety is achieved within boundaries limited by nature of music: all more or less light and delicate songs.

Group 2: Since Schumann is the quintessential Romantic composer, artists wish to inject an element of variety into his group by ending it with an archetypal Romantic song that should, however, be uncharacteristically soft and sentimental rather than the usual loud and rhapsodic ending. Therefore "Alte Laute" must be placed last. Since both "Meine Rose" and "Melancholie" are intense, they must be separated by "Singet nicht" (needed for variety earlier in the group) and "Schneeglöckchen" (as remaining song falls into slot 4).

Group 3: Artists revel in the fact that the original choices from the Bizet and Gounod repertoires netted two Bizet songs that are unusually calm and lyric, and two Gounod songs that are atypically exotic and rhythmically exciting. Thus the group perforce ends with Gounod. Unity achieved in fact of two major composers.

Group 4: Having recognized that all the Verdi songs chosen are character songs, the artists decide upon a simple musical order: position 1—exciting; position 2—charming; position 3—robust. Unity is assured by facts of one composer and three light character songs.

Group 5:   Order is preset by song cycle form.

4. Seems unquestionable that Weber is still the only proper choice for Group 1. Appears equally obvious that only Dvořák or Verdi can occupy Group 5 slot. Possibility of Verdi filling slot 3 briefly discussed; conclusion: because of the frivolous and salon-like quality of these songs, they are not sufficiently serious in quality to end the first half, or, for that matter, the entire program. Therefore, the totally romantic mood of the Dvořák cycle should end the program. Furthermore, the slightly superficial and gay flavor of the Verdi songs act as a divertissement at the beginning of Part II where needed. Remaining problem: what should follow Weber? In as much as the Schumann group is deliberately arranged with a decrescendo of emotional means, it is deemed best to place it second, thereby highlighting the exotic and bright color of the French group as the best ending for Part I.

5. Although at no time was a change contemplated from the above arrangement, the eye interest afforded the appearance of the program by the indentations of the guitar group and the cycle are very pleasing.

Responses and Results: Did It Work?

In general, all the carefully structured contrasts (serene Weber to sensitive, evocative Schumann, to brilliant French, to piquant Verdi, to lush and exotic Dvořák) worked very well. The audience was delighted by the gentle, lovely Weber songs because of the unexpected ensemble quality given by the sound of the guitar and the German language in these unfamiliar compositions. Verdi, too, was unknown to them as a song composer, and they enjoyed the light quality, but strong personality of these character songs. The reverse climax scheme of the Schumann group was very successful. The "in-joke" embodied in the Bizet-Gounod group was appreciated by musicians and sophisticates, and the songs were enjoyed by others simply for their beauty.

As to the artists' most compelling reason for programming an entire recital of Romantic music, for the most part the community's elite musicians stayed away, seemingly repelled rather than attracted by such literature. Those who did come, however, liked it, and a large crowd of non-professionals did attend, presumably drawn at least partially by the program. Their response, which was overwhelmingly favorable, served to underline one fact. For a long time the profession had regarded performers who dared to specialize in unfairly neglected Romantic music as vaguely disreputable, whereas those who delved deeply into the works of

Gesualdo or Luzzascho Luzzaschi were given enthusiastic and unstinting respect by professional musicians.

Perhaps a year after this decidedly out-of-step program was done for the first time, references to Romanticism as "fashionable" began to be seen in publications such as the Sunday edition of the *New York Times*. The artists felt supported in their beliefs as to the neglected state of Romantic compositions. Raymond Lewenthal, together with several colleagues, held a "Romantic Revival." Their common conviction was that Romantic performance practices were condemned as wild exaggerations without being fully understood. These feelings were bolstered by several media pieces written in the same vein, which pointed out that there were beginning to be vague stirrings in the direction of removing this onus by clarifying some of the legendary romanticisms. Some change of attitude has indeed come to pass, culminating in a most welcome new musicological journal, *Nineteenth-Century Music*, published by the University of California Press at Berkeley, which addresses itself to nineteenth-century performance practice.

Great efforts were made to adopt some cosmetic effects that could dress up the "Romantic Music" idea as much as possible within the bounds of taste. The advertising poster incorporated a period silhouette of a singer and pianist at the piano. The singer's recital gown was unusually elaborate, with a slight bustle effect, a small but wide train, and fur and gold embroidery on sleeves and train—very Romantic. Hair was done in a period style with ringlets on the side; an ornament was added. The accompanist was attired in a tailcoat worn with a ruffled period shirt. The hall was, although intimate, not too small for this picture to be effective.

How the French Program Was Constructed

I. Deciding on the overall theme.

   A. The survey session.

   2. a. Singer has never sung here before, but in this locality many innovative programs of predominantly French music have been presented, since the organization has a deep interest in French culture.

      b. This audience, being thoroughly cultivated, could hardly fail to appreciate an all-French program.

      c. Not only has neither artist any limitations in this repertory, but both feel very strong disposition toward the French repertoire and possess a real proficiency in it; singer's language skills are sufficiently advanced for such a specialized audience and program.

AN EVENING OF FRENCH MELODY

I. Mélodrame, Recitatatif and Air d'Ina   Etienne Méhul
     (from *Ariodant*)

II. Tristesse (Gautier)   Gabriel Fauré
     C'est l'extase (Verlaine)
     L'absent (Hugo)
     Arpège (Samain)

III. Le Papillon et la Fleur   Gabriel Fauré
     Automne (Silvestre)
     Mandoline (Verlaine)
     Notre Amour (Silvestre)

INTERMISSION

IV. *Chansons Madécasses*   Maurice Ravel
     (trad. Madegascan, trans. Parny)
          Nahandove
          Aoua!
          Il est doux de se coucher
               voice, flute, cello, piano

V. Le Chapelier (Chalupt)   Erik Satie
     Trois Chansons (Morax)   Arthur Honegger
          Chanson des Sirènes
          Berceuse de la Sirène
          Chanson de la Poire
     Il était une petite pië (Hirtz)   Georges Auric
     Les pâquerettes (Hirtz)
     La poule noire (Hirtz)
     Les petits ânes (Hirtz)

VI. La Dame de Monte Carlo (Cocteau)   Francis Poulenc

    d. Both artists feel an equal interest in French repertory and consider the challenge to construct an innovative French program to be timely.

    e. Not à propos to program topically or locally.

    f. Accompanist has had life-time ambition to do all-French recital because of love of the language and repertoire.

    g. No moral commitments at this time.

    h. Hall is relatively small, excellent for such a program.

Since there are no valid objections, the choice of an all-French program seems logical.

    3. There can be no doubt as to either the worthiness or the enjoyment ratio of this major repertoire.

    4. a. Unity is provided in overall theme.

       (1) French music offers a wealth of styles.

It becomes obvious that examples of Renaissance, Rococo, and Baroque styles will be simple to find, as well as Romantic, impressionistic, and modern. The problem will likely lie between Rococo and Romantic eras.

Medieval and Renaissance:	Machaut, Couperin
Baroque:	Lully, Campra, Monsigny
Rococo:	Gluck, Méhul
Romantic:	Fauré, Bizet, Massenet, Roussel, Duparc, Saint-Saëns
Impressionistic:	Debussy, Ravel
Twentieth century:	Satie, Honegger, Poulenc, Auric, Messiaen, Sauguet, Ibert, Milhaud, Françaix, Boulez

    (2) Taken care of by (1).

    (3) Impossible to vary languages.

    (4) This problem solved at II–B–3.

    (5) Such a wealth of material negates the problem of familiar and unfamiliar repertoire.

    (6) Fauré seen as only difficulty. At II–B–3 will seek as much variety as possible.

A major effort must be made to search out works by composers other than the familiar Debussy, Ravel, Fauré, Duparc, Poulenc, for example.

    b. (1) No problem with variety when using chronological order.

        (2) It is believed at this time that chronological order will take care of climaxes; see Responses and Results at end of outline.

        (3) Group 5, which looks long on paper, contains very short individual songs; "La Dame de Monte Carlo" is only seven minutes in duration.

B. Research.

1. a. Given both artists' vast knowledge of French repertoire, it seems necessary to research these periods only: Renaissance, Baroque, Rococo, some twentieth century.

    b. All composers easily available.

        (1) Fauré songs (*Madécasses*) and Satie songs are in personal libraries.

        (2) (b) In looking through Baroque repertoire, happen to find Méhul piece that is chosen immediately for obvious suitability, it having a declaimed recitative, a sung recitative, a slow section, and an allegro section for the aria; much additional Honegger, Auric and Poulenc is found; also Satie, Ibert, Françaix.

        (3) Unnecessary to look further.

II. Exploration.

    A. Screening.

    B. Final choices.

    3. Group 1: The Méhul is so large a work that it can be programmed for Group 1 alone.

    Groups 2 and 3: Being stubbornly wedded to the idea of using two groups of Fauré (in order to demonstrate our belief in the versatility of his song-writing), the only solution necessary is variety and juxtaposition of his songs, not necessarily to be done in chronological order of their composition. A decision is made that a chronological order would imperil the cause of showing Fauré's versatility, since the early songs are many of the "um-pa-pa" variety of accompaniment. Decided to build to climax through both groups rather than each single group at one time. Consequently the richest, most exciting, or heaviest songs are saved for Group 2, although variety is sought in each group singly. Song 2 and song 4 in each group chart the controlled crescendo of stimulation. Yet . . . (see Responses and Results at the end of this outline).

    Group 4: Order is predetermined.

    Group 5: The Honegger small cycle, being of a quiet, intimate nature, finds a natural placement in the center of the group. Since each song is fragmentary, the piquant Auric group that is set to children's poems is inappropriate to begin this section. This leaves "Le Chapelier" as a delightful and substantial opener. Unity is provided by the similarity of styles and the fact that all songs are sophisticated children's songs.

Group 6:   A dramatic monologue.

4. Entire program was originally conceived as chronological. Upon reeval-
uation artists decide to keep chronological order. The only problem is
the effective arrangement of music from second half. "Chansons
Madécasses" has to be followed by material demonstrably more, or less,
dramatic. It is deemed better to separate the two extended and heavily
dramatic works by the fragmentary Satie–Honegger–Auric group.

5. The Méhul piece is very effective to the eye, especially since the Fauré
looks dull. The indented Honegger breaks up an otherwise straight line
of eight songs.

Responses and Results: Did It Work?

In general, this program included a good deal of theatricality, which
the audience especially enjoyed. The Méhul spoken mélodrame and "La
Dame de Monte Carlo" in particular were a success; the Chansons Madécasses and the very sophisticated mixed group a little less so. (The artists
realized that much of this had to do with the French culture itself, which
so venerates the French language.) These works were programmed to
compensate for the comparatively static quality of the two groups of
Fauré. Although the second group of Fauré was pleasantly accepted, the
impression received by the artists was that they could have done better.
In retrospect, their blind insistence upon programming two groups of
Fauré may have been a mistake. Each group had its own effective peak,
but as a whole they might have provided a better climax for the entire
program had they researched the period between Rococo and Romantic
for some interesting choices.

"La Dame de Monte Carlo" offered the audience—some of whom
had never witnessed a "dramatic monologue" (Poulenc's subtitle) or
scena before—an interesting and real change of pace. (Audience comments included: "Too bad it is rather short; you could take this on
tour.") Much effort went into theatricalizing the event. To the recital
gown were added some extras to point up the lady's sleaziness—a long
feather boa, excessive and vaguely cheap jewelry. A green felt cloth was
laid on the piano to make an allusion to the gambling tables. At times the
singer related to the accompanist as if he were the croupier. The singer
entered normally and then, clearly and abruptly, assumed the role of "La
Dame." Treading the thin line between opera and recital was accomplished very well, judged by audience response and favorable reviews.

The recital gown was made of cool, elegant, pearly-grey fragile
China silk; sleeves alone were ornamented with individual two-inch cas-
cades of clear crystal beads, which gave a deliberately retreating, undra-

matic but soignée look that bolstered subliminally an impression of "Frenchness." The intentional understatement of the gown was not lost in the hall since the hall was very small and intimate.

How the Twentieth-Century Program Was Constructed

I. Deciding on the overall theme.

    A. The survey session.

        2. a. Previous program was standard; therefore, this should perhaps depart from the traditional.

           b. Large segment of this audience deeply interested in twentieth-century music and New Music.

           c. No restrictions musically speaking for either artist; some vocal limitations due to singer's voice category (lyrico-spinto) since contemporary music is generally better suited to a lyric soprano.

           d. Artists would welcome challenge to exploit their extensive twentieth-century repertoire.

           e. Possibilities for programming works of topical or local interest are few.

           f. Both artists have affinity for New Music.

           g. Commitment exists to show enormous breadth of variety within music of this century by programming specific examples of the best.

           h. Fairly large hall, but acoustics excellent.

Decision is made to construct a twentieth-century program that does not limit itself to 1960s and 1970s contemporary repertoire. Decision based on makeup and special interests of audience for most part.

        3. Interests of this audience focus strongly upon contemporary music. This twentieth-century program will satisfy their musical preferences and give them enjoyment.

Choice of twentieth-century program remains intact because audience's enjoyment of the contemporary music will be matched by exploring worthy music from all seven decades.

        4. a. Unity is guaranteed in overall theme.

           (1) Easy to find.

Can choose from (1) late Romantic feeling held over into twentieth century, (2) nationalistic trends, (3) Oriental and exotic influences, (4) Wagnerian extensions, (5) aleatory compositions, (6) electronic and surrealis-

A TWENTIETH-CENTURY PROGRAM

I.   *1830* (Musset; 1925)   Mario Castelnuovo-Tedesco
     Chanson de Barbarine
     Chanson de Fortunio
     Chanson de Bettine

II. From *Songs of the Passionate Muezzin*   Karol Szymanowski
     (Iwaszkiewicza; 1922)
     Allah Akbar
     O, O, Olio!
     Midí

III. The Rose Family (Robert Frost; 1947)   Elliott Carter
     Meditation (Gertrude Stein; 1964)   Gunther Schuller
     Pagan Saint (Consuelo Cloos; 1960)   Alan Hovhaness
     On the Beach at Fontana (James Joyce; 1964)   Roger Sessions
     Paracelsus (Robert Browning; 1921)   Charles Ives

                        INTERMISSION

IV. Quatre Chants (Jean-Aubry, Chabeneix; 1927)   Jacques Ibert
     Romance
     Mélancolie
     Familière
     Fête Nationale

V.   The Wonderful Widow of Eighteen Springs   John Cage
     (James Joyce; 1961)
                    voice and closed piano
     Forever and Sunsmell (e.e. cummings; 1940)   John Cage
                voice, Chinese gong, and tom-toms

VI. A Tavasz (Bersenyi; 1914)   Zoltán Kodály
     Imhol nyitva én Kebelem (anon.; 17th century)
     Várj meg Madaram (anon.; 17th century)

tic experiments, (7) compositions featuring jazz elements, (8) compositions with folk elements and influences, and (9) immense variety in poetry set by composers.

(2) Variety of historical periods is not applicable.

(3) A variety of languages is very necessary but easy to find.

(4) Variety within the oeuvre of one composer not necessary here.

(5) Small possibility for familiar music.

(6) There should be no problem exploiting tempo and key variety at II–B–3.

Familiar compositions from twentieth century include: some Barber, some Poulenc, Ravel, Debussy, some Ned Rorem, much Britten, Dvořák, Vaughan Williams, Respighi, and Falla.

    b. Chronological order not necessary. Problem of Group 1 remains: audience should not be required to participate emotionally to any high degree this early in the program.

(1) Group 1 must be rather low-key.

Extremely difficult task to begin rather dispassionately in twentieth-century repertoire. Search must be made for group that fits this description. No creative thought is forthcoming. Research will be necessary.

(2) Climaxes must come at end of each half.

Decision made to choose (from two poles of New Music—highly intellectual and highly emotional) to start each half intellectually and finish each half on high emotional plane.

(3) No problem encountered, but there was room in each half for almost any kind of groups as regards length.

  B. Research.

   1. a. On this occasion, advance knowledge is somewhat limited; therefore exploration proceeds along nationalistic divisions.

Italy:	Castelnuovo-Tedesco, Pizzetti, Malipiero, Dallapiccola, Berio
Germany:	Henze, Schoenberg, Křenek, Webern, Stockhausen
France:	Messiaen, Honegger, Auric, Poulenc, Satie, Boulez, Ibert, Francaix, Sauguet
England:	Britten, Musgrave, Birtwhistle, Searle, Berkeley, Davies, Bliss, Tippett
America:	Carter, Ives, Wagenaar, Bacon, Barab, Sessions, Babbitt, Rorem, Schuller, Cage, Chanler, Thomson, Bar-

ber, Copland, Diamond, Weber, Weisgall, Gideon, Dello Joio, Persichetti, Foss, Fine, Hovhaness, Riegger, Cowell, Brant, Crumb, Rochberg, Feldman, Trimble, Flanagan, Pinkham

Other countries: Berg, Bartók, Kricka, Janáček, Kodály, Martinů, Moniuszko, Skalkottas, Szymanowski

    b. (1) From personal libraries: Honegger, Satie, Auric, Ibert, Messiaen, Britten, many Americans plus aforementioned familiar repertoire.

        (2) (a) From reference books found what works existed, then searched them out.

            (b) Found Castelnuovo-Tedesco, Kodály, Szymanowski, Hovhaness, many Americans, Dallapiccola.

        (3) Found contemporary music not on library shelves: Carter, Schuller, Cage, Crumb, Berio, Partch; also out-of-print works in stores specializing in this material.

II. Exploration.

    A. Screening.

    B. Final choices.

    1. Great deal of time spent playing through vast materials of the composers and eliminating some composers from consideration.

1830 of Castelnuovo-Tedesco found rather by accident. All other Italian composers abandoned in favor of Castelnuovo-Tedesco because *1830* judged ideal for Group 1. Judging from vocal, musical, and program demands, Szymanowski and Kodály judged best of nonorthodox composers. Desire to use as many American composers as possible dictates use of composite American group with only one song from each composer. French cycle previously performed falls easily into place. Cage pieces answer need for contemporary music in an aleatory style. All familiar repertoire excised because other values so impressive in their drama and variety that absence of familiar in this case is considered not so important as other factors.

    3. **Group 1:**   *1830* already preset as to order by composer.

       Group 2:   Order preset by composer.

       Group 3:   Choice to use five songs since preceding groups fairly short and there is room for five different composers. "Paracelsus" should be last because it has morally uplifting quality suitable for last song. Also singer has special affection for Ives and would like to end with him as symbol of where it all began. For the other songs there are many possible arrangements. Final decisions based on these facts: extreme difficulty of "Meditation" dictates that it would be better early in the group. "On the Beach" is best separated from "Meditation" in order to serve variety. Of

"Rose Family" and "Pagan Saint," the Carter song is more suitable for first song. There is some lack of unity here, although none of the composers is completely avant-garde and this ties them together. But artists wish to use as many Americans as possible. Keys are arranged for variety.

Group 4:   Order preset by composer.

Group 5:   First Cage piece shorter, slighter, fewer performers involved. Second piece longer, more serious, and augmented by two percussionists. Considered anticlimactic to arrange in reverse order.

Group 6:   Obvious arrangement: middle one slow, desperately sad, and minor key; other two faster tempos, extravagantly lush and basically major. Thus slow minor one put between two faster ones for logical contrast.

4. Obvious that Group 1 must be Castelnuovo-Tedesco. Kodály best for last group because of highly emotional singing required and rich key changes. Of remaining groups, Szymanowski is only possibility for Group 2 since it is one degree higher than Castelnuovo-Tedesco in emotional involvement. Also, Szymanowski is of an exotic nature due to the Oriental themes, style, and keys used. In addition, since the Szymanowski is to be sung in French it is wise to separate the two French groups. French cycle or Cage unsuitable to end Part I, leaving mixed American group only choice to end Part I. French cycle very good to begin Part II, leaving Cage as very good contrast between charming French group and rhapsodic Kodály.

5. Program ideal for visual look; only two groups are listings of separate songs.

With this program order, each group benefits from its juxtaposition to the next. Part I moves to climax in the American group; Part II moves toward climax with Kodály group at the end.

Responses and Results: Did It Work?

Although it was well known that this locality supported New Music of the twentieth century with great enthusiasm, the artists were surprised to learn, too late, that the majority was inimical to John Cage's work. It was then that they regretted once again that there had not been enough time to learn Berio's "Sequenza" as planned. (The singer was not experienced in working within his techniques but interested and determined to acquire the capability. Two months time had been spent in this attempt, but there was simply not enough time to be sufficiently secure for public performance.) Thinking that they had chosen worthy music by an acknowledged master of that genre, and knowing that *all* twentieth-century music is somewhat controversial, even among aficionados, they were nevertheless amazed to see the extent of the reaction against the Cage pieces by the professionals in this locality.

The lay members of the audience clearly liked the percussion effects in the early and late Cage pieces. In the "Widow" the artists chose to use a percussionist for the "piano" part (none of which is played on the keys but with fingertips and knuckles on various parts of the closed keyboard) for two reasons: the accompanist was relieved of a portion of this especially taxing program, and visual variety was heightened.

The audience was pleased that the precaution had been taken to program the Cage pieces between two groups of easier approachability, since the majority of the audience was not dismayed, but, rather, found them a refreshing change. A critic who praised the performance said, "To see Miss Emmons's program is to strike fear into the soul."

The look of the gown was specially fabricated to connote "the twentieth century" with bold strokes visible everywhere in the large hall. A geometric design of bias-cut triangular sections (a triangular version of Mondrian) was executed in a slender gown of crepe, predominantly white, accented by black and shocking pink sections.

How the Cycle Program Was Constructed

I. Deciding on the overall theme.

    A. The survey session.

    2. a. A traditional program had been done by the singer before in this locality.

       b. The booking agent informs us that this city—population 100,000—is highly musical, cultured, willing to accept a program slightly offbeat.

       c. The skills of both artists are advanced.

       d. Both artists are at a point in their experience when they are looking for a new challenge that might well be a different kind of program.

       e. No possibilities for programming works of topical or local interest.

       f. Artists speculated whether this would be the time to do *Frauenliebe und -leben* which they both had wanted to do; singer felt that this work was now completely within her understanding because of personal maturity.

       g. No moral commitments at this time.

       h. Large hall with acoustics good only if piano placed well forward; singer must modify dynamics to a slightly fuller sound.

Decision is made around the pivotal choice of *Frauenliebe* to try to assemble a program totally composed of cycles.

A PROGRAM OF SONG CYCLES

I.   *Three Songs from Ecclesiastes*   Daniel Pinkham
           Vanity of vanities
           Go thy way, eat thy bread with joy
           To everything there is a season

II. *Frauenliebe und -leben* (Chamisso)   Robert Schumann
           Seit ich ihn gesehen
           Er, der Herrlichste von Allen
           Ich kann's nicht fassen, nicht glauben
           Du Ring an meinem Finger
           Helft mir, ihr Schwestern
           Süsser Freund, du blickest
           An meinem Herzen, an meiner Brust
           Nun hast du mir den ersten Schmerz getan

                        INTERMISSION

III. *Le Petit Cours de Morale* (Giraudoux)   Arthur Honegger
           Jeanne
           Adèle
           Cécile
           Irène
           Rosemonde

IV. *Ludions* (Fargue)   Erik Satie
           Air du Rat
           La Grenouille Américaine
           Air du Poête
           Chanson du Chat

V.   *Village Scenes*   Béla Bartók
           Haymaking
           At the Bride's
           Wedding
           Lullabye
           Lad's Dance

3. The enjoyment value will be high due to the unusual format. It only remains to choose cannily for variety. One prerequisite of a cycle recital would obviously be to choose carefully cycles of very high musical caliber. (A single song within a standard recital might very well be chosen in spite of lesser musical worth—perhaps even advantageous because of this—whereas an entire cycle of lower musical merit would clearly not be advisable.)

Choice of cycle program remains intact because all conditions are met.

4. a. Unity guaranteed in theme.

(1) Easy to find but requires some research as to nature of cycle form (see Chapter 13).

Can be chosen from any style after Beethoven's time, up to and including contemporary styles. Since *Frauenliebe* is definitely included in the program, all other cycles chosen must exclude Romantic style.

(2) Highly important to assemble cycles from as many periods as possible.

Possibilities limited by definition of cycle to post-Romantic, modern, and contemporary periods.

(3) Since *Frauenliebe* definitely included, prefer to use other languages than German—Italian, French, Spanish, Czech, Portuguese, Hungarian, English are possibilities.

Composers possible are Debussy, Fauré, Ibert, Ravel, Messiaen, Satie, Roussel, Honegger, Malipiero, Castelnuovo-Tedesco, Respighi, Kodály, Bartók, Britten, Finzi, Vaughan Williams, Turina, Rodrigo, Falla, Dvořák, Rorem, Floyd, Barber, Weber, Weisgall, Cage, Gideon, Musgrave, Blitzstein, Chanler, Griffes, etc.

(4) Not possible to vary within the oeuvre.
(5) *Frauenliebe* represents the familiar, therefore the search should include less familiar repertoire.
(6) Cycle eliminates any problems with variety of tempos and keys.

b. Chronological order not necessary; however, problem of first group remains as always. (Audience should not be required to participate emotionally to any high degree so early in the program.)

(2) With definite presence of *Frauenliebe* on program comes realization that this cycle should be one of the two climaxes.

Extremely difficult task to begin rather dispassionately, given the limitation of choosing from the Romantic era onward and *Frauenliebe* already occupying Romantic and climactic slot. Also decision made that *Frauenliebe* should not be Group 1 since too personal. Search must be made for cycle fitting this description. Research is the answer.

> (3) Deliberate choice to choose two short cycles for keeping length of program in bounds.

B. Research.

1. a. Realizing that other slots could be easily filled from broad personal repertoire of both artists, the larger part of the research concerns slot 1.

By process of elimination, based upon knowledge of musical styles, Italian or English-language composers seem to be most likely to produce right piece.

> b. (1) Many French, British, Spanish cycles known to artists, plus considerable amount of modern American choices.
>
> (2) From library shelves find Italian music by Malipiero and Respighi.

Singer chances to be reading Bartók biography at the time. *Village Scenes* mentioned there seems to be perfect choice for climax of Part II.

> (3) Search is made but nothing found of use.

II. Exploration.

A. Screening meeting.

B. Final choices.

3. Since cycles are already self-contained groups, no individual song choices are necessary; unity is also guaranteed.

4. Slot for cycle 1 is given to Malipiero's *Quattro Sonnetti di Burchiello* so that *Frauenliebe* can end Part I. Bartók has to end Part II. Lightness and extreme brevity of French (*Petit cours de morale* and *Ludions* last fifteen minutes together) is ideal to begin Part II. Thus the program includes the sophistication of French and the peasant-quality of Bartók, but *Frauenliebe* and Malipiero are judged too close in style and effect. Also Malipiero is not as good quality either as music or poetry. Therefore, being unsatisfied with Malipiero as slot 1, both artists are on lookout for a better work. Another singer happens to bring the Pinkham *Songs of the Ecclesiastes* to the accompanist for rehearsal prior to performance. He realizes immediately that this cycle would be ideal to begin the program: (1) religious text offers more formal mood; (2) music is of excellent quality; and (3) length is exactly right.

5. Cycle "look" is excellent.

Responses and Results: Did It Work?

The audience response to each cycle was better, truthfully, than actually expected. The artists were pleased at this compliment to their careful preparations. Special attention had been paid to sustaining the dramatic connection between the songs within each cycle, with an emphasis on the silent time between songs, whose length had to be expertly crafted by both, and executed faithfully by the accompanist.

4 More Sample Programs

A GOETHE LIEDER-ABEND FOR MEZZO-SOPRANO

I. Drei Gesänge   Ludwig van Beethoven
      Wonne der Wehmuth
      Sehnsucht
      Mit einem gemalten Band
  Es war einmal ein König (Faust)

II. Nähe des Geliebten   Franz Schubert
    Gretchen am Spinnrad (Faust)
    Hin und wieder fliegen Pfeile
      (Claudine von Villa Bella)
    An den Mond
    Der Musensohn

INTERMISSION

III. Two Goethe Songs   Paul A. Pisk
      Die Gondel
      Regenbogen

IV. Goethe-Lieder (Westöstliches Divan)   Luigi Dallapiccola
          mezzo-soprano, 3 clarinets

V. Heiss mich nicht reden   Hugo Wolf
    Nur wer die Sehnsucht kennt
    So lasst mich scheinen
    Singet nicht in Trauertönen
    Kennst du das Land (Wilhelm Meister)

A PROGRAM OF ENSEMBLE MUSIC FOR
SOPRANO AND TENOR WITH VARIOUS
INSTRUMENTAL COMBINATIONS

I. Se perfido amore   MarcAntonio Cesti
       soprano and tenor with strings and continuo
     How pleasant is this flowery plain and ground   Henry Purcell
       soprano and tenor with flutes and continuo

II. Die Amerikänerin   Johann Christian Friedrich Bach
       tenor with strings and continuo

III. Anonymous in Love (anon.)   William Walton
         tenor with guitar

IV. String Quartet #2   George Rochberg
         string quartet with soprano

INTERMISSION

V. Jazz-Koloraturen (vocalise)   Boris Blacher
       soprano with alto saxophone and bassoon
     Don't Let that Horse eat that Violin (Ferlinghetti)   Allan Blank
         soprano with violin and bassoon

VI. La Mort du Nombre   Olivier Messiaen
         soprano and tenor with violin and piano
     The Condemned Playground   Miriam Gideon
       (Horace, Milton, Baudelaire)
         soprano and tenor with flute, bassoon, string quartet

VII. Letters from Morocco (Bowles)   Peggy Glanville-Hicks
     tenor with flute, oboe, bassoon, trumpet, percussion, harp, strings

VIII. A Solo Requiem (Shakespeare, Hopkins,   Milton Babbitt
         Meredith, Stamm, Dryden)
             soprano with two pianos

A TRADITIONAL RECITAL PROGRAM

I. Non disperate, no   Alessandro Scarlatti
    (from the cantata *Entro romito speco*)
  Sí, sí, fedel
  Uccidetelo (from the cantata
    Tutto acceso a quei rai)

II. Frühlingslied (Robert)   Felix Mendelssohn
  Bei der Wiege (Klingemann)
  Andres Maienlied (Hexenlied) (Hölty)

III. *Chansons de Bilitis* (Louÿs)   Claude Debussy
    La Flûte de Pan
    La Chevelure
    Le Tombeau des Naïades

INTERMISSION

IV. Five *Epigrammas ironicos e sentimentaes*   Heitor Villa Lobos
  (Carvalho)
      Eis a vida!
      Sonho de uma noite de verão
      Epigramma IV
      Imagem
      Verdade
  Passarinho esta cantando (Mignone)   Francisco Mignone
  Vou-me embora (Guarnieri)   M. Camargo Guarnieri
  Quebra o côco (Galeno)   M. Camargo Guarnieri

V. Three contemporary religious songs
      David Weeps for Absalom   David Diamond
      Crucifixion (12th century Irish)   Samuel Barber
      Alleluia   Ned Rorem

A PROGRAM OF MUSIC BY
WOMEN COMPOSERS

I. 1650–1729
Soccorrete, luci avare	Barbara Strozzi
Amor dormiglione	Barbara Strozzi
La Flamande	Elisabeth Jacquet de la Guerre

II. 1815–1850
Three Romances
Mélodie en imitation de Thomas Moore	Pauline Duchambze
L'Hirondelle et le Prisonnier	Pauline Viardot-Garcia
La mère du matelot	Loïsa Puget

III. 1759–1896
Morgenlied eines armen Mannes	Maria Theresia von Paradis
Verlust (published as No. 10 of Opus 9 by Felix Mendelssohn)	Fanny Mendelssohn
Er ist gekommen in Sturm und Regen (published as No. 2 of Opus 37 by Robert Schumann)	Clara Schumann

INTERMISSION

IV. 1857–1918
L'été	Cécile Chaminade
Les Rêves	
From Les Fleurs de France	Germaine Tailleferre
Rose d'Anjou	
Coquelicot de Guyenne	
From Clairières dans le ciel	Lili Boulanger
Elle était descendue au bas de la prairie	
Deux ancolies	

V. The Twentieth Century
Five Love Songs for soprano and guitar	Thea Musgrave

A JOINT RECITAL FOR
SOPRANO AND BARITONE

I. Pur ti miro, pur ti godo (from *L'Incoronazione di Poppea*)
Claudio Monteverdi
Il giocator sfortunato   Giovanni Clari
soprano and baritone

II. Più m'impiaga quel ciglio (anon.)   Alessandro Scarlatti
Quanto peni, anima mia (anon.)
Siete estinte, o mia speranza (anon.)
Marmi adorati e cari (anon.)
soprano

III. Io mi levai (from *Poesie*   Francesco Santoliquido
Persiane) (Khayam)
O Luna che fa Lume (trad. Tuscan)   Vincenzo Davico
Nebbie (Negri)   Ottorino Respighi
La Ermita di San Simon (folkverse) Mario Castelnuovo-Tedesco
baritone

INTERMISSION

IV. Gott, ach Gott, verlass die Deinen   Johann Sebastian Bach
nimmermehr (from Cantata 79)
soprano and baritone

V. Minnelied (Hölty)   Johannes Brahms
Sonntag (Uhland)
Waldeinsamkeit (Lemcke)
Botschaft (Hafiz, trans. Daumer)
baritone

VI. From *Sieben frühe Lieder*   Alban Berg
Schilflied (Lenau)
Die Nachtigall (Storm)
Sommertage (Hohenberg)
soprano

VII. Trost im Unglück (*Des Knaben Wunderhorn*)   Gustav Mahler
(traditional German, trans. Armin, Brentano)
soprano and baritone

A TRADITIONAL PROGRAM FOR
CONTRALTO WITH STRING QUARTET

| I. | O rendetemi il mio bene (*Amadigi*) | George Frederic Handel |
| | Furibondo spira il vento (*Partenope*) | George Frederic Handel |

II. *Tote Blätter,* Opus 52 (N. Minsky,   Alexander Gretchaninoff
    trans. by von Lagin-Calvocoressi)
        Falling Leaves
        The Whirlwind
        Appeasement
                contralto with string quartet

III. *Quatre Chansons pour voix grave*   Arthur Honegger
        La douceur (Tchobanian)
        Derrière Marcie (Aguet)
        Un grand sommeil (Verlaine)
        La terre (Ronsard)
   Chansons de Négresse (Supervielle)   Darius Milhaud
        Mon histoire
        Abandonnée
        Sans feu ni lieu

INTERMISSION

IV. Stabat Mater   Julia Perry
           contralto with string quartet

V.	Go Tell it on the Mountain	(arr. John Work)
	This Little Light of Mine	(arr. Hall Johnson)
	Give Me Jesus	(arr. Hall Johnson)
	Many Wore Three Links of Chain	(arr. George Walker)

A PROGRAM OF EARLY
TWENTIETH-CENTURY MUSIC

I. From *Das Marienleben* (1923, Rilke)   Paul Hindemith
  Maria Verkündigung
  Geburt Christi
  Vor der Passion
  Pietà
  Stillung Maria mit dem Auferstandenen
  Vor Tode Maria III

II. Le Bachelier de Salamanque (1919, Chalupt) Albert Roussel
  Jazz dans la nuit (1920, Dommange)

  Chasse (1945, Rouart)   Henri Sauget
  Printemps (1936, Rouart)

  Prière Exaucée (1937, Messiaen) Olivier Messiaen

III. Tom Sails Away (1917, Ives)   Charles Ives
  Paracelsus (1912–1921, Browning)
  Cradle Song (1919, Ives)
  On the Counter (1920, Ives)
  Charlie Rutlage (1921, ballad)

INTERMISSION

IV. San Basilio (1912, trad. Greek, Ildebrando Pizzetti
   trans. Tommasèo)
  La Madre al Figlio Lontano (1910, Pàntini)
  Passeggiata (1915, Papini)

V. *Siete Canciones Populares Españolas* (1914) Manuel de Falla
   El Paño Moruno
   Seguidilla Murciana
   Asturiana
   Jota
   Nana
   Canción
   Polo

A SEASONAL CHRISTMAS JOINT RECITAL
FOR SOPRANO AND MEZZO-SOPRANO

I. Three Christmas Anthems   Robert Powell
            soprano and mezzo-soprano duets

II. Bereite dich Zion   *Johann Sebastian Bach*
            (The Christmas Oratorio)
     Jauchzet, frohlocket   *George Philipp Telemann*
            (Christmas Cantata)
     Alleluia   *Antonio Vivaldi*
            (Dux Aeterne)
                        mezzo-soprano

III. Nun wandre Maria (traditional Spanish,   Hugo Wolf
            trans. Geibel)
      Die ihr schwebet (traditional Spanish, trans. Geibel)
      Ach, des Knaben Augen (traditional Spanish, trans. Geibel)
                        soprano

INTERMISSION

IV. Villancicos Españoles   Joaquín Nin
            Villancico Gallego
            Villancico Vasco
            Villancico Castellano
            Villancico Andaluz
                    mezzo-soprano

V. Carols from Southern Appalachian   *(arr. John Jacob Niles)*
        Mountains
                The Seven Joys of Mary
                The Cherry Tree
                Jesus born in Beth'ny
                Jesus the Christ is born
                        soprano

VI. The Spirit of God   Paul Pisk
            soprano and mezzo-soprano duet

A PROGRAM FOR TENOR AND PIANO WITH
CHAMBER ENSEMBLE

I. Ich weiss, dass mein Erlöser lebt   Johann Sebastian Bach
    (Cantata 160)
            tenor with violin, cello, harpsichord

II. Three Sonnets by Petrarch   Franz Liszt
            Pace non trovo
            Benedetto sia, o giorno
            I vidi in terra

INTERMISSION

III. Serenade, Opus 31 (Cotton, Tennyson,   Benjamin Britten
     Blake, Jonson, Keats)
            tenor with horn and string ensemble

A PROGRAM OF TWENTIETH-CENTURY
AMERICAN MUSIC

I.   Into the Garden   Ben Weber
     Lament
     Five Short Adelaide Crapsey Songs

II. *Love Songs of Hafiz* (Hovhaness)   Alan Hovhaness

INTERMISSION

III. *A Net of Fireflies* (17 Haiku poems)   Vincent Persichetti

IV. *Block Songs* (Lomax)   T.J. Anderson
            voice, jack-in-the-box, pitch-pipe, musical busy box

A TRADITIONAL PROGRAM FOR BASS

I. Recitative: Alcandro, lo confesso   Wolfgang Amadeus Mozart
    Aria: Non so donde viene

II. Drei Gesänge von Metastasio, Opus 83   Franz Schubert
    L'incanto degli occhi
    Il traditor deluso
    Il modo di prender moglie

III. *Songs and Dances of Death*   Modest Moussorgsky
    (Golenischef-Kutusof)
        Lullabye
        Serenade
        Trepak
        Commander-in-Chief

INTERMISSION

IV. *Four Ladies* (Pound)   David Diamond
        Agathas
        Young Lady
        Lesbia Illa
        Passing
    Flight for Heaven (Herrick)   Ned Rorem
        To Music to becalm his Fever
        Cherry-ripe
        Upon Julia's Clothes
        To Daisies, not to shut so soon
        Epitaph upon a Child that died
        Another Epitaph
        To the Willow-tree
        Comfort to a Youth that had lost his Love
        To Anthea who may command him Anything

V. Four Welsh folk songs, sung in Welsh
        David the Bard
        Watching the White Wheat
        Lullabye
        Men of Harlech

A PROGRAM OF QUARTETS AND DUETS

I. Vier geistliche Quartetten   Franz Schubert
    quartet and piano

II. Duets: Robert Schumann
    Erste Begegnung (traditional Spanish, trans. Geibel)
    soprano and mezzo
    Intermezzo (traditional Spanish, trans. Geibel)
    tenor and baritone
    Ich bin dein Baum (Rückert)
    baritone and mezzo
    Unterm Fenster (Burns)
    soprano and tenor

III. Caro mio Druck und Schluck   Wolfgang Amadeus Mozart
    (a nonsense quartet)
    quartet and piano

INTERMISSION

IV. Duets: Camille Saint-Saëns
    Enfant, je te donne l'example
    tenor and baritone
    O mon maître et seigneur
    soprano and baritone
    L'amour divin
    mezzo and tenor
    Aime! Eros
    soprano and mezzo

V. Quartets: Gerald Ginsburg
    anyone lived in a pretty how town (cummings)
    Recuerdo (Millay)
    The Great Hunt (Sandburg)

A DUET RECITAL (FOR SOPRANO AND
MEZZO-SOPRANO)

I.	Ho nel petto un cor si forte	Giovanni Pietro Franchi
	Quando lo stral spezzai	Giovanni Päesiello
	La mia Fille	Luigi Cherubini
	Canzonetta II (from *Six Italian Duets*)	Johann Christian Bach
	Canzonetta VI (from *Six Italian Duets*)	Johann Christian Bach
II.	Si l'éclat du diadème (from *Reine de Golconde*)	Pierre Alexandre Monsigny
	Ni jamais, ni toujours (Noctourne)	M. Delieu
	O ciel! dois- je croire mes yeux (from *Le Prisonnier*)	Domenico della Maria
III.	Act I Duet from *Der Rosenkavalier* Marschallin and Octavian	Richard Strauss

INTERMISSION

IV.	Three Duets, Opus IIIA (Rafael) Waldesstille Frühlingsfeier Abendgang	Max Reger
V.	On the Raft (Strombeck)	Charles Wuorinen
	The Door in the Wall (Strombeck)	Charles Wuorinen
	Two Duets by a local composer	
VI.	La Pesca (Metastasio)	Giacchino Rossini
	La Regata Veneziana (Pepoli)	
	Duetto buffo di due gatti	

A SCANDINAVIAN PROGRAM FOR DRAMATIC SOPRANO

THE SCANDINAVIAN EXPERIENCE

I. From Sweden (from *Fredmans Epistlar*)   Carl Michael Bellman
   Hjärtat mig klämmer   (1740–1795)
   Drick ur ditt glas
   Fan i fåtöljerna
   Liksom en herdinna
   Vila vid denna källa!

II. From Sweden (from *Romantiska Visor* Carl Jonas Love Almquist
   ur Törnrosens Bok)   (1793–1866)
   Den lyssnande Maria
   Hjärtats Blomma
   Marias Häpnad

III. From Norway   Edvard Grieg
   Med en Primula Veris   (1843–1907)
   En Digters Bryst
   Fra Monte Pincio
   Eros

INTERMISSION

IV. From Denmark   Carl Nielsen
   Underlige Aftenlufte   (1865–1931)
   Aebleblomst
   Saenk kun dit hoved, du blomst
   Sommersang

V. From Finland   Jan Sibelius
   Till Kvällen   (1865–1957)
   Säv, säv, susa
   Var det en dröm?
   Flickan kom ifrån sin älsklings möte
   Höstkvall

**A PROGRAM OF MUSIC BY BLACK
COMPOSERS FOR SOPRANO,
MEZZO-SOPRANO, AND TENOR WITH
PIANO, CELLO, AND PERCUSSION**

I. *From the Dark Tower*   Dorothy Rudd Moore
   O Black and Unknown Bards (Johnson)
   Southern Mansions (Bontemps)
   Willow Bend and Weep (Johnson)
   Old Black Men (Johnson)
   No Images (Cuney)
   Dream Variation (Hughes)
   For a Poet (Cullen)
   From the Dark Tower (Cullen)
    mezzo-soprano, cello, and piano

INTERMISSION

II. *Heart on the Wall* (Hughes)   Robert Owens
   Heart
   Remembrance
   Havanna Dreams
   Girl
   For Dead Mimes
    soprano, piano

INTERMISSION

III. Sometimes   Olly Wilson
    tenor, tape
 And Death Shall Have No Dominion   Olly Wilson
 Wry Fragments
    tenor, percussion

ANOTHER TRADITIONAL
RECITAL PROGRAM

I. Quoniam tu solus (*Magnificat*)   Antonio Vivaldi
    Quia respexit (*Magnificat*)   Antonio Vivaldi
    Va godendo (*Serse*)   George Frederic Handel
    Alleluia (*Esther*)   George Frederic Handel

II. Six songs from the *Italienisches Liederbuch*   Hugo Wolf
        (traditional Italian, trans. Heyse)
                Gesegnet sei das Grün und wer es trägt
                Mein Liebster singt am Haus im Mondenscheine
                Mein Liebster ist so klein
                Wenn du, mein Liebster, steigst zum Himmel auf
                Du sagst mir, dass ich keine Fürstin sei
                Verschling' das Abgrund meines Liebsten Hütte

III. Chanson Perpétuelle Opus 37 (Cros)   Ernest Chausson
                          INTERMISSION

IV. Varen (Vinje)   Edvard Grieg
    Mens jeg venter (Krag)
    Julens Vuggesang (Langsted)
    Fra Monte Pincio (Björnson)

V. Paganini (*Metamorphoses*) (Vilmorin)   Francis Poulenc
    Il vole (*Fiançailles pour rire*) (Vilmorin)
    Violon (*Fiançailles pour rire*) (Vilmorin)
    Les gars qui vont à la fête
        (*Chansons Villageoises*) (Fombeure)

VI. La Dame de Monte Carlo (A dramatic scene   Francis Poulenc
        for soprano with words by Jean Cocteau)

A BICENTENNIAL PROGRAM OF
AMERICAN MUSIC

I. The Founding Years

I Have a Silent Sorrow (Sheridan)	Alexander Reinagle
Beneath a Weeping Willow Shade (Hopkinson)	Francis Hopkinson
When Icicles Hang by the Wall (Shakespeare)	Benjamin Carr

II. The Sentimentalists

Tyrant Love (MacDowell)	Edward MacDowell
Dearest (Henley)	Sidney Homer
The Poet Sings (LeGallienne)	Wintter Watts
Hymn to the Night (Longfellow)	Louis Campbell-Tipton

INTERMISSION

III. The American Impressionists

Les Silhouettes (Wilde)	John Alden Carpenter
Les Paons (Kahn)	Charles Loeffler
Elfe (Eichendorff)	Charles Griffes
The Rose of the Night (MacLeod)	Charles Griffes

IV. American Folk Songs Arranged by Contemporary Composers

Fare You Well	John Edmunds
Common Bill	Ernst Bacon
Long Time Ago	Aaron Copland
Ching-a-Ring Chaw	Aaron Copland

INTERMISSION

V. The Twentieth Century Classicists

On Death (Clare)	David Diamond
Memory (Blake)	Theodore Chanler
The Dying Nightingale (Young)	Norman dello Joio
hist whist (cummings)	William Bergsma
Wild Swans (Millay)	John Duke

VI. Contemporary

Three Sonnets from *Fatal Interview* by Edna St. Vincent Millay	Miriam Gideon

A JOINT PROGRAM FOR MEZZO-SOPRANO AND PIANO OF THE MUSIC OF TWO COMPOSERS: HAYDN AND LISZT

I.   Canzonettas: Joseph Haydn

        Mermaid's Song (Anne Hunter)
        She Never told her Love (Shakespeare)
        A Pastoral Song (Anne Hunter)
        Sailor's Song

mezzo-soprano

II.   Variations in F minor, Opus 93   Joseph Haydn

piano

III.   Cantata: *Arianna a Naxos*   Joseph Haydn

mezzo-soprano

INTERMISSION

IV.   Songs: Franz Liszt

        Comment disaient-ils (Hugo)
        O quand je dors (Hugo)
        Die Lorelei (Heine)

mezzo-soprano

V.   Années de Pèlerinage (1 Année, Suisse)   Franz Liszt
        Les cloches de Genève
        Orage
        Vallée d'Obermann

piano

GUIDELINES FOR PRACTICE

1. In order to augment the information gleaned from Chapter 3, analyze the programs in this chapter to determine why the groups were arranged in the order in which you find them.

5 The Unique Needs of the Young Artist

When it comes to the total package of voice, musicianship, personality, projection and so on, I cannot think of any recitalist who is her superior.

The Cleveland Plain-Dealer

ESSENTIALS

What follows is a sampling of opinions elicited from colleagues around the country in response to the question: "What do you want from a good recital?"

Primarily an emotional experience, secondarily an intellectual one. Voiceless "artists" usually bore me although of course the degree of voice required does vary according to repertoire.

DONALD READ
Mannes College of Music

A good voice, a good technique, but most of all joy in singing. To be touched and moved.

INGRID SOBOLEWSKA, PRESIDENT
New York Singing Teachers Association

Entertainment, enrichment of mind and ear.

MARTIN KATZ

Presentation of familiar and less well-known music with a pleasing sound in a variety of tempi, moods, and languages, performed with authority, authenticity of style and musical accuracy; interesting personality; some display of virtuosity and imagination.

ANN MATHEWS
Dickinson College

The very best! But at least: a good voice, excellently trained in vocal technique, languages, projection, ease, style.

CATHERINE ASPINALL
Vassar College

In addition to the thrills I have received for diverse and at times unexplained reasons when attending recitals given by Lotte Lehmann, Maggie Teyte, I want an insight into the songs, a personal insight which is "more than singing" and not only voice, but more than mind. It is a combination of music and theater, though not opera.

RICHARD FLUSSER

Good music, performed well.

BETHANY BEARDSLEE

I want a variety of styles, presented in a proper idiomatic fashion or a program devoted to one style or school. I would want to hear an agreeable voice—not necessarily a sensational one—singing with imagination and polish in a variety of repertoire. Finesse and penetration of the text and the music are essential.

WILLIAM GEPHART
Hartford Conservatory
Dalcroze School of Music

Sensitive response to poetry, secure, relaxed, yet with an animated presence, serviceable technique.

LESLIE BENNETT
Ithaca College

Variety, balance, taste. Proper execution as regards language, diction, understanding both text and context. Above all, proper understanding of the works, and *life* in the presentation.

PAUL HARTMAN
Regina Symphony Orchestra,
Saskatchewan, Canada

I would like ideally to be entertained, emotionally moved, and musically and intellectually stimulated.

VALERIE GOODALL
Douglass College

I want poetic dramatization through intensified musical and vocal expression; communication and beautiful singing. In short, *artistry*.

CESARE LONGO
New York University

A voice needless to say, exciting programming, imagination, appearance, and a fine accompanist.

RUTHANN HARRISON
Trenton State College

Enjoyment, variety, education in style, and the opportunity to hear new music as well as earlier music of good taste.

ELIZABETH WRANCHER
Florida Technological University

Not one of these musicians responded with the single phrase "good singing." The quoted critique of Judith Raskin with which the chapter begins is undoubtedly what any singer would term "a wonderful review," because the critic neatly sums up the qualities of a fine recital singer and tells us succinctly that Ms. Raskin's skills embrace them all.

Surely an aspiring recitalist acknowledges that, in order to be deserving of a comparable accolade, he or she must either possess naturally, or acquire through study and experience, this "total package," not just part of it. In surveying the attributes and skills expected of a finished recitalist, however, one's first reaction is to be overwhelmed, perhaps even intimidated, by the length and comprehensiveness of the list: a well-trained voice of some natural beauty, with a wide range of color and the ability to spin long phrases without inordinate effort; secure musicianship accompanied by dedication to the art and a sincere reverence for the composer (often the poet as well); the discernment to make details fit into the musical whole, finesse in vocal, musical, and dramatic execution; insight and imagination permitting deep penetration of music and text; versatility of styles (which Americans, especially, cannot do without); a strong and attractive personality; musical and intellectual flexibility; self-confidence; technical acting skills with which to express personal convictions about the music (sometimes described as projection or communication); an ability to work concomitantly on many levels; and the capacity to seize what has been taught, then to go beyond that, forging it into a personal style and presence.

In some respects such a list is a list of ideals. But not quite unreachable ideals. The list also describes all the attributes of a great singer—of whatever kind, specializing in whatever type of music. Just to *aspire* to these standards of excellence is to live a life of happy artistic dedication. To *live up* to these ideals is to have the power to sway an audience, to thrill them, to give them an unforgettable experience. To go *beyond* these ideals is to accomplish the ultimate as a singer. The joy of performing in command of self, in control of resources, is an artistic satisfaction truly immeasurable.

This immense list of personal and musical disciplines is, happily, not without rewards equal to the labor expended in cultivating them. Those students who do recitals will, as they emerge from the crucible, be able to assess very accurately their musical capacities, perhaps even to the point of deciding that they have no talent for recital. They will lay bare their strengths and weaknesses precisely because recital is an acid test of musical artistry. Recital practitioners will, if they continue, acquire vocal stamina and a sense of how to use their resources—when and why to husband them or lavish them upon the audience.

Even for those directing their careers toward opera, recital performance provides specific as well as general dramatic training. In a recital, the singer must carry the whole show alone. In opera, a singer sooner or later tends to be stereotyped—always an adorable soubrette, or always a ponderous king. Versatility of dramatic skills and breadth of stylistic experience gained from concentrating upon vital details in recital singing is a useful accessory in preparing operatic roles. Cesare Longo of New York University says, "Recitals, in the best artistic sense, add to opera singers' in-depth internalization of their operatic roles."

In his acting classes, Stanislavski himself stressed the efficacy of learning dramatic skills through songs. He required his budding opera singers to learn their acting technique by singing songs because he believed that each song has within it "the seed of a larger work," a plot, a conflict, a solution—a miniature drama. A song, being so short, is packed tight with images, ideas, and sentiments. Learning to find the core of a song sharpens the singer's artistic eye and musicianly sensitivity. When the composer's intent is communicated through the singer's own emotions, the singer becomes a singing actor.

In addition to these general advantages which accrue to the singer from recital work, there are a few specific ones. There is a strong resemblance between the requirements of operatic aria and simple song, not to mention other lyric moments of opera, such as duets. Furthermore, skills learned in recital work convert without exception to auditioning skills. The essentials of singing opera in small houses are also very close to the requisites for recital. Simply from the way an aria is sung during an opera performance, one can often deduce recital experience. Best of all, since the qualifications demanded of a good recital singer are so stringent, he mysteriously but surely acquires through this recital experience a strong platform presence. One might even hope that this personality could develop into the elusive quality—magnetism—often branded as missing from the current crop of singers.

English-speaking, Scandinavian, Spanish, and Russian singers must know a minimum of three non-native languages, and at least as many musical styles, before they are equipped to be recitalists. French, Italians, and Germans, on the other hand, perform recitals almost exclusively in their own language and within that style, venturing only rarely out of their own culture. For this reason, young American singers often feel burdened by the need to learn four sets of language skills and, correspondingly, even more than four musical styles. Feeling hemmed in by all these disciplines, skills, traditions, and rules, it is small wonder that opera appears more attractive to them. Opera, as drama, is easier to understand than poetry. Opera appears easier to perform, supporting as it does the artist with a network of other singers, props, costumes, conductors, and prompters. And most of all, it appears more glamorous!

Overwhelmed by the magnitude of what is to be learned, young singers, under the all-important guidance of their teachers, must be encouraged to believe that, after mastering rules and traditions, they can then use their newly learned competence to experiment within tradition or to transcend it. Why not? Those who know the rules well are best equipped to break them imaginatively and beneficially for us all. Teachers and coaches have the opportunity to convince young artists that immense satisfaction is to be gained by high standards of research and program-building, that a song recital is the equivalent in music of the one-man show in theater,[1] that recital acting requires mastery of communication that is at once intense, sincere, and subtle. Stimulated by such dedicated work with their teachers young singers will begin to rise to the challenge.

PREPARATION AND TRAINING

Young singers are preoccupied with perfecting their musicianship, stabilizing their vocal technique, learning their languages, and immersing themselves in musical styles, to the exclusion of their dramatic skills. Because singers begin their vocal training some ten years later than in-

---

1. The vocal recital finds its spoken equivalent in the monologue, often billed as the "one-man show." A single actor or actress entertains his or her audience with several character sketches, unencumbered by props or scenery. It is a difficult art form, rarely seen today. The brilliant career of the American Ruth Draper, whose five extraordinary recordings of her best monologues remain with us, best exemplifies this art. Cornelia Otis Skinner, Joyce Grenfell, James Whitmore, and Lily Tomlin have followed in her footsteps.

strumental musicians do, they naturally must give precedence to singing lessons once they begin. Soon, however, interpretive demands assume equal importance. Suddenly, students are asked for dramatic techniques with which they are ill-equipped. Suddenly they are vulnerable to criticism as actors.

In the words of Stanislavski, "The creative capacity of an actor and a singer is a science. You have to study, develop it, as you do other forms of science."[2]

We strongly believe in the importance of equal dramatic training for a singer. In the following paragraphs Walt Witcover and Leyna Gabriele (co-founders and directors of Masterworks Laboratory Theater in New York) have graciously allowed us to quote them as we address ourselves to the ramifications of becoming a singing actor.

The recital, despite an audience that, in the twentieth century, has come to want more theater and larger forces in its musical entertainments, has stood still. Only a few exceptional attempts have been made to revitalize the drama of recital. Why, then, have young singers not been motivated in this direction?

> First, of course, is the rarity of both first-rate singing and first-rate acting talent co-existing in the same human being. [Secondly,] the lack of motivation; why should our singers learn or try to act any better when they are hired on their vocal prowess alone? When their uncritical fans loudly applaud and reward inept acting masked by seeming assurance and ringing top notes? Next, singers are conditioned to receive their vocal score complete at the hands of the composer; coaches pass on "correct" interpretations. Therefore the . . . singer assumes that his acting "score" is similarly given and concrete, and only needs coaching to form a "correct" interpretation. Unlike the stage actor, who creates his own melody, pitch, tempo and dynamics of his vocal line in expressing the words of his text, the . . . singer has all of this expression beautifully and meticulously done for him. The proficient stage actor knows that he himself (with the director's guidance) will work out his acting "score" in rehearsal—and that this "score," a sequence of inner and outer concerns, problems and intentions, will be highly personal, fresh in form, and truly his own. . . . Finally, and perhaps most profoundly, is the singer's lack of true acting training.

Why have most singers not pushed for a revitalization of the recital? Without enough real acting training, they cannot even know what more to expect from the form, unless of course they have been so fortunate as to attend the performance of a truly great recitalist.

2. Constantin Stanislavski and Pavel Rumyantsev, *Stanislavski on Opera.* New York: (Theater Arts Books, 1975), p. 31.

Frequently a recital accepted as "good" is—though accomplished and professional in a musical sense—aimless, conventional, and inexpressive dramatically. Recitalists' attitudes toward the art of acting in no way match their musical and vocal standards, which have kept pace with the latest research. Having no real acting tools,

> but determined to act, inexperienced singers substitute conventional planned gestures and facial expressions for true spontaneous feeling . . . or, the singer may truly experience real feelings, but his lack of acting training has given him no channels of his own for its expression. . . . Finally, the singer plays to the house because his entire training and performing experience has been audience-directed. He has been taught to "express," to "project," to "communicate," so he develops an overriding concern for immediate audience response,

Or he gives up at the enormity of the problem and does nothing, which is only slightly better than doing something "hammy." The results of these misconceptions are unfortunate and embarrassing on the recital stage: they rob the artist of the inner truth and concentration that is the hallmark of a great artist.

As important as it is, the understanding of the song's inner life is not the whole story (see Chapter 6, Recreating the Song, and Chapter 10, Text and Subtext). In order to *communicate* this understanding, the singer needs acting technique. The ability to discover the inner score is fed by musical, vocal, and literary maturity, but to *execute* it takes dramatic ability.

> The key word on stage is *spontaneity*. To create that spontaneous moment is the actor's task. His technique, training, and experience teach the actor to recreate each event as something new and fresh. Acting is a constant re-discovery.

To be sure, a well-trained singer may be able to convey passion with his singing voice, and very well, too, but he would have more to give if he were trained to summon it. A singer who has neither flair nor experience can, with acting training, *learn* to create spontaneity on stage. Because the recital is made up of a series of small dramas, the recitalist has an obligation to make each song seem to be born of the moment. This is the essence of artistic spontaneity. The singer is often led, by the surge of the music he sings, by the sensuous sound of his own voice, and by the effort he makes to sing, to believe erroneously that he must be communicating. Moving beyond this barrier to real communication necessitates some schooling.

Young singers often feel a compelling need for high artistic standards to which they can aspire. Rightly so. Yet the problem of avoiding out-and-out imitation of an acclaimed artist's interpretation while at the same time putting together personal criteria for styles of performance and worthy musical practices is a perplexing one. Many singers make it a point to avoid listening to recordings until their ideas about interpretation have been fully formed. Others deliberately listen to every recording available before beginning work on a new piece. Soon after winning a prestigious international piano competition, one young artist defended the latter procedure by declaring that he must hear what other artists have done with music before setting to work on it. He described his philosophy thus: let the music speak for itself. Therefore, he does whatever he has to do to entertain his audience on the highest possible artistic level. Nevertheless, emulating a mature artist's command of style must not be confused with copying his interpretation. Young singers seem to have more of a problem with this than more mature and experienced artists. Perhaps each method should be tried and the results weighed by the student and his teachers.

Methods for vocal training are different than those for acting instruction.

> The training for the singer is almost the antithesis of the actor's training. The singer is trained to place each note in its correct place; the breathing must be precise, the pitch accurate, the rhythm exact. The voice must have the technique to execute the detailed musical demands of the composer. . . . Control is the key word for the singer. . . . But the very controls so needed for singing seem to get in the way of good acting. Ideally a . . . singer ought to be spontaneous in his acting and still be able to maintain necessary vocal control.

It rarely happens that natural singing and acting talents are present in the same person. This capacity for "controlled freedom" cannot be regarded as something that goes hand-in-hand with a singing voice. It is foolhardy to rely on a miracle, rather than real training. Would a singer try to learn to sing, avoiding vocalises throughout the process, and trusting to public performances to teach him his craft?

Where and how does the young singer get acting training? Let us tread on a few toes by stating that the usual workshop is usually not sufficient. This does not reflect on the director's ability, but on the exigencies of time. There is not enough time in the usual workshop class to teach acting skills because the public performance toward which the instruction is heading is so critical. Students and young singers are most apt to find proper acting guidance in the systematic training courses of professional acting schools. The vocal and musical needs of students are served in colleges, but if professional acting training is not available students should take advantage of the resources of the drama department.

How will good acting instruction serve the singer in arenas geared largely to musical and vocal values?

> First, the actor-singer will learn how to prepare his acting instrument as he prepares his vocal instrument; second, he will learn the basic principles of good acting as he learns the basic laws of good singing; and third, he will learn how to perceive and solve for himself the dramatic problems of the music he undertakes. . . . Moreover, this preparation will be both solid and flexible enough to permit him to carry out any interpretation. . . . He will no longer ask such questions as, "What do I do with my hands?" "How do I stand?" "Where do I look?" "What should I think about?" He will have learned to answer them himself or even never to have to ask them.

We believe that this training should initially be carried on separately from singing, beginning with the first intimations of serious interest in a singing career and continued through the time when a singer is capable of managing the two disciplines together. We suggest that in a four-year drama course for singers the freshman year should ideally teach acting techniques and body freedom, not singing; the sophomore year should teach acting in songs only; the junior year should teach acting in arias, duets, and ensemble scenes; and the senior year should find the student capable of anything from opera to full recitals.

One cannot ignore the belief shared by some teachers and coaches that, unless a student is gifted with both talents, it is neither possible nor necessary to combine great acting with great singing. Even Stanislavski suffered from the proponents of pure singing who did their best to prove that a singer with a real voice does not need any training in acting. We believe, as do Mr. Witcover and Ms. Gabriele, that "good acting coming from a totally free and expressive body truly helps the singer to sing better." The subject of dramatic training cannot be left without mentioning body movement and dance classes that are so important to the actor/singer's free and expressive body. (See Chapter 6.)

The artistic demeanor expected of a singer is an elusive combination of dignity and glamor; the same might be said for the singer's physical appearance, social demeanor, and apparel, on stage and off. What the public expects of a singer in terms of social obligations and attitudes is probably best learned from experience or from one's teachers. Personal recital strategies (which are outside of musical, vocal, and dramatic skills) include all the attributes of acknowledging the accompanist, speaking from the platform, dealing with stage fright, and learning correct health habits. Stage presence, that most intangible element of recital conduct, depends not only upon competence but also such individual qualities as flair, ease, and charm. All of these can be learned the hard way, by experience, but the more sensible way is to learn them from your teacher, reinforced by the discussion of recital tactics in Chapter 8. Practice them during the rehearsal-concerts, then improve your command of them by actual performance experience.

These types of learning and preparation are often emphasized by the teacher. While accepting this in theory students often choose to ignore or delay this type of structured preparation either because of lack of judgment as to time priorities, or because of simple youthful overconfidence. Instead of practicing how to bow, students in many instances prefer to extemporize at the concert. Instead of memorizing their programs early in the game and routining them for the sake of security, students often opt for cramming during the last week. Instead of studying the text in depth to identify completely with the emotional content of the song, students frequently choose to "wing it," believing that the audience will provide inspiration. ("When I get in front of an audience, it just comes to me!") Indeed, some of it may, but never as well as it might have, given repetition with guidance.

Such behavior is risky business for a young singer! It is folly to take these professional and procedural matters for granted. Wearing concert attire at least once while rehearsing (and certainly for the rehearsal-concert!) is absolutely necessary, if only to make sure that the stresses and strains of the fit do not interfere with the singing. The easy grace so vaunted by the audience and the critics does not come to one who is struggling for the first time with a new, confining gown or dress shirt.[3]

Entering and leaving the stage are not matters best left to chance. Nor should bowing or acknowledging the accompanist be totally improvised on stage by a young singer. In the absence of recital experience, only practice will give ease and authority, buttressed, of course, by experience and time.

The same can be said for talking from the stage. An easy naturalness seems simple to achieve, but young singers must not rely totally on the inspiration of the moment. Routining these procedures and disciplines repeatedly during rehearsal-concerts will give the same results as learning them in public—but much earlier.

Nervousness can be dealt with at least partially by design. What does not solve the problem is ignoring it, with the hope that experience will solve it. (See Chapter 8 for a fuller discussion of all procedural matters.)

During the rehearsal, it is essential to check the lighting and acoustics. It disturbs one's preconcert equanimity to deal with these details

3. An outside opinion (perhaps even professional help) should be sought when there are any questions relating to questions of dress.

under the stress of the last moments. Looking into spotlights while sing-ing and communicating must be practiced *before* the concert! What exer-cises and how long to vocalize on the day of the concert must be prac-ticed *before* the concert! What exercises and how long to vocalize on the day of the concert must be practiced *before* the recital! Planned encores must be practiced *before* the recital! All elements of the interpretation—truthfulness, motivations, plastics—must be practiced repeatedly *before* the recital!

The natural singer, because of a genuinely superior talent, is probably the personification of youthful overconfidence that leads to optimistic assumptions of infallibility. Yet the record demonstrates that such vocal (or pianistic) facility may prove under nervous stress to be fallible. Lest these exhortations to prepare carefully seem unceasing and doomsaying, we hasten to offer suitable retribution. Youthful overconfidence has its virtues. Audacity, sensory and mental flexibility, courage, alertness, and resiliency, not to mention physical endurance, the ability to learn quick-ly from mistakes, nimble reflexes, energy and enthusiasm, eager accept-ance of challenge—all of these qualities bespeak youth.

PROGRAMMING

The Young Singer

Standards of good programming apply as consistently in young per-sons' recitals as in those of more mature artists. Thanks to the wealth of great song materials in all languages, dull programs can easily be avoided. At the same time, care must be taken not to tax young singers' technical capabilities. It is cruel to expose students to the public when they are not yet qualified.

Teachers of those very young singers who have no knowledge of lan-guages other than English should refrain from crowding them with a wearying weight of study which might possibly negate their enthusiasm for singing. Songs in Italian, a language relatively easy to learn, should be used early in their development since they parallel their vocal growth. Songs in French and German may be added in time, as students, their in-terest sparked by language courses, become capable of assimilating them. During these formative years, songs drawn from such collections as the Weckerlin "Bergerettes," old Italian classics, Elizabethan songs, and English folk songs, are best for the young singer.[4]

4. One of the better collections of songs for young singers is Arthur Ward's *Singing Road* series available for all voices from Carl Fischer.

We do not feel that Schubert Lieder, which are often given to young students, are the best choice for their earliest forays into song literature. To sing a Schubert Lied in a manner befitting its substance demands the ultimate in interpretive ability. Most of Schubert's songs are strophic or at least semistrophic in form, as opposed to the songs of Wolf, for instance, whose texts are vividly and specifically illuminated by the music and whose musical and interpretive markings are abundant and explicit. A personal approach to dramatic accent, rhythmic inventiveness, imaginative dynamics, and dramatic involvement, are just some of the demands required of the singer who performs the music of Schubert. Sung without an insightful and original analysis of the text and music, even this great composer's works are rendered dull. Old Italian arias and songs are traditionally given to young singers precisely because these songs depend for their effect upon the very attributes most likely to be found in a talented young singer—vocal beauty and musicality.

Many great composers have written songs specifically for young singers. They have also composed songs that only coincidentally require fewer skills. Why ignore the easy songs of composers whose vocal music is generally thought of as difficult?[5] When searching for repertoire for young singers, do not assume limitations that may not in fact exist, especially since young singers respond with great enthusiasm to songs by the major composers.

A traditional program is well suited to young artists. Its demands can be regulated. Its fixed format guarantees variety in languages and style. Although another language and another style add to his burden, their presence on a program effectively relieves young singers of another difficult responsibility, that of having unremittingly to maintain audience interest. Young recitalists are simply not ready for a specialized program that demands advanced ability in all disciplines. The traditional program, on the other hand, works to their advantage.

When young singers choose to compile a group of American songs as their last group, they must be careful that it does not become a catch-all of time-worn, overly popular, and often musically poor songs. This practice yields a group fatally without unity. On the contrary, the group should be a miscellany of good songs that ensures a climactic arrangement, variety with unity, and a good fit within the program design.

As a singer matures in years and experience, beginning to realize that she is in every way best suited to one particular musical style within the recital sphere, she may decide to specialize. She may also be in a position because of her ethnic alliances, her association with universities, her so-

---

5. Bach's *Anna Magdalena Notenbuch* is one such example, even though some of the songs included are wrongly attributed to Bach. *Mikrokosmos* (Béla Bartók), which children seldom consider difficult, supplies an example of piano music in this category.

cial background, her national or local origins, or her former travels, to create a good following for her special art. It is then that she may realistically envisage becoming both expert and recognized within her chosen musical sphere. When such a decision toward specializing is made, it is important that the singer accept these three responsibilities: (1) to search out her special audiences; (2) to intensify her intellectual involvement in that special field; and (3) to immerse herself completely in that specialty.

It does not make good sense for a young singer to decide to specialize too early, however. She should sample all performance styles and gain what overall versatility she can. Then she will be equipped with the judgment to assess carefully in what area to specialize, mindful that only in large cities and universities can she find an audience for specialized programs.

Home-made cycles described in Chapter 13 are immensely valuable for young singers. Not only do they introduce the young singer to the performance practices of the song cycle form, but they also challenge his imagination by offering him a chance to invent a cycle idea. Renaissance and Baroque music are equally valuable because these styles engender less emotional involvement than, say, songs from the Romantic era. Ensemble music from whatever period (as described in Chapter 12) benefits the young singer in many ways, such as teaching him how to share performance responsibilities. Most of these benefits could be described as the theatrical possibilities of ensemble music—the larger number of participants, the potentialities for visual techniques (such as lighting), and the integration of more than one art (such as dance). Other types of ensemble music such as joint recitals and duet recitals offer similar challenges to the young singer, such as relating plastically and textually to another singer.

What is the optimum length for a beginner's recital? The oft-quoted cliché, "Leave them wanting more!" is probably more à propos to the young singer than the older one. The young artist need not be in a hurry to construct a monumental program. He has time. Later in his career, having attained greater versatility born of his artistic and vocal maturity, he may expand his musical horizons and risk a longer program. Meanwhile, shorter is better.

The Studio Group Recital

In the opinion of Paul Hartman, former manager of a professional opera company, "young singers are ill-advised on such matters as program-selection, proper research, and presentation approaches, if they are advised at all." How *does* a young singer improve herself in the absorbing but difficult art of the recital? Only an exceptionally foolish teacher would allow a very young singer to perform a complete recital of any kind before years of steady application. Such a climate for development can be found in the studio recital—the place of apprenticeship where a singer begins to learn her craft. Her progress closely watched by her teachers, she learns recital procedures and begins to acquire confidence. Here she experiences for the first time the satisfaction of achievement and the frustration of failure. Here the teacher measures change and takes mental notes of areas that need further work.

The best private teachers and coaches schedule a yearly or semi-yearly student recital, usually in their own studios, to be performed for families and guests. Colleges do the same, utilizing the libraries, the dormitory parlors, the lecture halls, or the auditoriums. Students of one or more voice teachers perform under semiformal conditions. Each performs one, two, or at most a group of songs, depending upon his graded ability. The studio recitals are primarily useful for students in freshman or sophomore terms.

In his junior year, an exceptionally talented student may share a recital program with another student. This may well be their first experience in a formal situation. Colleges generally require voice majors to perform a full solo recital. In any academic year, most serious young singers wisely take advantage of studio recitals whenever they can in order to sharpen their performing confidence.

Programming of the studio recital presents only one problem. Having on hand some twelve to twenty young singers, all of whom have chosen songs independently, unity of any kind is practically impossible to achieve. Many audiences understand this and accept it. Still, principles of good programming should apply whenever possible.[6]

Visual and vocal variety are supplied by the very number of singers. Unity is the problem. The following are offered as unifying themes:

1. A studio group recital devoted to the music of one composer, such as Schubert, or any composer whose work is prolific and diversified

2. A studio group recital devoted to the music of one country, such as Italy, or any country whose song output is extensive

3. A studio group recital devoted to the music of one era, such as the Baroque, or any other era

4. A studio group recital devoted to one or more literary characters who appear in many songs, such as one half devoted to songs about

---

6. In a studio recital a familiar operatic aria is acceptable because its inclusion serves a special purpose; that is, it affords a singer whose operatic studies coincide with his song studies an opportunity to make a trial-run in a public concert.

Mignon (or Gretchen) and one half to songs about Orpheus (or Bacchus), thus serving both male and female voices

5. A studio group recital devoted to religious literature, such as geistliche Lieder by various composers, together with obscure cantata and oratorio arias, or religious songs of any kind, including contemporary versions

6. A studio group recital devoted to groups of songs, each sung by a different performer, each in a differing language or musical style, each group following the same specific design, such as: (song 1) a love song; (song 2) a fun song; (song 3) a narrative song; and (song 4) a character song (the advantage here being the possibility of culminating with a group in like pattern chosen from worthwhile popular songs, for those students who are interested in this literature)

Debut Recital

A debut recital differs somewhat in its requirements from other recital programs for young singers. Each of the two debut recitals that follow will be preceded by some hypothetical data on the singer's background and succeeded by a short analysis of why the program chosen is suited to his or her particular capacities and professional situation. An examination of these two programs and the relevant data leading to program choices will serve to point out the criteria critical to these decisions. In a debut recital, the program should be tailor-made to highlight the talents of the singer while not inviting invidious comparisons with more established artists.

A REASONABLY WELL-ESTABLISHED YOUNG ARTIST

Ann Rodén, a lyric soprano, was the only child of two professional parents, born in a small, East Coast university town that supported many musical activities. She played the flute and sang during high school and college. At a major university she took a graduate degree in musicology, specializing in the Baroque era. Turning not away from musicology but toward singing, she immersed herself in acting training and dancing instruction to complement her already excellent musicianship and superior linguistic talents. She achieved notable success and some reputation in Baroque opera performance before leaving for Europe, where she sang oratorio and opera, principally Strauss roles and contemporary repertoire. She has since returned to America, where her prestige has mounted. Sponsorship by a private individual has made it possible for her to make a New York debut recital. Thirty-two years old, she is married, has no children, has a beautiful, graceful figure and an attractive, strong face that reveals her intelligence and artistic nature. She is elegant, extremely feminine, and has a somewhat cool, patrician personality.

Program Organization for Ann Rodén's Recital

The choices made for the first half of this program made it possible to showcase Ms. Rodén's phenomenal fioratura, superior musicianship, as well as her true dedication to and expertise in Baroque music. The Babbitt composition, showing her grasp of contemporary literature, is wisely placed between the quiet and wistful Ravel that highlights her beautiful command of French and the full-throated Strauss that serves as a powerful ending. The special training for Strauss roles that she received during her operatic sojourn in Germany equips her with a better than average feeling for the Strauss style.

A RECITAL-AWARD PROGRAM

Gary Lethbridge, a tenor, comes from a large family that shares an amateur interest in music. He was born in a small mountain town in New Mexico. He attended the University of Colorado, where he began his real singing and musical training. He later went to San Francisco to continue his studies. During his army duty in peacetime Korea he was fortunate enough to be able to study with a German-trained Korean mezzo-soprano and to travel to Japan, where he also studied. Encouraged by his success in singing Western opera in Korea, on his return to the United States he relocated in New York City, where he promptly won an award entitling him to a New York debut recital. At the age of twenty-six Mr. Lethbridge is handsome, intense, and intellectually curious. He has a natural flair as an actor and is extremely personable, with an easy and eloquent speech. He is determined to achieve success in a singing career.

Program Organization for Gary Lethbridge's Recital

Mr. Lethbridge's intellectual curiosity has equipped him with a fair amount of versatility within the vocal repertoire of someone of his age. He himself searched out the Scarlatti, for which his excellent coloratura makes him especially well-qualified. His French is good and his communicative skills are excellent—hence, the sophisticated Poulenc. The Haiku group is included for several reasons: (1) he has studied the form

**A DEBUT RECITAL FOR A REASONABLY
WELL-ESTABLISHED YOUNG ARTIST**

Ann Rodén
LYRIC SOPRANO

I. Exulta, filia   Claudio Monteverdi
                    soprano and continuo

II. Lucrezia (cantata)   G.F. Handel
                    soprano and continuo
                    INTERMISSION

III. Three Songs   Maurice Ravel
              D'Anne qui me jecta de la Neige (Marot)
              D'Anne jouant de l'Espinette (Marot)
              Manteau de Fleurs (Gravollet)

IV. Phonemena   Milton Babbitt
                    soprano and tape

V. Befreit (Dehmel)   Richard Strauss
        Hat gesagt - bleibt's nicht dabei
            (Des Knaben Wunderhorn)
        Cäcilie (Hart)

A DEBUT RECITAL-AWARD PROGRAM FOR
A YOUNG ARTIST
Gary Lethbridge
TENOR

I. Vinto sono (*La Statira*)   Alessandro Scarlatti
    Mostri dell'Erebo (*La Fede Riconosciuta*)
    Non vi vorrei conoscere (*Griselda*)
    Ergiti, amor (*Scipione nelle Spagne*)

II. Five Blake Songs   Ralph Vaughan Williams
                      tenor and oboe

III. Métamorphoses (Vilmorin)   Francis Poulenc
        Reine des Mouettes
        C'est ainsi que tu es
        Paganini

                    INTERMISSION

IV. Haiku   Robert Fairfax Birch
        Spring:
            First Dream; New Clothes; Rainfall in April; Even
            the Baby; On How to Sing
        Summer:
            What a Cooling Breeze; The Night was Hot; The
            Firefly; A Woman in the Twilight; Moonrise in the
            Eastern Sky
        Autumn:
            Autumn Breezes; Willows Weeping; The Cat; Au-
            tumn Leaf Temple; The Haunted Hut
        Winter:
            Last Night a Snowfall; Crescent Moon; Ah yes,
            Man and Wife; Waiting; Soft Snowflakes

V. I Pastori (D'Annunzio)   Ildebrando Pizzetti
    Passeggiata (Papini)
    San Basilio (traditional Greek, trans. Tommasèo)

in Japan; (2) he frankly wishes to speak just a bit from the platform and (3) he would like to include a section by an American composer. The Haiku are an ideal solution. They represent an uncommon area in which he is unusually well-qualified; they are American compositions; and they afford him an opportunity to use his platform ease and personal charm in a logical and informal moment (even to the explanation of where applause should not interrupt these exceedingly short pieces). The Italian songs are extremely well-fitted vocally to a young tenor, as well as unusual enough not to invite comparisons with other, more experienced singers. Moreover, they are beautiful, worthwhile compositions that are, unfortunately, seldom performed.

SAMPLE PROGRAMS
FOR YOUNG SINGERS

The following recital programs (followed by a commentary) are intended to be helpful in planning programs for young singers of various levels of undergraduate recital experience.

A TRADITIONAL PROGRAM FOR
A YOUNG LYRIC SOPRANO

I. A chi sempre ha da penar   Alessandro Scarlatti
    (from *Esagerazioni d'Envilla*)   (ed. Crussard)
    Ne men per gioco
        soprano with violin, double bass, and piano

II. An Chloë (Jacobi)   Wolfgang Amadeus Mozart
    Als Luise die Briefe ihres ungetreuen Liebhabers
      verbrannte (Baumberg)
    Warnung (anon.)

III. Mandoline (Verlaine)   Gabriel Dupont
    Prends garde! (Barbier)   Charles Gounod
    Psyché (Corneille)   Emile Paladilhe
    Ils étaient trois petits chats blancs (Lorrain)   Gabriel Pierné

INTERMISSION

IV. *Five Poems by Emily Dickinson*   Ernst Bacon
        It's all I have to bring
        So bashful
        Poor little heart
        To make a prairie
        And this of all my hopes

V. From *Chansons d'Auvergne*   Joseph Canteloube
        Baïlèro
        L'aïo dè Rotso
        Brezairola
        Passo pel prat

Responsibility is shared with two instrumentalists in Group 1. The French songs are not excessively demanding. Although the young singer is exposed in familiar repertiore during the Mozart group, she could, if necessary, manage with good singing only.

A TRADITIONAL PROGRAM FOR
A YOUNG MEZZO-SOPRANO

I. Mermaid's Song (Hunter)   Franz Joseph Haydn
    She never told her love (Shakespeare)
    A Pastoral Song (Hunter)
    Fidelity (Hunter)

II. *Due Canti Persiani* Opus 8 (Khayham)   Luigi Cortese
              mezzo-soprano with flute and piano

III. *Zigeunerlieder* Opus 103 (Conrat)   Johannes Brahms
              He, Zigeuner
              Hochgethürmte Rimafluth
              Wisst ihr, wann mein Kindchen
              Lieber Gott, du weisst
              Braune Bursche
              Röslein drei
              Kommt dir manchmal
              Rothe Abendwolken

INTERMISSION

IV. *Antica poesia populare Armena* (Zarian)   Ottorino Respighi
              No, non è morto il figlio trio
              La Mamma è come il pane caldo
              Io sono la madre
              Mattino di luce

V. *Childhood Fables for Grownups*   Irving Fine
              Polaroli
              Tigeroo
              Lenny, the Leopard
              The Frog and the Snake

   The Cortese pieces are unusual and interesting; they also provide a rather unfamiliar ensemble sound—mezzo and flute. The Brahms cycle gives an effect of vocal and dramatic prowess without being as exigent as they sound. The Respighi folklike songs are extremely beautiful but vocally simple.

**A TRADITIONAL PROGRAM FOR
A YOUNG BARITONE**

I. Villancicos from the 15th and 16th centuries
       Dame acogida en tu hato (anon.)   Esteban Daza
                                                (arr. Tarrago)

       Duélete de mí, Señora (anon.)   Miguel de Fuenllana
                                                (arr. Tarrago)

       Tres moriscas m'enamoran   Anonymous
                                               (arr. Lamaña)

       Gentil dama, non se gana (anon.)   Juan Cornago
                                                (arr. Tarrago)

II. *Cinq Mélodies Populaires Grècques*   Maurice Ravel
        (Calvocoressi)
           Le Réveil de la Mariée
           Là-bas vers l'Eglise
           Quel galant
           Chanson des cueilleuses de lentisques
           Tout gai!

III. Silent Noon (Rossetti)   Ralph Vaughan Williams
      Orpheus with his Lute (Shakespeare)
      The Water Mill (Shove)

                        INTERMISSION

IV. Meerfahrt (Heine)   Robert Franz
     Was pocht mein Herz so sehr (Burns)
     Wandl'ich in dem Wald des Abends (Heine)
     Umsonst (Osterwald)
     Die Liebe hat gelogen (Osterwald)

V. *Sea Chanties*   Celius Dougherty
           Rio Grande
           Blow, ye Winds
           Across the Wide Ocean
           Mobile Bay
           Shenandoah

**The early Spanish pieces are used because they are unusual and
because Spanish is a language that is easy to learn and comfortable for
singing. The Franz songs, too often neglected, are useful to beginning
Lieder singers.**

A TRADITIONAL PROGRAM FOR
A YOUNG TENOR

I. I saw my lady weep   John Dowland
    Fine knacks for Ladies
    Flow my tears
    What if I never Speed?

tenor with guitar

II. Geistliche Lieder   Carl Philipp Emanuel Bach
     Morgengesang (Gellert)
     Passionslied (Sturm)
     Der Frühling (Sturm)

III. Chevauchée Cosaque (Alexandre)   Félix Fourdrain
      Les Abeilles (Alexandre)
      Carnaval (Alexandre)

INTERMISSION

IV. L'eco (Poliziano)   GianCarlo Malipiero
     Stornellatrice (Zangarini)   Ottorino Respighi
     Ninna Nanna (traditional)   Mario Castelnuovo-Tedesco
     Riflessi (Santoliquido)   Francesco Santoliquido

V.   Twilight Fancies (Björnson)   Frederick Delius
     The Nightingale (Henley)
     Young Venevil (Björnson)

Not only is it helpful to begin the program with an instrument rather than voice alone, but the guitar sound in the untaxing Dowland songs allows the young tenor voice to be favorably shown in relief. Although all the repertoire used on this program is good for the lyric voice, which weight is typical of the young tenor, variety and interest come from the different dramatic outlook of each style and language.

A TRADITIONAL PROGRAM FOR
A YOUNG LYRIC SOPRANO

I.   Un certo non so che   Antonio Vivaldi
     Chiare onde
     Viene, vieni o mio diletto
     O servi volate

II. Schenk mir deinen goldenen   Arnold Schoenberg
         Kamm (Dehmel)
     Waldsonne (Schlaf)
     Erhebung (Dehmel)

III. Black is the color of my true love's hair   Howard Boatright
     Rose is a rose   Vernon Martin
     One morning in May   Howard Boatright

                    soprano with violin

                    INTERMISSION

IV. From Four Exotic Countries
                 Arabia: Adieux de l'hôtesse arabe (Hugo) George Bizet
                 China: Réponse d'une épousse sage   Albert Roussel
                     (Roché)
                 Greece: Tout gai! (Calvocoressi)   Maurice Ravel
                 Spain: Les Filles de Cadix (Musset)   Leo Delibes

V.   Irish County Songs
                 The Lover's Curse   (County Donegal)
                 I Know My Love   (West Irish)
                 I know where I'm goin'   (County Antrim)
                 When through life unblest we rove   (Old Air)

**This program is essentially traditional. Yet interest is created by the
addition of a Schoenberg group, the inclusion of an ethnic group and a
home-made cycle (From Four Exotic Countries), and the use of an instrument. Romantic to a considerable degree, the Schoenberg songs are
surprisingly undemanding both vocally and musically.**

A TRADITIONAL PROGRAM FOR
A YOUNG BASS-BARITONE

I.	Bois Epais	Jean-Philippe Rameau
	Air de Caron	Jean-Baptiste Lully
	Air de Mars	Jean-Baptiste Lully
II.	Minnelied (Hölty)	Johannes Brahms
	Sapphische Ode (Schmidt)	
	Mein Herz ist schwer (Geibel)	
	Ständchen (Kugler)	
III.	The Ballad of William Sycamore (Benet)	Douglas Moore
	bass-baritone with flute, trombone, and piano	

INTERMISSION

IV.	The Fair Garden (Borodin)	Alexander Borodin
	Snowflakes (Brüssof)	Alexander Gretchaninov
	Oriental Romance (Pushkin)	Alexander Glazunov
	Pilgrim's Song (Tolstoi)	Peter Tchaikovsky
V.	when life is quite through with (cummings)	Marc Blitzstein
	Green Stones (Harper)	Alan Hovhaness
	Two Epitaphs (Herrick)	Ned Rorem
	Epitaph upon a Child that Died	
	Another Epitaph	
	Valentine to Sherwood Anderson (Stein)	William Flanagan
	O When I Was in Love with You (Housman)	Juli Nunlist

The Moore piece offers something unusual after the familiar Brahms. The Russian songs are done in English since it is doubtful that a college-age singer would be accomplished in Russian.

**A JOINT PROGRAM (TENOR AND
BASS-BARITONE) FOR TWO YOUNG ARTISTS**
The Man's Life

I. FAITH
    [From *Saint Paul*]   Felix Mendelssohn
                Now are we ambassadors for Christ
                For so hath the Lord commanded
                            tenor and bass-baritone

II. JOY IN LIFE
                Provenzalisches Lied (Uhland)   Robert Schumann
                Mein schöner Stern (Rückert)
                Hinaus ins Freie (Fallersleben)
                Der Hidalgo (trad. Spanish, trans. Geibel)
                            tenor

III. DEDICATION
                Don Quichotte à Dulcinée (Morand)   Maurice Ravel
                    Chanson Romanesque
                    Chanson Épique
                    Chanson à Boire
                            bass-baritone
                    INTERMISSION

IV. LOVE
                There Is a Lady (anon.)   Norman dello Joio
                Sing Agreeably of Love (Auden)   Daniel Pinkham
                Don Juan Gomez (Coatsworth)   Richard Hageman
                            tenor

V. FUN AND ADVENTURE
                Colorado Trail   Celius Dougherty
                Blow Ye Winds
                The Golden Willow Tree   Aaron Copland
                I Bought Me a Cat
                            bass-baritone

VI. ROVERS ON LAND AND SEA
                Les Gendarmes   Jacques Offenbach
                I Pescatori   Gioachino Rossini
                            tenor and bass-baritone

Although music for this program is drawn mostly from the Romantic or neo-Romantic styles, interest and variety are achieved by the sound of two male voices singly and in duets, and by the use of group titles. The Rossini duet can easily be transposed into any comfortable key, should it prove a bit high for a young tenor.

A DUET PROGRAM (MEZZO-SOPRANO AND BARITONE) FOR TWO YOUNG ARTISTS

I. Herr, ich hoffe darauf   Heinrich Schütz
    Musette   François Couperin
    Capriccio   Antonio Lotti

II. Sound the Trumpet (*Ode for the Birthday*   Henry Purcell
    of Queen Anne, 1694)
    My dearest, my fairest (*Pausanias*)
    No. Resistance is but Vain (*The Maiden's Last Prayer*)
    Shepherd, leave decoying (*King Arthur*)

III. Heimat gedanken   Peter Cornelius
     Ich und dir
     Der beste Liebesbrief

INTERMISSION

IV. Ich wollt', mein Lieb'   Felix Mendelssohn
    Gruss
    Abendlied
    Lied aus Ruy Blas
    Herbstlied

V. Two Old Irish Airs   Norman Peterkin
    Pastorale
    Soontree

Group 1 is unified by the use of one early duet from each of three countries. The Purcell group furnishes an emotional change of pace. Two German groups are separated by an intermission. The final group provides duets on the light side and a second group in English.

GUIDELINES FOR PRACTICE

1. A church group in your home town has asked you to give a recital after your college graduation. Write your publicity biography for this occasion.

2. Arrange a student recital program for three undergraduate-age singers—soprano, mezzo, baritone—that opens and ends with a group of trios and includes a group of solos for each singer.

3. From the programs given above, choose a program that is either suitable for your voice or simply interesting to you. Write appropriate program notes for it.

4. Even if you dislike the idea of speaking from the platform, you may well one day find it necessary to do it. Choose from the programs in this chapter a group that lends itself for any reason to speaking. Prepare remarks containing information you wish to communicate. Create a clever, interesting, or charming way of conveying the facts that fits and reveals your personality. Make an outline of your remarks on file cards. Standing in your room (sitting will not do), practice *aloud* improvising on these notes. Soon, after some trials and many errors, this improvisation will take on a pattern that satisfies in its effectiveness. Using information from your voice teacher or speech teacher (a speech course is highly recommended), practice in a larger room. Make your voice project to someone present. (For a real recital preparation from this point on, in each rehearsal routine your spoken words at the proper place with your accompanist.)

6 The Singing Actor

RECREATING THE SONG

There was a time when a singer was not necessarily expected to be an actor, but this is no longer acceptable. A singer must be at once a musician, a singer, an actor (an interpreter, or a communicator, if you will). Music is an art that exists in time, an art that is always expressed in the present. A listener cannot, as can a viewer of a piece of sculpture, pause to converse, then come back to attentiveness later. Since written music exists only as a sort of blueprint, there must be a third person to re-create what happens between the composer and the listener. That person is you, the performer. Music, a circular art, begins with those who compose it and ends with those who receive it. As the performer, the intermediary, you must be skillful, creative, and perceptive. The renowned director Felsenstein defined this philosophy during a lecture in 1963: ". . . . everyone taking part in a performance is concerned with something so unspeakably significant and moving that he can communicate in no fashion other than by singing."[1]

We define the word "re-creator" used in reference to a singer as one who communicates what he or she believes is the essence of the music's meaning in such a way as if creating the song spontaneously at the moment of performance.

Any great performance is unique. To make this happen, the singer, like a musically sensitive detective, must ferret out the composer's per-

1. "Putting the Human Being Back in Opera," *New York Times*, October 26, 1975.

sonal feelings toward the chosen text and the musical means chosen to set it. The recital singer must be conversant with various motives that have guided the composition of songs. Let us mention a few opposing philosophies.

1. In the sixteenth century madrigal, the sound commonly reflected the word. William Byrd wrote that "there is a certain hidden power in thoughts underlying words themselves. As one meditates on words and constantly considers them, right notes suggest themselves spontaneously."

2. Brahms constructed his melodies so that they would somehow represent the number of metrical feet in the poem.

3. César Franck believed that form and treatment should come out of the thematic material only.

4. The Germanic tradition takes the position that the artist communicates ideas by means of aesthetic measures that reflect his inner emotions and sensations.

5. Impressionism asserts that it tries to render impersonally and with a minimum of infused thought the immediate sense impression of the composer.

6. Schoenberg eschewed the "primitive imitation" betokened by the "outward correspondence" between text and music, taking his inspiration from the "inward correspondence" that he found in the sound of the text's first words—the idea behind the poem.

7. Moussorgsky declared the task of music to be a musical sound-reproduction of not only the mood of passion, but also the mood of human speech.

8. Wagner drained the values of dramatic speech into an abstract symbol, the leitmotif.

9. Debussy felt that music began where words were impotent, that music expressed the "inexpressible."

10. Appearing to take his inspiration from the text and its inner meaning, Hugo Wolf fused words and accompaniment into a single experience.

11. Stravinsky warned that music only *seemed* to express something, but that in actuality it expressed only the present musical moment.

12. Christian Wolff feels that music must be a "collaboration and transforming activity" turning "performer into composer into listener into composer into performer."[2]

13. Chou Wen-Chung finds single tones "endowed by nature with their own attributes and expressive potential.'[3]

2. *Peters Catalogue of Contemporary Music*, p. 106.
3. Ibid., p. 23.

That which separates the task of an instrumental re-creator from that of a vocal recreator is the existence of a text. Although the influence of the text on the composer may well have been one of degree, as noted above, it is virtually impossible for him to have been totally uninfluenced by his text. Alfred de Musset, the great French Romantic poet, declared: "In the best verse of a true poet there is always two or three times more than what is actually said; it is up to the reader[4] to supply the remainder according to his ideas, his drive, and his tastes."

A singer's attitude toward words must therefore vary widely with epochs, styles, and composers' intentions. Theories of interpretation—how much and what kind—must be linked to the type of text employed and the composer's philosophy commanding his methods. Thus the singer's first task is to pinpoint exactly the composer's text-setting intentions. Oriented, he can then make the necessary and proper demands upon himself as a singing actor.

Historically, the traditional procedures of text-setting never really obviated a singer's emotional involvement, just varied the degree. When compositional and poetic concepts changed radically in the twentieth century, however, such techniques as tone painting, vocal ornamentation to illuminate certain words, musical expression of the subtext, musical personality expressions, and programmatic representations of the actual and subtext gave way to various sorts of nonverbal meanings. (For a fuller discussion of all text-setting techniques, including twentieth-century methods as they relate to interpretation, see Chapter 11.

For practical purposes, this chapter will only discuss techniques serving repertoire written mainly with traditional text-setting devices, where verbal meaning or connotation is central to the composition. The most important reason for limiting our discussion to music where interpretation is fitting rests upon our conviction that the singer cannot function well as an interpreter without emotional commitment. Therefore, we will focus on how to plumb your own interpretational depths and those of the text and the music.[5]

The text presents at once the greatest glory for and the heaviest burden on the singer. Every vocal technical decision to be made must be filtered through the demands of the text. This is the singer's responsibility to the poet. *The singer must communicate to the audience what he believes the composer believed the poet meant.* (And he must come to a clear understanding of what means the composer adopted to illuminate

---

4. Here, substitute "composer" and then "singer."
5. We make no effort in this chapter to identify subtle but critical differences between interpretive demands exacted by, let us say, Baroque and Romantic styles. (These come better in person from the vocal coach.) This is not to deny that these demands must mesh with dramatic techniques in the final performance.

this meaning as he saw it.) To do this the singer must solve the literary meaning of the words and then relate them to the music. A singer is touched by a poem only if he truly comprehends the poet's unique experience described in that poem. If his understanding of the words, their inflection and their nuance conflicts with the musical means selected by the composer, the singer must find a new solution. In addition, the text involves the singer with languages other than his own, with diction, pronounciation, nuance, and with relating his actual life-experience to a literary or poetic medium. In view of this, is it any wonder that singers differ so much from one another in their composite skills?

The text provides impressive advantages, too. First, an empathy with the audience is easily and quickly created, since the words provide a clear common ground. Second, the range of possible meanings being somewhat circumscribed by a text, the music becomes more easily intelligible to an audience. It takes considerably longer for a French horn soloist, for example, to build a rapport with his audience, but the possible meanings of his music are limitless.

Of the three kinds of vocal performance—opera, oratorio, and recital, mastery of which is sought by the well-rounded singer—the last is the most complex due to its wide range of musical styles and their possible expositions.

THE SONG AS A MICROCOSM
OF DRAMA

Believing that a song is a "microcosm of drama," Stanislavski insisted that students who would be opera singers begin their dramatic studies with songs. Many contemporary singers accept the dictum that an operatic singer must obviously be an actor but that "acting" is a dirty word where songs are concerned, "interpretation" somehow being accepted as a more noble description. This stand is based upon such admittedly incontrovertible statements as "the body will reveal what is on the mind." While we agree in principle, let us point out that the mind must first understand and the body must first be freed in order to reveal. Such technique is not a natural gift. Real acting training equips a singer to be able to search out the inner meanings of the text and to communicate these meanings to the audience. Why must one be an actor when performing songs? Because there are words.

Consider for a moment that in the course of a normal recital, a singer is as many people as there are songs on that program. The object of this "acting" exercise is to communicate a two- or three-minute slice of the life of a particular human being in a certain mood atmosphere. Put another way, during the moments of the song the singer must be a specific human being in a specific mood, expressing specific thoughts. If that specific person can be seen to possess traits in common with the singer himself, then, as any actor knows, the job is far easier. All of the song's particulars are perceived by the singer through the clues provided by the music and text of the song. In short, he must seek out the human being! (For a thorough discussion of how to elicit, identify, and weigh the importance of these clues to the subtext, see Chapter 10.) This perception, together with the ability to communicate it to an audience, roughly equates to the elusive quality described as "artistry."

As we have seen, Stanislavski believed that all songs, no matter how brief, contain the seed of a larger work. In every song is to be found a plot, a conflict, a solution, and an undeviating line of action, plus certain given circumstances, all leading to a "super-objective." Each singer-actor aims to gain the right understanding of the inner circumstances and to know how to choose the right colors—vocal, musical, verbal—in which to reproduce them.

A narrative song is perhaps the easiest type of composition to cope with. It requires that you determine who you are, to whom the story is being told, and that you tell the story as that narrator. In a character song, to penetrate the meaning of the verses is comparatively simpler. The part one is playing and the emotions one is expressing are usually rather obvious. (A warning: playing a stereotype will not suffice as a solution!) The lyric song proves the most difficult to "unriddle" (a word coined by Stanislavski). Whereas a clear picture of who you are is rarely provided, the mood and the message are more apparent. To make such a song your own requires the utmost imaginative insight, clues to which are supplied by sensitivity to the words and music. Special attention ought to be paid to the dramatic exigencies of strophic songs. Each verse must be examined for the special characteristics that differentiate it from the others.

Spontaneity and Planning

The skill with which to communicate this essential core to your audience is, however, quite another matter. Most singers untrained in drama have ample means to convey drama with their voices. But lacking dramatic tools they fall back upon substituting planned gestures and facial expressions for true spontaneous feeling, or they cannot find the channels for the true feelings they are experiencing during performance. The very controls required of trained singers make twice as difficult the spontaneity so avidly sought. Very few talented singers are born with an equal talent for drama. For those who lack a singularly rich dramatic talent or musical/literary perception, real acting training is the only way for them to truly overcome these limitations. The goal of simplicity and honesty espoused by conscientious actor-singers is just not *given* to all who acknowledge the objective.

Stage director Frank Corsaro bids us to examine the history of famous singers. More than half of them were not paragons of flawless vocal excellence; they took vocal risks in order to suggest personal involvement with their songs. This is not to intimate that a flawed vocal instrument is necessary to communicative resources, but rather that perfect singing is only one part of what an audience prizes. In order to escape being merely half a singer, vocal skills must share the honors with the "human being housing (the musician)."[6] A pity that neither Stanislavski nor the great singing actresses such as Mary Garden wrote down somewhere a description of their innovative techniques for relating the actor's art to the art of music. Such a manual could compete for attention against the singer's other hallowed reference books—mostly vocal methods and anecdotes of backstage trickery.

A pitched battle is sometimes fought by singers over the issue of how much of the song's interpretation should be prepared and how much room should be left for spontaneity on the occasion of performance. Actually, the experienced singer knows that there is little to argue. To leave the interpretation in the lap of the gods, waiting for the audience to "inspire" you, is courting artistic disaster. We must not fear that by acknowledging the place of reason and effort in the artist's work we divorce that work from artistry. A totally unprepared moment before an audience inspires only frantic thoughts such as "I ought to be doing something!" An artist can ill afford such indulgence. In our opinion, to plan or not to plan is not the question, but *how much* and *how to prepare* is well worth discussing.

One might profitably pause here to relate the discussion about spontaneity to a favorite thought of Stanislavski's, that a singer is more fortunate than an actor. The composer provides him with the rhythm of his inner emotions. Actors must create this for themselves out of a vacuum. The singing actor listens to the inner rhythm of his song and makes it his own. The written word is the author's theme, but the music is the emotional experience of that theme.

The crucial difference, therefore, whence springs the actor-singer's dilemma, is the very fact that, unlike the nonsinging actor who can create his own flexible time and space, the singer's far more complex chain of command insists that musical correctness govern dramatic truth. Even

6. Frank Corsaro, *Maverick* (New York: The Vanguard Press, 1978) pp. 95–97.

if one admits that in the vocal arts a proper balance should give equal importance to music and drama, the implementation of this philosophy requires new investigation and stringent training.

Viewed from this vantage point it seems ridiculous to assume that total spontaneity alone would ever tap the essence of a song. On the other hand, having done your preparatory analysis correctly and thoughtfully, and having uncovered the complex subscore of a song, you are then free to polish it, to render it more beautiful and lustrous. In short, take care to develop the sharp eye of an artist and the sensitivity of a poet–musician; then you will be able to go unerringly to the core of your song.

The Iceberg Theory

Part of the renowned Stanislavski Method embraces what is sometimes known as the iceberg analogy. An iceberg has roughly seven-ninths of its mass under the water and two-ninths above the waves. Yet, when one regards the small chunk of iceberg, why the feeling of imminent danger? Because the visible part does not move lightly in the water as an object of such small size ought to move. The viewer senses the danger and infers the existence of the hidden seven-ninths. Applying this iceberg analogy in reference to a song, two-ninths of a song's meaning is clearly presented to an audience by virtue of the words and the music. In an opera, the inferred seven-ninths portion of the meaning is perceived by the audience in the way the singer moves in costume among the props and relates to the other characters. In a song recital, the weight of this hidden seven-ninths is sensed rather than seen. Yet the audience will know when the interpretation has depth even though they may not be sure why they know it.

Let us take, for example, the part of a young girl in an opera. Her youth is visible to the audience by the costume she wears, how the other characters treat her, how she walks, "pieces of business" given her by the director, even though the words of the libretto may not describe her as young. In a recital, even if a particular song is intended to appear as if sung by a young girl, none of the above methods are permissible within the recital tradition. Rather, you must rely on your own acting skills: you must *know* that you are young; you must *feel* young; you must *sing* as a young person. The audience may not be able to identify with any precise or realistic evidence that you are young, but it will be transmitted to them in that mysterious way born of your interior conviction. Here again is the hidden seven-ninths of the iceberg.

Thus, an essential part of your dramatic preparation is to delve deeply into all possible ramifications of the character and mood of your song. It matters not a bit whether all this will *show* to the audience. *You* will know it and your interpretation will undergo a major change because you do know it. What you express (within the circumscribed tradition of recital) will be true and sincere. With this groundwork you can truly trust in yourself and your spontaneous reactions.

With regard to preparation, you must learn from experience to use your interpretive self *under discipline*. Sooner or later you will push your emotions all the way to real tears, discovering too late that you must tread the very delicate line between being uninvolved and being too involved. Mastery of your personal emotions must be carefully gauged in this preparation time so that you can be emotionally truthful but at the same time able to function. Virtuosity in the handling of your emotions is required. Entering into verses so completely that you begin to weep implies hysteria, not art, says Stanislavski. The creative capacity of a singer is a science. It requires study and development. Controlled "uncontrol" must take its place alongside public "privacy" and "artless" art.

TECHNIQUES

In a song recital, when entering and departing the stage, and while accepting applause you are yourself, but while you are singing you are whoever the song calls upon you to be. When you play La Traviata, you are Violetta throughout the performance, but you may be twenty-four different people in the course of a recital program. Your goal is to take the audience with you—without benefit of scenery, sets, props, costumes—to that specific fantasy land belonging to each new character.

What actor's techniques are available to you as a concert singer? Your palette of actor's skills is very small, more limited at some times than others, and always dependent upon the particular musical style. Those actors' skills include the eyes and face, which should always be communicating; gesture, which is often not suitable; and body movement, which should be used very discreetly until later in the program, when informality increases.

One can see that economy of means is highly important. In a way, dramatic techniques in recital and opera are as different as they are between movie acting and stage acting; that is, one lifted eyebrow is immensely effective in a movie closeup but does not project with the same force from a stage. Dramatic means in recital work must not be used in a profligate and wasteful way. Subtlety is not merely tasteful; it is indigenous to the recital style.

The concepts of subtlety and economy, however, too often translate into repression and constraint, which are but one step from inhibition. The following suggestion will allow you to commence your in-depth interpretive work on a broader, and therefore freer, scale. Practice the song as a dramatic scene at first. Use props, even a costume of sorts. Move about freely. When satisfied with this scena, reduce its size. Stand only in the piano curve and allow the experience of the larger scena to influence your interpretation, now considerably more subtle.

Before proceeding to survey specific techniques, we remind the singer that the voice must always come first. Nevertheless, the blame for the occasional failure of song recital can be attributed partially to bad communication with the audience. Our methods are not meant to be a substitute for good singing; they are designed only to "prime the pump," to stimulate the flow of your own imagination. The following discussion of dramatic means is not intended to encourage the American singing population to execute the same body movement on the same specific bar of the same specific song. On the contrary, each example is merely an attempt to demonstrate precisely one *possible* use of the various actor's tools and to motivate the young singer's imagination to further self-directing use of these tools. Yet, we say again, these tools employed mechanically in an empty, mannered show will accomplish nothing. They can only articulate a personal dramatic truth and sincerity already arrived at by hard work. (See Chapter 10 for a more detailed discussion of text and subtext.) When this basic work has been done faithfully, the body *will* reflect what is on the mind, as proponents of "natural" singing rightly insist. However, the personality will be highlighted only when artistic development and acting technique have released it.

Since the body *is* his instrument, it behooves the singer to make it as responsive as possible. One of the methods used for this purpose is the acclaimed Alexander Technique, followed by such greats as George Bernard Shaw, Aldous Huxley, and John Dewey. American actors' training organizations today use F. Mathias Alexander's discipline to achieve head-neck-torso alignment, which gives physical freedom, which in turn gives psychological freedom. Since singers, perhaps more than actors, urgently need physical freedom as well as psychological freedom, it seems very foolish for them to resist such necessary training.

The Alexander Techniques embrace the following basic vocal principles:

1. the relaxation of all unnecessary tensions
2. attention to posture
3. breathing
4. establishment of automatic reflexes

5. guiding the development of the intrinsic muscles of the larynx

6. the working concept of the independent functions between vowel and consonant formation and phonation.

Although Mr. Alexander began his work in England, the American Center for the Alexander Technique is now located in three cities in this country: New York (227 Central Park West); San Francisco (931 Elizabeth Street); and Santa Monica (853-C 17th Street).

Eyes and Face

Let us now survey the various ways that the eyes and face express and communicate. First, if through nervousness or even by design the singer's eyes are frenetically moving about, the observer equates that helter-skelter movement with insincerity. In truth, of course, a singer could be totally sincere—but nervous. This movement gives the impression, however unfairly, of not wholeheartedly believing in the words.

≫   Remember that the eyes can move separately from the head, or that the head can move and the eyes stay pinned. It is not necessary that they always move together; separate movement is very effective.

Wolf's "Du sagst mir, dass ich keine Fürstin sei," from the *Italienisches Liederbuch*, furnishes an excellent example. As one studies the poem, the slight petulance of the protagonist's argument becomes evident. It is clear that she is really speaking in person to the one who is, in modern vernacular, "putting her down." In a real-life situation one would vacillate between eye contact with the person being lectured and not looking at him directly. In order to prompt truthful petulance and anger, one can use to advantage the technique of placing the imaginary fellow to the left, keeping the head facing forward, letting *only the eyes* stray toward the left at salient moments to see how he is taking the nagging remarks, and letting the head turn left together with the eyes only when direct confrontation is logical.

≫   Eyes need not always be fixed at the audience's head level, or, for that matter, fixed at any particular level. On such a small scale, up-and-left gazing means something very different from down-and-center.

One of the ways to build reality for yourself in singing Wolf's "In dem Schatten meiner Locken" is to consider where the loved one is sleeping. Logically, the singer (speaker) observes him from a bit above, and shadows the beloved with her tresses. There are two "places" identified in the words: the lower couch level where the beloved is asleep and the slightly different level occupied by the singer (speaker). What is more logical for the singer and supportive to her inner realism than to look slightly down and to the side while addressing the sleeping lover?

Similarly, in "Wenn du, mein Liebster, steigst zum Himmel auf" there are two "places" clearly indicated: the feet of God where the lovers will offer their love, and God's beneficent eyes from which He regards them and makes the miracle of one heart out of two loving hearts. It is helpful to see inwardly the relative physical positions of what you are describing. The plastic reaction follows naturally.

≫   Abrupt changes of eye position signal something very different from slow traveling of the eyes.

In the second song of Rossini's "Regatta Songs" the slow-moving eye positions dictated by the logic of the words are quite overt. This song describes the race itself. A slow sweep of the eyes beginning on the far right at the moment of the starting gun, continuously shifting leftward by minute degrees as the race progresses, and finishing on the far left imaginary finish line only at the final moment of the contest—this slow sweep clearly delineates the singer's interpretive powers.

In Brahms's "Vergebliches Ständchen" a case can be made for the dramatic efficacy of placing "Sie" in an upstairs window and "Er" down on the street near the front door. Thus there will be more abrupt changes of eye focus without gross head movement as "Er" speaks looking up at the window and "Sie" calls downward to "Er."

≫   Eyes can focus far as well as near, and many points in between. In real life we do it constantly and unconsciously. This change of focus is very meaningful to the audience when the singer really sees his imaginary person or thing and truly relates to it.

In the Rossini "Regatta Songs" there are many logical shifts from far-focused observance of the race off in the distance to close-up focusing on the gondolier's sweaty face.

The beginning of Pizzetti's "I Pastori" (the poem written by Paris- exiled Gabriele d'Annunzio) describes in the present tense how it must be now (September) in the poet's beloved native Abruzzi mountains. This is incontestibly a moment where a reminiscing, nostalgic exile would gaze off into the distance conjuring up beloved memories.

≫   There are times when your eyes ought not contact the eyes of the audience.

When the singer, for example, is busy in her dramatic and musical imagination being Gretchen at her Spinnrade, there is in her scenario no audience watching her. Therefore, the audience is, in a sense, a voyeur unseen by Gretchen. How the mood would be shattered if she were to signal abandonment of dramatic sincerity by looking into the eyes of her audience! On the contrary, in one of those narrative ballads of Loewe, to contact the audience directly as the story is being told to them would support the truth of the song. Here the audience is part of the nary scene as well as the real one.

Gestures

What about gestures? Whether or not permitted by tradition in recital, a gesture is never successful unless it begins with a true, sincere intention. Only a consummately skilled actor can *plan* to use the same gesture in the same place and repeat it without looking faked and staged. Laurence Olivier managed to do this superbly in each of many performances as Oedipus putting his eye out; the late, distinguished recital singer Jennie Tourel magnificently repeated the exact drunken movements each time she sang the aria from *La Périchole*. This practice, however, is not for everyone to try. We suggest the following rule to solve the dilemma of the gesture in recital: If in this song it is traditionally and stylistically feasible to use a gesture, and if in the moment of performance it seems natural to gesture, *allow it to happen*. Planning and/or practicing a gesture for a specific place is almost never successful. In addition, the less formal second half of the program, if anywhere, is traditionally and logically the more likely place for gestures. The end result of many motions and gesturing is random and trashy. Restraint is utterly necessary. Most important, there is no beauty in a gesture or pose done for its own sake; there must be a compelling reason behind it. Stanislavski referred to beautiful poses that lacked all inner meaning as "ballet," an uncomplimentary description.

The Body

≫   The subtle use of the body gives the audience subliminal messages throughout the program, but big body movements must not be distracting or ludicrous. They are permissible only in certain songs, and then only in highly charged moments. "To insist that the body is not used in recital is nonsense," says Richard Flusser, director of the famed After-Dinner Opera Company. The free body emphasizes the points made by the mind. It is the singer's job to make these messages contribute to the interpretation rather than detract from it.

It is almost unthinkable to contemplate beginning or singing through "Verschling der Abgrund meines Liebsten Hütte" (Wolf) from a passive body position. The song is all fury and attack; there is no retreat in the entire thirty-two bars. The forward, active body positionnaturally expressing this mood transmits the anger and threats to the audience distinctly, without requiring gross movement.

The shifting of body weight, without moving the feet at all, from a forward position implying activity to a backward position implying passivity is eloquent in another way.

In Debussy's "Chevaux de Bois," if one imagines himself to be riding on the merry-go-round horse, it is logical for the body to be forward, with the weight on the balls of the feet during the moments of enjoying the fast motion, as if urging the horse ever faster. Then the imagination can be fed further by retreating to a passive position, with the body weight on the heels during the introspective moments at the end.

≫   Equalizing weight on both feet gives the audience a different message.

In the fifth song ("Evening Prayer") of Moussorgsky's cycle, *Nursery*, keeping the feet absolutely together and aligned reinforces to the audience not only childishness (adults scarcely ever stand with feet perfectly even) but the formal position of prayer (even adults consistently address God from a physically symmetrical and formal position.)

≫   Actually moving the feet as well as shifting the weight gives an even bigger effect.

Schubert's "Ganymede" furnishes an à propros example. At the end of the song, after articulating his wish to rest in the strength of his god's arms, the protagonist, just before he says "Ich komme!" can make a small step forward in his eagerness to ascend and to be united with his god.

≫   Touching the piano or, alternatively, standing well away from it sends a subtle, wordless message to the audience.

A fitting example might be the Brahms "Lullabye." The bouyant touch of your fingers against the piano wood as the music begins feeds your inner dramatic image of touching the cradle whose rocking is distinctly identifiable in the accompaniment figure. "I'll Sail upon the Dog Star" (Purcell) is regarded by most interpreters as a song showing unremitting masculine strength. Standing well away from the piano will bolster this rugged independence in the eyes of the audience, whereas holding onto the piano would assuredly diminish such an impression.

≫   Actually leaning on the piano encourages an impression of indolence, casualness, perhaps even sophistication.

Consider Poulenc's "Hôtel" from *Banalités*. One fine way to put the audience and yourself into the "paresseux" mood marked above the first bar is to show by your indolent body position your intentions for today: "I do not wish to work; I wish to smoke."

≫   Touching the piano very lightly with one hand and then removing that hand is an intensely personal response to the inner life of the song, and, as such, is very evocative for the audience. The moments of touching are in a way indicative of a need for support, sometimes imitative of an actual contact described in the words.

Although very difficult to describe adequately (and impossible to plan), let us attempt to explain one singer's personal reactions to a very lyric song, "La Flûte de Pan," from Debussy's *Chansons de Bilitis*. During the initial part of the song, recollections of how the story started are in the past tense. Quite naturally, as the recitation of past emotions continues, the emotional involvement heightens and the verb changes to present tense as the protagonist relives the story. During the description "he teaches me to play seated on his knees, but I am a bit trembling," the need for a slight support calls for a gentle touching of the piano; when, finally, the loving moment "bit by bit our mouths meet on the flute" gives its own support, the hand leaves the piano. That hand does not describe anything specific; it simply underscores the singer's emotional life underlying the words. Somehow the audience empathizes.

≫   Leaning back against the piano curve ever so weightlessly supports the dramatic message of a song.

In "La Chevelure" (Debussy), for example, this action supports the sensual feelings described in the music and the poem—as if the piano were the bed upon which the couple reclined.

Summing up the influence upon the audience wielded by body movements, we must not neglect the dramatic force an initial body stance taken upon or even before the opening bars can transmit. Passive or active, sad or happy, contemplative or desperate—all of these mental states can be transmitted with that first body position. This "body language" can be a great help to your interpretation and thus to your audience's perception of the inner meaning or subscore that you have created for the song.

One can surely hear, at this point, a mighty chorus of protestations indignantly insisting that Johannes Brahms, Claude Debussy, and Hugo Wolf do not need such assistance. True, but the *singer* does. The modifiable physical aids for recital stage acting discussed here do two things for the singer: they help him to strengthen the truth of his inner dramatic convictions and they elicit from the audience a greater response than from severely limited traditional recital acting.

To sum up, the ideal condition for you as a singing actor is one in which your have complete command of the musical and mechanical elements (pitch, rhythm, ensemble, language skills) and almost total command of the vocal technical requirements (what singer feels he or she has *total* command?) Now you are free to give ninety percent emotional sincerity, reserving five percent for those moments where you must bluff dramatically in order coldly and technically to control your voice or the musical ensemble, or cope with some difficulty of memorization, and dedicating the remaining five percent to inspiration. One of the truly great recitalists, Gerard Souzay, says, "Much as I believe in preparing a piece very well, I also believe in leaving a margin for last minute inspiration."[7] The real performance is the present occasion, not an idealized perfect performance. Leave room for spontaneity. Do not try to be "great"; just be real.

7. *The New York Times*, February 16, 1975.

Aphorisms setting forth the path for earnest and dedicated musicians abound. They state, for example, that one must seek out and observe with scrupulous fidelity all composer's intentions and that only virtuosic performance skills can properly illuminate these intentions. A heretic thoroughly briefed in the scientific method might suggest, however, that these statements are not incontrovertible.

To illustrate the first point, let us refer to a venerated accompanist of many internationally acclaimed singers of the past. Coenraad Bos has recounted experiences with Clara Schumann and Johannes Brahms that bely the sacrosanct quality of the composer's written notation. In "Frühlingsnacht" and "Widmung," even though a diminuendo had been marked by Robert Schumann, Mr. Bos was counseled by Mme. Schumann to continue the ecstatic intensity of the last vocal phrases through the piano postlude to the end. Speaking from long practical public experience, she explained that otherwise the total artistic result would be weakened.

On two other occasions within one month, Mr. Bos played the Brahms "Vier ernste Gesänge," at which performances the composer himself assisted. At the first performance the last bars were sung in a diminuendo as marked. On the second occasion, the singer felt it necessary to his interpretation to sing the last bars as a cumulative intensification, with even the piano continuing his crescendo, against the music as marked. Brahms, in his own words, found both renditions magnificent! All of which simply suggests once again that, however morally important it may be as a prerequisite, it is not sufficient to do the preliminary work correctly. One must learn to trust in the self and soar creatively.

GUIDELINES FOR PRACTICE

1. Stanislavski is described by Pavel Rumyantsev[8] as making a differentiation between "working contractions" (those of the diaphragm, the intercostals, and the larynx, necessary for singing) and superfluous tensions, in his search for complete freedom from involuntary body tensions and pressures. To music providing eight beats for raising arms and hands and eight beats for returning them to original position, work to achieve—

    a. the relaxation of wrist muscles until the hands freely hang;
    b. the relaxation of finger muscles until they dangle freely;

8. Constantin Stanislavski and Pavel Rumyantsev, *Stanislavski on Opera* (New York: Theatre Arts Books, 1975), p. 4.

c. the freedom from tension while the arm raises to shoulder height;

d. the ability to freely shake the lower arm from the elbow joint.

Now return to the start and repeat with the other arm. To the same number of beats work on your legs.

a. Stand on one leg and relax the foot of raised leg, especially the toes.

b. Rotate the free foot.

c. Relax the whole leg; rotate the knee gently.

d. Raise the leg at the knee; relax the whole leg.

Now put the weight on that leg; repeat with the other leg. Work on the neck and body trunk in movements tuned to the music.

a. Throw the head front and roll it side to side by body movement only.

b. Seated on a chair, relax the neck; throw the neck backward and let it roll, simulating a state of sleepiness.

c. Seated, bend the body forward, waist free, arms dangling.

2. It is clearly not possible to write as efficaciously about muscular awareness as it is to experience it first-hand from a skilled practitioner. Nevertheless, we present the following two exercises from the Alexander Technique (which we hope will stimulate the student to seek out the Maisel book [see Bibliography] or a class where it is available).

a. Posture and alignment

Let the neck be free to go forward and up out of the shoulders (up to the ceiling if standing; if reclining, back to the wall).

Let the neck be free to let the head go forward and up out of the neck.

Let the neck be free to let the back lengthen and widen.

Let the neck be free to let the shoulders lengthen out of a free trunk.

Let the neck be free to let the upper arm lengthen out of free shoulders.

Let the neck be free to let the forearm lengthen out of free elbows.

Let the neck be free to let the fingers lengthen out of free wrists.

b. Relaxation

Lie on a firm surface on your back.

Start with a book about 1 and 1/2 inches thick under your head. Do as above.

After completing the section concerning the back, start with one arm at a time.

Lengthen fingers into infinity.

Above your waistline, let your stomach fall through to the floor.

Raise the legs at the knee. Then lengthen from the pelvis to the knee.

Lengthen from ankle to knee.

Let the knees fall up to the ceiling.

Lower the legs.

Lengthen from the pelvis to the knee.

Lengthen from the knee to the ankle.

Lengthen the toes to infinity.

Let the knees fall up to the ceiling.

3. We remind singers who would not dream of trying to learn to sing without vocalizing that acting training relies on exercising, too. Stanislavski prescribed exercises in walking to slow music.[9] Take only one step to two bars of an adagio tempo. Your objective is to change body weight without the slightest visible interruption, so that if you had a glass of water on your head you would not spill a drop. Gradually increase the number of steps per bar, maintaining smoothness, until your are almost running. Your aim: to walk with controlled and graceful pliancy.

4. A brilliant stage director, costume designer, master lighting engineer, professional scenic designer, and respected acting teacher, the late Elemer Nagy of the Hartt College of Music in Hartford, Connecticut, gave an exercise to his New York class that he called "the Jesuit exercise." His master, the great Max Reinhardt, had used it to extend the student's awareness of himself and others. The exercise supposedly served the Jesuit Society as a means of honing their capacity for insight into the other person's feelings. Nowadays, termed a "consciousness-raising device," it would probably serve the purposes of an encounter group. At the end of a day of normal activity, sit down alone and re-live each one of that day's encounters with other human beings. Repeat the conversations aloud, trying to remember every word. Then try to fit yourself into the other person's body. Imagine that person's thoughts and reactions to the encounter. Search for possible hidden responses to the conversation, unsuspected by you at the time. The exercise will lead, in the absence of an acting class, to a sharper ability at discovering, understanding, or creating an inner life for your song's text.

5. Examine your mind: what relationship do you see between singing and acting in a recital situation? Write a hundred words on the sub-

9. *Ibid.*, p. 6.

ject. This will clarify your convictions and opinions. We trust that you will then act upon them.

6. Stanislavski recognized no beauty in the fact of a gesture or pose. An inner purpose was mandatory.[10] Choose a gesture at random. Mentally create a set of given circumstances that provide a real purpose for this movement. Follow through with a completed gesture which is a total action, paying close attention to muscular smoothness and lack of superfluous tension. Try, for example, the gesture of reaching directly forward. (a) You are walking through an old-car lot; mountains of partially dismantled and wrecked cars surround the paths through which you walk; depressed by the sight, you suddenly come across a large, beautiful, red flower growing in the weeds between the two wheels of a car; finding it hard to believe, you reach forward to touch it. (b) You have been confined to your bed for several months with an illness; after a slow recuperation in the house, today you are permitted outside for the first time; spring has arrived; the day is warm and fragrant with scents of blooming flowers and new grass; you walk slowly and weakly behind the house where the rose bush is covered with blooms; you reach forward to touch a beautiful rose, as if it will reassure you of your "aliveness." This procedure is, of course, the converse of that in song preparation where the situation is at least partially given by the text and the music.

7. Imagination can be extended by exercising it. Choose an everyday routine action (e.g., shaving or making the bed). Do it twenty different ways, each one impelled by a different set of circumstances that you create. Extend your fantasy as far as you can. For example (if you are a man): (a) you have been out drinking all night; you are far from sober; you have just time to clean up before going to work; you shave or (b) you are going out to meet a girl who has made you wait six weeks for a date; you shave. Or (if you are a woman): (a) you are sixteen years old; your mother has given you an ultimatum: one more day with the bed unmade and you cannot use the car for one month; you make the bed or (b) you are a poetess; you are composing a poem while making the bed.

8. Choose an insignificant object on your person. Give it your sharpest attention. Articulate with imagination several relationships you might have with respect to it (e.g., shoelace). You see that it is very long; it often comes undone because the material is slippery; you remember the last time it untied itself in the presence of the girl next door you tripped on it and you were embarrassed; you castigate yourself for not replacing it earlier; you ruminate on this reinforcement of your known laziness.

9. Choose a recording of a piece of nonvocal music that is not too familiar to you. Decide on a simple scenario. Listen to the music well, because its "tone" gives you the reason for doing what you will do and

10. *Ibid.*

how you will do it. Search out your harmony with the music while acting out your scenario. Improvise. Let the music lead you to an idea of the type of human being you might be. Now create another scenario entirely different from the first. Proceed as before. Try to attach more than one possible meaning to the rhythms and melodies. Bear in mind that we are not hereby trying to put a program to absolute music. This is simply a method for extending your sensitivity to musical elements. You wish to find the thing that arouses your emotions, giving them fervor and vigor. You wish to truthfully evoke these feelings.

10. Choose a song with which you are not too familiar that is in a language you speak. Read the text aloud. Now consider: by these words what do you wish to convey to those who are listening? Analyze all the ramifications of this text's meaning to you—the overt thoughts clearly articulated by the text, but especially its inner life. Shape with your imagination the state of being called forth by this poetry. Read the words aloud again. Continue until you are satisfied that the fantasy life you have created is as complete as you can make it. Now play and sing through the music and ascertain whether the composer agrees with you. Is your version of the logical significance of the text completely reflected by the music? If not, adjust your personal understanding of the subscore to reflect the message of the actual score. Remember that you are the poet speaking and the music is your means of communicating the inner life of these words. You must render the author's and composer's intent through your own emotions. This is why artists refer to this process as "making the song your own." Begin with these broad-based questions— they are the minimum list of questions to be answered about your song— and continue to the smallest details until you have sought every subtlety your mind can winnow out. Some answers will be facts; some must be intuited. First list what you *know* from the text in answer to the questions. Then go back and write next to each answer what you *believe* is connoted by the music or your intuition, although unarticulated by the text.

Who is it who speaks the words?

Exactly where is he as he speaks?

What does each of his five senses perceive of his surroundings as he speaks?

Does he stay there throughout the song?

If not, where does he go?

Why does he go?

What happened before he spoke?

To whom does he speak?

Is that person or object present?

Exactly what does this person or object look like?

What is the relationship between the speaker and the person or object addressed?

Why does the speaker speak when he does?

Why does he say what he does?

What is his emotional and physical state at the beginning of the song?

When does this change?

Why does it change?

Does the object addressed or observed stay the same throughout the song?

If it changes, what is its exact description?

What is the speaker's mental and physical condition at the end of the song?

What happens after the text stops?

What happens after the music stops?

11. Choose a group of songs. For each song find all the concrete, overt images and pictures the poet has used. How does the composer show these in the music, if indeed he does? (For example, the text of "Wohin" speaks of a brook and you hear a brook. In Wolf's "Lied vom Winde" a wind is described in the poem and you hear a musical allusion to wind.)

12. Choose several songs. Find the core of each song, that is, the essential element without which the heart of the song cannot be communicated. (For example, in Wolf's "Du denkst mit einem Fädchen" the words clearly seem to be spoken with sarcasm, but aimed at getting attention rather than taking revenge with wounding remarks. In Debussy's "La Chevelure" the passion clearly felt with both words and music must be heavily *sensual* passion. In neither song is it sufficient to presume a general and simplistic attitude—the Wolf piece is not about sarcasm and the Debussy piece is not about love. Absolute specificity is necessary. Come to your conclusions by trying out the words in various ways. What does the music tell you about the inner meaning that the words do not spell out but that the composer who then wrote the music perceived accordingly? In this way you can zero in on the core of your song.

13. These three songs contain poetic images for which you must have a real understanding.

De Grêve (Debussy)

Les Roses d'Ispahan (Fauré)

Le Paon (Ravel)

If you have *seen* the seashore at twilight, the clouds gathering for a storm, an English watercolor, you have no problem. If not, you must *go* to the seashore at twilight (one being nearby) and see for yourself, or you must seek out a description or a painting that makes you understand this image completely. What does the city of Isfahan look like? Have you been to Iran? Can you find a picture of these famous roses? Have you seen a peacock? You can easily find a color picture. Can you find a recording of a peacock's cry? These inner images, in the absence of first-hand knowledge, might come from poetry you have read, a ballad you have heard, books read, pictures seen, tales recited. The important thing is to leave no poetic image unexperienced by your inner eye.

In the following songs where would *you* go to find the real experience of these images?

Der Feuerreiter	Wolf
Die Zigeunerin	Wolf
The Lordly Hudson	Rorem
Wild Swans	Duke
Die Zeitlose	Strauss
Frühlingsfeier	Strauss
Ablösung im Sommer	Mahler
Lob des hohen Verstands	Mahler
A Swan	Grieg
Proud Songsters	Britten
Seascape	Britten
Gruppe aus den Tartarus	Schubert
Nachtviolen	Schubert
Der Atlas	Schubert
Fantôches	Debussy

Check through your own songs for images for which you must find a personal experience.

14. Using the traditional programs given in Chapter 4, discover the human being in each song, his characteristics and his background, both those given by text and music and those intuited by you. From this list try to formulate what qualities *you personally* have in common with each one.

15. The verses of strophic songs are usually very similar in tone, one to the other. It takes hard work to find subtle distinctions between them. Analyze the text of the following two strophic songs. Now differentiate in any way possible between the verses—mood, plot, etc.

Litanei	Schubert
Meine Wünsche	Mozart
(*Ein deutsches Kriegslied*)	

16. Choose a song on which you are currently working. Make a list of:

a. what facts are *given* by the words;

b. what facts are *connoted* by the words;

c. what facts are *implied* by the music.

Obviously your imagination and sensitivity must work harder to find implied meanings and implications as opposed to clear facts supplied by text.

17. Using songs on which you are currently working, examine the songs for answers to the following questions:

a. What is the object of your attention in each? (What exactly are you looking at or talking to or concerned with?)

b. Does this change anywhere? If so, to what?

c. Where might your eyes logically be on each occasion?

18. Take a current song and answer the following questions:

a. What does the music and text lead you to believe is the condition of this human being at the time of singing?

b. What body stance might logically convey this emotional condition?

c. Does this condition change during the song? If so, to what?

d. What might the body stance be that reflects this emotion?

19. Take a current song and, having come to grips with your understanding of the words and music, sing it *down an octave* without relinquishing any sincerity or expressivity.

7 The Accompanist

The mode and manner in which Vogel sings and I accompany him, the way in which, during such moments, we seem to be one is something quite novel and unheard of for these people.

FRANZ SCHUBERT

GENERAL RESPONSIBILITIES

A beautiful recital results from a cooperative effort among singer, accompanist,[1] and voice teacher. The accompanist's work is to help the singer in preparation of all matters of interpretation, musical and literary. In order to accomplish this, the singer's musicianship should ever be his concern. Paramount here is the matter of rhythm—the backbone of all music. Because the rhythm is often taken for granted by the singer it is frequently misused. It is within the realm of rhythm that most atrocities and many displays of bad taste occur.

Every accompanist finds much joy in the work he does with a singer who is already a good musician, not only because he is spared the drudgery of pounding out the tune but also because he can get quickly to the

---

1. The talents and equipment of both the vocal coach and the accompanist are usually combined into one person, the coach-accompanist. While respecting each profession as singular, from now on, for the sake of simplicity, we shall refer to the combined talents as one person, the accompanist.

131

more fascinating work of detailed interpretation. The valuable rehearsal time is thereby put to better use.

A singer is, of course, within his absolute rights when he asks for extensive musical repetition in order to routine himself thoroughly. Singers, possibly more than any other musical performers, are in need of adequate routining time. They depend upon repetition to gain security, and to find a balance among all the elements that constitute their performances: vocalism, acting, body control, and, above all, memory. As many performance elements as possible should become automatic in order to free the singer for those that are paramount at any given time. It is à propos to note that the German and French words for coach are *Korrepetitor* and *répétiteur*, meaning "a pianist who repeats music." No good accompanist will ever begrudge his partner hours spent on necessary routine. If he does, he invites risks that may easily disturb his own performance as collaborator. (See Chapter 10.)

Perfect teamwork between the accompanist and singer may not always be noticed by the audience—it all seems so easy; but lack of teamwork will be quite apparent. The amount of time the singer and the accompanist spend in rehearsal is directly proportional to the success of the recital. There is no short-cut to the creation of a team—time and toil are the only ingredients. Commercial recordings of piano accompaniments without voice cannot substitute for teamwork. An impersonal disc cannot collaborate with a singer. Neither can two hours of rehearsal time with a local accompanist supplied for a visiting artist bear appropriate fruit, no matter how talented the two artists may be in other respects.

Taped accompaniments made specifically for the singer by the actual recital accompanist to aid the singer in the process of memorization may prove of some help. At the very least, the musical ideas are made evident. In the long run, however, nothing can really supplant live hours spent building true musical collaboration.

The best vocal accompanists will readily admit that they have an abiding love for the human voice, believing it to transcend all other means of musical communication. An accompanist who is concerned with the song's piano part only is destined for failure in his work. Singers totally disdain the type of recital accompanist who would have preferred to be a piano soloist but was obliged to accompany in order to make a living. A love for the vocal line should indeed be present in actual performance since it is necessary for fully half, if not more, of the accompanist's attention to be riveted there. It is only then that he can be aware of every infinitesimal detail of the singing, whether it be a momentary vocal annoyance such as phlegm, a lapse of memory, a slight tempo adjustment, an inspired interpretive improvisation, or—if the preparation was thorough—a flight of unexpected musical magic, unprepared but insightful. Moments of controlled freedom like these are worth all the work involved.

The intelligent singer considers his accompanist his teammate in the recital. The singer will discuss both the music and the poem with him and ask for an opinion or two. In suggesting interpretive points, the accompanist should be constantly aware of the technical resources of the singer, lest he at any time unwittingly interfere with vocal production. There may be occasions when he requires a fuller knowledge of his singer's vocal status. Some discussion with the voice teacher often smooths the way.

A good accompanist will have a deep loyalty to his singer in the studio and in performance. Because the accompanist wants his singer to appear in the best possible light at all times, he prepares himself to handle any musical mishaps, and in their work together he accentuates the singer's artistic strengths. Whereas in the studio the accompanist owes the singer the benefits of his opinions, in performance his demeanor must not so much as hint at criticism of any detail. His conduct there, demonstrating an obvious admiration and respect for the singer's artistry, must bolster the ego, and his attitude must radiate enthusiasm, cheer, and optimism, giving comfort to those stressful moments before and during performance.

Languages

Singing in a given language presents several special problems that the qualified accompanist must be able to solve for his singers if called upon. The accompanist, therefore, should acquire a practical knowledge of the main singing languages: Italian, French, German, and Spanish. Without command of these languages he will be unable to deal with such important problems as metric spacing of words with double consonants, the complexities of elision, their metric spacings, the dramatic accent of anticipated first consonants, the correct execution in meter of vocalized consonants, problems arising from diphthongs, and problems of Italian triple syllables on one note.

Sara Knight neatly summed up the accompanist's responsibility with regard to languages in a speech before the New York Singing Teachers' Association, entitled "What the Vocal Coach Listens For":

> He should open the singer's ears to the challenge and pleasure of absorbing the unique modes of expression in each language. For example, in English, not to accept the prosaic use of words, but to listen to the poetic imaginative expression of the great range of accents and colors in

our native tongue; in Italian, to hear the fluidity of tone, to understand the use of portamentos; in German, to understand the sentence structure which often places the activating verb at the very end of a complicated thought and therefore demands of the singer great carrying stamina and to master the art of the Luftpause; in French, to hear and create a fine-line spinning of tone which is intense and concentrated without being tight and constricted.

The average accompanist who collaborates with several singers and who has accumulated a large repertoire of song material becomes a valuable source of music when the singer is in need of suggestions. David Garvey, the eminent American coach-accompanist, reminds us that the accompanist is in the best position to offer recommendations on matching personality with repertoire since he is both objective and aware of the singer's particular strengths. In program building he should be as involved in the exciting search for the best music as is the singer himself.

The Page Turner

The subject of the page turner, that quiet but alert body to the left of the accompanist, is a controversial one. Some advise the use of a page turner to facilitate the work of the accompanist. Others think that his presence on stage is an unneeded distraction for the audience. In any case, an accompanist who prefers to turn his own pages is compelled to find ways to execute the troublesome duty without mishap. Various partial solutions are to—

1. memorize passages of music on the succeeding page until a convenient pause, stop, fermata, or chord of long duration allows easy turning;
2. write out on staff paper those passages and place it to the right of the score;
3. carefully and cleverly fake the left or right hand passage while the other turns.[2]

Performance Mishaps

An accompanist uses music in a recital performance for two reasons. If he is a busy accompanist he will never have time to memorize all the

2. Those who adamantly eschew faking of any kind should see Gerald Moore's book *Singer and Accompanist*, for the greatest accompanist's advisable fakings. (New York: Macmillan, 1954.)

music he must play. Secondly, he plays the important role of guardian against any mishaps during the performance. With the score before him he is better able to remedy the situation. During rehearsals he must ensure a smooth public performance by noting various danger points in advance.

Mr. Sonntag tells of a harrowing occasion: a well-known soprano who was singing "Ah, perfido" by Beethoven took a wrong turn due to a memory lapse and jumped two entire pages to an identical musical phrase. Mr. Sonntag, forewarned by a similar lapse during a previous rehearsal, turned to the final page without blinking and finished off the truncated aria with great flourish. Only those who knew the music well ever suspected the mishap, although the soprano on the way to the wings commented sotto voce, "That certainly seemed short tonight."

Nevertheless there are those occasions when any attempt to maintain a refined and dignified atmosphere is doomed to failure. Mr. Sonntag, in the story now to follow, takes full blame for what happened. The tenor William McGrath, having completed a noble Handel aria, was launching into a serious and difficult Hugo Wolf group. In the middle of the beautiful "Lied von Winde," Mr. Sonntag suddenly stopped playing. Nervous titters swept the audience. At the moment he had turned a page—and there was only a split moment to do so, due to a tricky chromatic run coming up—the loose page, caught by a momentary updraft, had sailed high into the air, landing some fifteen feet away from the piano. There was nothing to do but stop, recoup the errant page, and wonder whether to start again. Mr. McGrath calmly said to the audience, now close to hysterics, "I really don't think there is much point in trying that one again."

The moral to these two tales is, of course: Be prepared.

It is sometimes the practice for singers traveling on extensive recital tours to allow their accompanists to perform a group of piano solos at a given point during the recital. Reasons advanced for this practice are that the singer is thus afforded a moment or two of rest during the recital and that the audience is offered a bit of variety.

If indeed any singer feels the need to rest during a recital (we don't believe it; most good singers want to sing on forever) then his technical equipment might be insufficient. Also, if he feels that some variety is called for during the program, then his ability to arrange an interesting and absorbing program might have been limited originally. Such practice is as much an affront to the ideal song recital as the addition of several familiar operatic arias. This unfortunate practice, though certainly not as common as it once was, disturbs and weakens the song recital by injecting a foreign element into the evening's entertainment. Most acccompanists are rarely good solo pianists due to the nature, not the degree, of their talent. They are in these circumstances set at some disadvantage.

Also, the public has bought tickets for the vocalist's recital and is thereby deprived of hearing a full and comprehensive evening of song from the artist.

When maximum rewards are the objective, collaboration is the key word. This implies a relationship somewhat like an ideal marriage—sharing points of view, weighing them, discussing amicably, occasionally giving in on a point with the sincere hope that the other way will work as well. But, as in any profession, one hundred percent perfect collaboration between two workers is rare indeed. A realistic goal is to aim for the highest possible percentage. Far too often singer and accompanist do not in their discussions come to grips with just exactly what it is that they seek from one another.

If a singer engages a pianist, wishing that he accompany and not coach—an unfortunate relationship in our opinion—it behooves the singer to make this wish known at an early date. If he does not clarify his wants at the outset he will consider any proffered suggestions as to interpretation a complete waste of time. Granting a more fruitful and happy collaboration between the two, wherein singer and accompanist listen, weigh, and accept each other's remarks, there still remains a need to explain individual problems, set priorities, and agree upon certain time allotments for particular objectives. One of the best ways to insure a good working relationship is to start by spending a full session, or parts of several sessions, to ventilate opinions and discuss methods of attack. The accompanist's question "What precisely do you want (or not want) from me?" is a valuable one. In response, the singer would do well to clarify goals and explain any individual methods of study, at the same time asking the accompanist about his methods. Periodic talks of this kind accelerate progress and propose mutual challenges for growth.

Other problems stemming from personality traits can be solved in similar discussion periods. A very young and inexperienced singer does not always know what to ask of his new accompanist, much less how and when to ask for it. Under such circumstances the accompanist had better assume leadership, albeit temporarily. One type of singer may feel shy, nervous, or fearful out of overreverence for an accompanist's musicianship. Another, resenting the manner in which an accompanist phrases his suggestions, may develop a defensive attitude.

Neither the singer nor the accompanist should ever dictate to the other. We speak, naturally of interpretive points. Incorrect rhythm or mispronunciations are quite another matter. To quote a singer of some renown: "I wouldn't give you two cents for an accompanist who has no ego, but I also wouldn't give you two cents for an accompanist who wouldn't coordinate his ego with mine. Notice that I said co-ordinate, not sub-ordinate."

As for those singers who are high in temperament, their rule ought to be: act like a prima donna only on stage. Most singers, we believe, are easy to work with and welcome suggestions, even demand them. Gerald Moore, in his excellent book *The Unashamed Accompanist*, states: "There are some singers, however, who know everything, and these are the birds that need watching. They will hate being corrected; they will resent being advised. True, this type of singer may not forgive such an attitude on the part of the accompanist and the result may well be that he will engage another pianist at his next concert. And a good thing, too!"[3]

Every singer has his own set of gifts and his own set of failings. Each one, by virtue of his existence as a human being, has some combination of weaker qualities within himself—lack of self-control, immaturity, inability to collaborate, sometimes outright fear of public performance, an inclination to be overly analytical or to be victimized by improper learning habits. In the presence of these weaknesses and career deterrents, the accompanist must often be a psychoanalyst. But he must first instill confidence. Criticism judiciously mixed with praise is mandatory. Making the learning of a recital as much a joy as an achievement helps. The ever useful sense of humor also goes a long way. If an accompanist through some personal deficiency of his own is truly unable to inspire confidence in a singer, then no matter how valuable he may be in other respects he should not continue working with that singer.

A complete listing of musical and interpretive aids for which the accompanist should be responsible would be prohibitive here, but we will discuss a few of the most prominent.

INTERPRETIVE CONCERNS

In the studio the singer's principal interests are vocal and technical. For this reason one of the accompanist's main duties is to know when to offer suggestions and to be tactful and succinct in his remarks. Yet, there are some areas where the accompanist properly involves himself directly in the singer's interpretive concerns.

Composer Markings

A singer constantly searches for further means of attaining dramatic accent. The guide most immediately to hand lies in strict observance of the composer's markings in both piano and voice lines. By making the most of his piano markings, the accompanist supports and heightens the singer's interpretive efforts. He must also remember that markings in the

3. *The Unashamed Accompanist* (New York: Macmillan, 1944), p. 36.

piano and voice parts are sometimes purposefully divergent. In Hugo Wolf's "Auf ein altes Bild" there are two occasions when the piano stabs out the mezzo-forte chords as if to underline the tragic nature of the poem, while the voice remains rapt and soft. Another kind of marking, the line accent, is used by Debussy in "De Grêve." During the last bars, while the voice is quietly chanting the words on low sustained pitches and the right hand of the piano part is creating the murmering sea motive, the left hand suggests the sound of the Angelus by repeating several E's marked with the line accent. Throughout Duparc's "Chanson Triste" the observant pianist will find hidden within the arpeggiated figures groups of double notes that are marked as slurred. The effect when played correctly produces a lulling sighlike pattern and helps to expose the song's inner life.

Vocal Effects

Notations of expression were few in the Renaissance but more common in eighteenth-century song. The Romantic composers of the nineteenth century used the entire battery of expressive markings, as did the Impressionists. Singularly, the Baroque era preferred to trust the performer in these matters as much as possible.

If the accompanist's career has involved him with some advanced professional singers, he will probably be in a position to pass on some highly valuable secrets of interpretation to his younger singers. He may even suggest to them vocal effects that he has found to be particularly impressive or effective.

A correctly executed slur is one such effect. Formerly, the use of the portamento was highly acceptable to the concert public, and indeed many fine singers used it to a degree that an audience today would find excessive or artificial. Performance styles change and we cannot hope to alter the cyclic patterns. Because of today's rather more austere standard with regard to slurs, we too often witness singers zealously ignoring portamentos that are actually designated. Taste today demands careful control and limitation of the slur. However, not to err on either side of the esthetic line, the accompanist must advocate the sparing use of this vocal effect only at most desirable times, thereby assuring that its value is not destroyed.

Possibilities for dramatic effect can be found in the use of vocal imagination applied coloristically to a particular note or combination of notes. Three illustrations are: the vibrato-less "dead" tone, effective when craftily used for words or phrases connoting weariness, poignancy, madness; the spoken or "breathed" tone (actually a forerunner of Sprechstimme), when a tone is almost completely spoken, but on pitch; and the colored tone, which is achieved by brightening or darkening the voice.

Many teachers believe that these effects are simply the direct result of involvement in the mood of the text. This may be true, but the accompanist should be acquainted with them in theory. He will then be able to point them out in practice when they do occur or should occur.

One remembers the great recitalist Jennie Tourel, who, when singing a tragic Russian song came to the word "death," sang it with a cold, vibrationless tone to which the entire audience thrilled, proving that an occasional ugly tone is perfectly admissible, even desirable, when artfully placed.

The recital art is closely wedded to the word. Inasmuch as the word or thought of the poet nevertheless is not always noble or beautiful, the accompanist might well advise the imaginative singer to adopt for an occasional effect a less noble or beautiful quality. The accompanist must not hesitate to offer such suggestions. All singers are fascinated to hear of vocal effects adopted by great singers. The prerogative remains to accept or reject such ideas.

Breath Markings

Notation practices differ widely from style to style. In playing music from those eras when breathing space was not notated, the accompanist may find it his duty to counsel the singer on the correct practice. Generally the singer should, to insure the onward pace of a song (when that pace is not retarded), breathe in the time value taken from the note that is left, not from the note that is approached.

Not all singers are blessed with great breath control. This limitation may be purely physical. The singer's accompanist may be able to offer a remedy to solve the breathing problems in music where long phrases might be considered to be idealistically written. Moreover, it is a fact that song composers have been very generous in allowing some license within their music when a more perfect performance is in this way made possible.

In measure 55 of Strauss's song "Beim Schlafengehn" the accompanist might advise that the word "tausend" be completed on the last note of the bar (F-flat), a breath taken, and on the next measure the word "tausendfach" re-stated. A second breath will allow a fuller and more effective climax.

Phrasing

We are all aware that a series of notes does not constitute a musical idea without the element of phrasing. Why, then, is this so often forgotten by the young singer? He must be reminded that a sensitivity to the art of phrasing is really an advantage to his vocal technique insofar as it telegraphs disciplinary messages to the breathing apparatus, thereby conditioning its use.

In a sense, the accompanist has two duties related to phrasing. For the singer who already understands phrasing, the accompanist need only be a watchdog, but for one who is not so accomplished, he may be called upon to teach phrasing. This task is not as difficult as may be believed, provided the singer has some intuitive musical sense. By strict analysis of the composer's markings and the text, find at what point or points the shape of the music rises and falls in musical intensity. Remember that these moments may not of necessity be moments of high dramatic force. Discipline the breath to this shaping, and the phrasing will improve, because breath *is* phrasing.

Harry Plunket Greene, in his charmingly written book *Interpretation in Song*, speaks of the "long phrase" in relation to music that calls for it.

> Long phrasing—that is, long phrasing not only achieved but assimilated and reveled in—is the essence of big singing. Small phrasing narrows the range of vision. The power to phrase in large exalts phrasing to a higher plane. The knowledge of its possession enables the singer to think in large and therein, automatically, phrasing becomes interpretation—the means becomes the end.[4]

Performance Practice and Composer's Intentions

A dedicated accompanist ought to equip himself with a broad background knowledge relating to historical details of performance practices as well as performance suggestions offered by composers during their lifetimes. From this font of information he then can offer to the singer advantageous performance advice.

Stylistic approaches to singing differ greatly in performance between, say, Bach's religious works and eighteenth-century Italian vocal music. In the former an instrumental style of singing produces the desired effect. Some of the objectives in the latter are bel canto line, vocal display, and ornamentation (consisting of embellishing or adding notes and altering notated rhythm). Scholarly choices concerning which embellishments to make, how to place added notes, and where to use altered rhythms must frequently be made or facilitated by the accompanist. He must be reasonably competent in this area. Knowledge of his singer's preferences and abilities will guide his choices. For a comprehensive

---

4. Harry Plunket Greene, *Interpretation in Song* (New York: Macmillan, 1940), p. 65.

study of vocal and instrumental ornamentation the accompanist is advised to seek out *Interpretation of Early Music* by Robert Donington and the same author's smaller and more practical book on the same subject, *A Performer's Guide to Baroque Music* (see the bibliography).

Although the study of ornamentation is highly complex, Mr. Donington explains that it is the few plain and relatively straightforward ornaments, not the many complicated variants, that are needed and will ordinarily suffice. "The impromptu ornaments of today become the written figurations of tomorrow," Mr. Donington states. He clearly defines such matters as appoggiaturas, the slide, trills, acciaccaturas, and the mordent. The problem of the Baroque figured bass is also explained with such interesting advice as: Baroque composers trusted the accompanists not only with a simple figured bass but also with ornamentation of their own. There is also a fine chapter on the study of inequality of rhythm (*inégales*), another feature of Baroque style.

Many informative statements by composers themselves are to be found in *Interpretation of Early Music*. Giulio Caccini, in his *Nuove Musiche* (1602), defines correct tempo: "I call that the noble manner of singing which is used without tying a man's self to the ordinary measures of time . . . whence proceeds that kind of singing with a graceful neglect."[5] This illustrates that most Baroque music thrives on considerable flexibility of tempo, although this is not always easy to accept.

Even though in our efforts to divine the composer's intentions we must treat the printed page as sacrosanct, it can be admitted that slavishly literal attention to the page is on rare occasions historically unwarranted. In his informative little book *The Well-Tempered Accompanist*,[6] Coenraad Bos relates instances when such composers as Brahms and Schumann (via Clara) gave full license to Mr. Bos to change completely the dynamics of a song when certain circumstances warranted it. From this book we learn that Richard Strauss himself recommended omitting the postlude of his song "Heimliche Aufforderung" on one occasion when the tenor Lauritz Melchior was performing it.

INDIRECT INFLUENCE

The accompanist often exerts subliminal influence on the singer's work through his pianistic artistry. A homily respected by recitalists asserts that the greatest songs are not written for voice *with* piano accompaniment but for voice *and* piano. The voice and piano parts are not

5. *The Performer's Guide to Baroque Music* (New York: C. Scribner's Sons, 1974), p. 161.
6. *The Well-Tempered Accompanist* (Bryn Mawr: Presser, 1949), pp. 45, 71.

each just half of the total; rather, each one is in a certain sense the whole. Therefore the accompanist must not be satisfied with pianistic skills alone; he must exploit every facet of his intrinsic musicality. He takes inspiration for his artistry in part from his understanding of the poem, since the piano part must be the inner life of the spoken (sung) words.

For example, accompanists must study introductions, interludes, and postludes not only from a purely musical standpoint but also from a poetic one. The greatest song composers always have a dramatic intention for solo piano sections within a song. For example, a given interlude may finish or develop a poetic thought that has already been stated by the singer, or it may introduce a new idea completely. The accompanist's effectiveness when playing these sections presupposes that he have a more than ordinary comprehension of the poem itself. (For examples and a full discussion of the accompanist and subtext see Chapter 10.)

GUIDANCE IN ENSEMBLE

It is the accompanist's responsibility to act as guide while both artists find and clarify the means by which total musical ensemble will be achieved.

Proper Coordination of Arpeggios

When arpeggios are found in piano accompaniments, it is wise, unless otherwise indicated by the composer or the performance practices of the period, to execute them so that the top note of the arpeggio falls on the sung note. Erratic rhythm and sloppy ensemble are avoided in this way.

Tempo Suggestions

When metronomic markings are not indicated by the composer, the possibility of conflicting views between the singer and the accompanist exists. Calm collaboration generally solves most conflicts of this sort. Even when the page offers a metronomic reading, it is sometimes rewarding to analyze the effectiveness and appeal of the song by trial-testing it in a variety of different tempi that approximate the one given by the composer. In this way, important differences of age, temperament, emotions, physical health, and voice weight are accommodated. Almost all songs allow some flexibility of choice. Wonderful revelations can occur when choosing the tempo with a trial-test. The artists gain by knowing the song more personally and deeply than before.

More often than not, the first bars of a song are written for the piano alone. Therefore, it is the accompanist's task to set the tempo. On this subject the great Stanislavski gives the following advice to his singers, "You need great inner technique in order to seize at once the intense inner rhythm of a song, but you do not get your rhythm after the song has begun. You must set your rhythm ahead before the music starts, as though you were determining it for the accompanist."[7] The great teacher's advice is both idealistic and practical; moreover, it is meaningful for the accompanist as well as the singer.

The Ritard, Accelerando, and Rubato

Every performance is unique. There are many reasons why it is often difficult to remember correct tempi. Beethoven himself once refused to believe his own previous tempo markings. Changes in interpretation, even slight ones, influence tempo. Time signatures and time words can be misleading or vague and very often have little resemblance to musical practices of a period. (For example, our visual reaction to the long notes written in sixteenth-century music can hypnotize us into playing them slowly.)

At least in theory, most singers know the meaning of the terms ritard, accelerando, and rubato. In practice, however, one too often hears what amounts to total ignorance of them. The differences between poco ritard, ritard, and molto ritard are often confused, often simply ignored. Then why should the composer bother to differentiate them in his markings? Aside from the matter of degree, the execution of these markings is a special study. The accompanist must again be a sentinel, reminding the singer as well as himself that any ritard implies a gradual change of tempo, not the sudden use of a new one. Another common bad habit is carelessness with regard to where the ritard is actually marked. Both artists must be on guard, too, against anticipating a fermata, since its sole purpose is to arrest tempo suddenly, not to slacken it gradually.

The rubato, usually not marked, is a more subtle device. Here the tempo fluctuation must be compensated for by a corresponding change in the opposite direction later in the phrase. Although Mozart himself was alleged to use rubato in playing his own piano music, its use is considered by experts to be of the most advantage in Romantic music.

7. Constantin Stanislavski and Pavel Rumyantsev, *Stanislavski on Opera* (New York: Theater Arts Books, 1975), p. 36.

STARTING A CAREER

At this point it might be of value to offer some advice to the beginning accompanist on the subject of how to start a career. When a young and able would-be accompanist has learned a broad repertoire of vocal music and when he has shown himself sufficiently eager to associate with singers and musicians, he will no doubt be drawn into the studios of voice teachers to play for lessons. His apprenticeship starts here. Some of the singers in the studio will be more advanced. In this way his apprenticeship will lead him also into studios of other advanced coaches and conductors, language coaches, and stage directors or drama coaches. He must understand the skills of each[8]—conceivably even learn them.

An accompanist's career advances inevitably through a network of personal contacts. Success then depends upon the state of his musical preparedness. If it is adequate, he will be able to take advantage of these professional relationships, and thus launch himself and his career.

One who wishes to become a recital accompanist must above all be fond of people, including singers—even tenors! He must have infinite patience. Without losing his own ego, he must adapt himself to each singer who enters his studio and he must be well content to do so.

A good piece of advice for any young accompanist is to recognize that most singers will not respect an accompanist who learns a song technically at the same time that he is coaching it. Most accompanists occasionally find themselves doing an unavoidable crash course on a piece of music. By burning the midnight oil, they will be able to hold their own with the singer the following day.

We submit a method of study for the young accompanist. It is designed primarily to initiate and/or accelerate proper learning habits, habits which may differ to some degree from those of singers or solo pianists.

A first step in understanding the musical setting of a song is to sight-read it for overall concept, stressing the harmonic and rhythmic skeleton only. Now leave the piano. At desk or table study the song, noting the following: form, harmonic structure, general tempo, metronomic marking, dynamics, changes of tempo within the song. Do not hesitate to mark with pencil strokes the boundaries of any beats that might need rhythmic clarification. Your eye will be aided when later you return to the piano. Mark subdivisions when you see the need. Observe both vocal

8. Fritz Lehmann, brother of Lotte and in his day an eminent German actor, had for several years coached singers, putting emphasis upon such matters as poet's lives, historical periods, customs of the poet's times, and local idioms. Pianists lucky enough to accompany at these sessions were treated to a wealth of information of inestimable worth in their future teaching.

and piano line and their relationships. Routine the rhythm, your most valuable consideration, by various means such as tapping silently or humming the rhythmic patterns.

Return to the piano. Play the song somewhat slowly and with scrupulously accurate rhythm, observing both lines. Repeat often without fretting about notes. Now study the song for correct notes. Mark your accidentals. Don't be afraid to use your pencil; so will your eye be routined. Now attend to fingering.

The next step is to analyze the song's vocal line. With your knowledge of tradition (and your singer's breath control) devise some useful breath marks which do not violate the grammar or intent of the poem. The final step is to make your own short study of the text of the song. (See Chapter 10.) Now, only now, are you ready to work with your singer. Not a moment sooner!

Artistry sometimes engenders a certain eager naiveté. Even as the child eagerly looks forward to his prize, the artist anticipates with childlike expectancy his reward—the beautiful musical moment. This rare quality of enthusiastic openness is a blessing to the accompanist. Those who possess it are fortunate in their work. Ultimately, good teamwork between colleagues who share the same ideals makes the preparation of a song recital such a satisfaction.

REPERTOIRE LIST FOR
BEGINNING ACCOMPANISTS

This list, comprised of music of various degrees of technical difficulty, is designed to acquaint the young accompanist with songs performed more often than others.

Italian Anthology (2 Volumes). G. Schirmer

Italian Songs of the 18th Century. International Music

Handel: *45 Arias.* International Music

Beethoven: *Songs* (complete). Kalmus or Peters

Mozart: *Songs*. Peters

Mendelssohn: *Selected Songs.* Schirmer

Mahler: *24 Songs* (4 Volumes). International Music

Strauss: *27 Songs*. International Music

Brahms: *Selected Songs.* Schirmer or International Music

Schubert: *24 Favorite Songs*. Schirmer or International Music

Schumann: *Collected Songs.* Schirmer

Wolf: *Collected Songs.* International Music

Grieg: *Selected Songs.* Schirmer

Fauré: *Songs* (3 Volumes). Marks

Debussy: *Collected Songs.* International Music

Duparc: *Collected Songs* (2 Volumes). International Music

Ravel: *Cinq Mélodies Populaires Grècques.* Durand

_____: *Don Quichotte à Dulcinée.* Durand

Berlioz: *Les Nuits d'Eté.* International Music

Poulenc: *Airs Chantées.* Salabert

_____: *Banalités.* Eschig

_____: *Deux Poèmes.* Lerolle

Obradors: *Canciones Clasicas* (3 Volumes). Union Musical Española

Falla: *Siete Canciones Populares Españolas.* Eschig

Granados: *Tonadillas.* International Music

Rachmaninoff: *Collected Songs.* Boosey and Hawkes

Dvořák: *Gypsy Songs.* International Music

Barber: *Collected Songs.* Schirmer

Copland: *Old American Songs.* Boosey and Hawkes

Purcell: *40 Songs.* International Music

GUIDELINES FOR PRACTICE

1. Try the following songs in different metronomic tempi—somewhat faster, then somewhat slower than the given metronomic number (or, if there is none, the traditional standard tempo). Compare the results of these tempi with the one requested by the composer, or in some cases by the editor. By means of reference to your text, establish the logic of the composition and stay within it.

Danza, danza fanciulla	Francesco Durante
Der Ring (*Frauenliebe und -leben*)	Robert Schumann
Was ist Sylvia?	Franz Schubert
Nell	Gabriel Fauré
Der Schmied	Johannes Brahms

Determine, after singing and playing these trial-tests (don't just start the song; do the entire composition!), which tempo in each case is most rewarding for you musically and dramatically. Write a paragraph to justify your reasons.

2. What part of the inner life of the following songs is in your opinion expressed by the accompaniment? How?

Meine Liebe ist grün	Johannes Brahms
Die Post	Franz Schubert
Die liebe Farbe (*Die schöne Müllerin*)	Franz Schubert
Polo (*Seven Spanish Songs*)	Manuel de Falla
Le Faune (*Fêtes Galantes*)	Claude Debussy

In the same way, examine the songs you are currently working on.

3. Obtain a Protestant hymn book. With reference to the eight points outlined in this chapter, analyze several hymns of your choice, the more dull the better. Prepare several of these as if they were art songs. You will of course appear eccentric should you attempt your own interpretation while in a church congregation, but your interpretive abilities for recital will be greatly put to the test.

4. Choose songs from the *Schirmer Anthology of Italian Song* and ornament them in several ways. Examine the texts carefully. Use your imagination while adhering to proper performance practice.

5. The following songs contain introductions, interludes, and postludes of various lengths and importance. Decide, as an accompanist, what the sections mean to you musically and dramatically. Into the music write a scenario, outlining what each section indicates. Mold your playing (not acting—leave that to the singer who has the words) accordingly.

Der Tod und das Mädchen	Franz Schubert
Ich hab in Penna (*Italienisches Liederbuch*)	Hugo Wolf
The Dying Nightingale	Norman dello Joio
La Flûte de Pan (*Chansons de Bilitis*)	Claude Debussy
Clair de Lune	Gabriel Fauré

Do the same for your current song repertoire.

6. All libraries contain some collections of folk melodies with easy-to-play, straightforward piano accompaniments. Choose several of varying mood and do the following.

    a. Arrange with your own harmonic and rhythmic invention attractive and colorful piano realizations for a particular singer with whom you are working. Refer to the stylistic piano literature of composers of the country you are drawing from. (See Chapter 14 for further discussion.)

    b. By using one or two instruments other than the piano, arrange some attractive realizations for the recital of a particular singer with whom you are working. Make a list of songs from other repertoires that are scored for the same combination of instruments to be included in the same recital. (It is sometimes good practice to use your instrumentalists more than once in the same program.)

8 Recital Tactics and Strategies

THE RECITAL FROM ITS INITIATION TO THE CRITICS' RESPONSES

I am concerned that there be a reasonable turn-out for my forthcoming recital. Can you help me with some ideas about publicity?

When you are engaged to perform a recital you are asked to submit a biography (a "bio"). This biography is made available to the local newspaper, television stations, and other media for publicity purposes. Normally, the duty of putting together the bio belongs to the singer's agent along with the rest of his responsibilities. Let us offer to the singer who is without management some advice on how to build a correct and effective biography.

Because the song recital is essentially an intimate performance, the bio assumes a double importance. Have no romantic illusions; this is purely a Madison Avenue advertising strategy. The product to be sold includes no chorus, no conductor, no corps de ballet, no sets or costumes—just two artists (two personalities), perhaps on occasion a third assisting artist, and the music scheduled for performance. The audience is to experience an evening of direct communication from this two-part artistic team only. Enjoyment of this intimate musical adventure can be expanded when it is accompanied by knowledge of the artists' backgrounds. This is one of the compelling reasons for putting together a program cleverly tailored to the singer. The program itself is one factor in the advertising of the singer's exploits. An eclectic and varied program should reflect the versatility and imagination of the singer and point up his special background and skills.

Most managers have two kinds of bios at hand for every artist they represent. The first, the large bio, lists all the pertinent facts about the singer in full detail. Care should be taken that all facts are constantly updated since recitals are often planned some time in advance. The list should include:

1. name, place of birth (state and country only)
2. type of voice
3. pictures (glossies)
4. where the artist has performed
5. listing of important performance dates (in order of importance)
6. nature of the recital program being offered (compositions of topical, ethnic, or locally special interest)
7. important musicians with whom artist has studied (voice teachers, conductors, drama coaches, famous singers)
8. artist's knowledge of a country (or composer from that country) whose music will be featured on that recital
9. any first performances offered
10. personal bits of information (husband, children, wife, degrees, hobbies, prizes, etc.)
11. interesting information as to attire artist will wear (make sure that these items, jewelry especially, do not appear too "show biz")
12. reviews (best ones only)
13. time and place for recital, ticket sale, etc.

The second kind of biography is called a program bio. It is sent to the sponsoring organization to be used in the actual program. It should include:

1. a short bio culled from the large bio, devoted to well-chosen highlights from the singer's career (best to ask in advance how many words are preferred)
2. the program itself
3. translations
4. program notes

I am preparing a recital and am a novice at making program notes. Do you have any general guidelines to help me organize my program notes?

Let us begin with the assumption that the program notes refer to any extra materials other than the program of the recital itself. Although the advantages of having program notes decidedly outweight the disadvantages, serious thought about the issue reveals two drawbacks.

1. No matter how good the idea behind them, or the notes themselves, they do distract the listener during the performance. The pages rustle; they divert not only the audience but the performer. Annoyed by paper noise, Toscanini once ordered programs made of gold silk, believing that they would not rattle; instead they rustled. Howard Shanet tried heavy cards for children's concerts, anticipating complete quiet; instead they were used as frisbees! It is especially distracting to hear pages turned during songs or during cyclic groups where no applause is expected. (The printer's dummy must be checked against such mistakes.)

2. To enable the audience to read program notes, some audience lights must be on, thereby negating the theatrical quality of the recital. We happen to be of the old school that considers every performance a theatrical event, even an orchestral concert. A theatrical event is a magical event; elementary psychology dictates that the performer be lighted and the audience darkened. This is not a critical factor if you sing for your own pleasure at home, but if you sing in public you should be more elevated and illuminated than the audience. The above discussion notwithstanding, a compromise—some dim audience lighting—must probably be offered for those who wish to read program notes during the music.

When weighing these pros and cons with a view to making a decision, practical matters must be taken into consideration. Can you afford the extra pages of printing? If finances are a problem one might weigh the advantages of (1) limiting program notes to short paraphrases of the texts and the minimal necessary information combined with the program listings or (2) printing the notes by a cheaper method than the program itself, such as mimeo or offset.

There are criteria other than financial that may influence your decision. Should the text be printed in toto? Should it be printed in both languages or only in translation? Should the translation be literal or paraphrased?

Howard Shanet, presently of the Columbia University music department, but whose long and distinguished career included an incumbency as writer of program notes for the New York Philharmonic Orchestra, answers these questions with a conviction born of experience. If you have the money, by all means print the complete text in both languages. As to what kind of translation, Mr. Shanet believes that the original language provides the poetic beauty; therefore the translation should be literal.

Elaborating further, Mr. Shanet reminds us that in the concert hall we are *reading* the translation for a quick understanding of the underlying meaning. We will *listen* to the poetic subleties of the original language as the singer performs. (In metropolitan centers there is a large public that listens in the original language. They understand the language and they know the literature and the tradition.) Unless the translator is especially gifted at combining poetic sounds and thoughts with a close-to-literal translation, it is best to settle for just a verbatim translation.[1] (For a thorough discussion of an allied subject—whether to sing an English translation or not, see Chapter 15, Innovations.)

If you cannot afford to print comprehensive notes and a choice is forced upon you, then the text and/or translation must gain the day. Given the unlikely circumstance of unlimited funds or an "angel," there are many other facts that belong in your program notes. What you put in the notes depends on several issues. Is your audience learned or unsophisticated? Is it a closed, popular, or university concert? Did the audience buy the whole series and happen to get you?

Pure musicology is always out of place, partially for reasons of time. Also, you must do what is most useful to most people while keeping the notes as compact as possible. Do not be didactic. It will not succeed in a few paragraphs anyway, and at the same time it will frighten and/or bore the untutored audience.[2] Cathy Berberian tells about writing program notes in the form of a chatty letter that described her interest in the fin-de-siècle program. In effect, she supplied swift information while making sure that the words reflected her personality. In this way the notes were not dry as dust, which insured their being read. The crucial information was transmitted in the most palatable way.

The minimal but essential program notes include such vital statistics as the full and real name of the composer and the poet,[3] the real title of the piece, the birth and death dates of the composer, and where he was born and died. These facts give the audience insight as to why the performer chose this composer's work and also places the composer chronologically. Any further comments do not have to be erudite. They can consist of a brief paragraph which offers:

> 1. some insight not evident from the performance (e.g., that a song is part of a collection that had such and such meaning to the composer, or this song was much valued by another great person, such as Goethe);

1. Surely it is unnecessary to repeat word for word each reiteration made by the singer in, for example, a repetitive Baroque composition.
2. Mr. Shanet once solved such a dilemma neatly by explaining the entire twelve-tone theory in a footnote!
3. If your program has no separate program notes, list the poets' names next to the titles of the compositions. Should you feel that a certain poet is unusually significant, you can put his name on the program as well as in your program notes.

2. some fact of human interest (e.g., this song was written just after the death of the composer's mother);

3. some charming or colorful detail (e.g., this song was dedicated to the composer's wife on her birthday);

4. some extra touch of liveliness, quaint or curious sidelight (e.g., this poem was set in four different ways by the composer).

In addition, some explanation ought to be made of areas in which people are less well-educated, such as medieval literature or Spanish repertoire. An example of such a special case is certainly afforded us by the twentieth-century repertoire. Frequently an audience is faced with an avant-garde piece of such complexity that they comprehend only one idea out of many that the composer is attempting to put across. Yet how much can be taught in a short paragraph or sentence? If it is a long paragraph of notes it may well defeat its own purpose.

The twentieth century sets a great value on innovation and novelty. First performances are treated very seriously; second performances, when and if they take place, slip by unnoticed. It is difficult literally to get to "know" a new composition by repeated hearings. Before Beethoven, novelty was not prized as such. Haydn knew just how far he could go with novelty within the rules Esterhazy set forth. No one minded that Beethoven innovated very little. If we could apply our twentieth-century standards to an unknown Beethoven we would have to say, "This composer owes more than fifty per cent of his inspriation to his towering predecessors, Mozart and Haydn!" The price for our modern love of novelty is the loss of an audience, most of which does not know what the composer is doing. Perhaps the best practical answer to the problem is this: if something can be said in a brief way to shed light on a complicated twentieth-century composition, then say it.

How do you decide what your recital gown should look like?

As we have said, the recital is a theatrical event, but the gown must escape being a costume by just the slightest margin. It must combine flair and practicality without making you feel ill at ease. It must in some respect complement your personality. Remember that the visual element is extremely important in your recital.

As the recital dress is such an important consideration, we have chosen to offer the following guidelines:

I. General remarks on male and female attire

   A. Caveats

   1. Lack of good taste and dignity will probably be noticed more than their presence.

   2. Clothing must be comfortable for wearing and for singing, as well as becoming.

      a. Check front and rear, walking and standing, and the effect of raising the arms.

      b. Consider size, height, bone structure, and coloring when making decisions.

   3. Do not fail to coordinate plans for dress with your accompanist. If accompanist and singer are both women, coordinate style and color as well.

  B. Practical guidelines

  1. Outside of metropolitan centers, audiences are more interested in dress.

  2. Do not be so far out-of-date that the effect is old-fashioned.

  3. Do not be so dignified that the effect is drab.

  4. Do not be so fashionable that the effect is bizarre.

  5. Sing, gesture, and walk in your clothing, watching the rear as well as the front.

  6. Keep a record of what gown was worn on each occasion so as not to repeat your wardrobe in the same location.

II. Daytime appearances (or auditions)

  A. Female dress

  1. A suit versus a dress

      a. A dress is better than a suit if your figure is full.

      b. A jacket must fit so that there is no need to tug it down after raising your arms.

  2. Skirts

      a. A loose one is usually better than a tight one.

         (1) A tight skirt wrinkles more easily.

         (2) A tight skirt calls attention to figure faults.

         (3) A loose skirt hides the bouncing breathing mechanism.

      b. Length

         (1) Make sure the length is suitable to your figure.

         (2) Keep it dignified even if you have no figure faults.

         (3) Be stylish, not faddish.

         (4) Check front and rear in the mirror for graceful sight lines.

         (5) Remember that a full skirt appears shorter than the same length in a slender skirt.

  3. Style or cut

      a. Waistline or crosswise seams cut figure and make you appear shorter and fatter.

  b. Princess lines lengthen and slim the figure.

  c. Flowing and loose fit tends to flatter any figure.

4. Belts

   a. A belt cuts your figure in half—not helpful for short or stout figures.

   b. Contrasting belts are only useful if you are very slim or tall and wish to appear shorter or wider.

   c. If you use a belt, make sure it does not hamper breathing.

5. Fabrics

   a. Stiff fabrics

      (1) Since stiff fabrics tend to be made into tight silhouettes, they are very hard for larger figures to wear gracefully.

      (2) When stiff fabrics are made into fuller silhouettes, they are helpful to painfully slender persons, though unbecoming to larger figures.

      (3) Stiff fabric wrinkles easily.

   b. Soft fabrics

      (1) These are more crease-resistant.

      (2) They are generally more becoming to larger figures.

   c. Patterned fabrics

      (1) Large patterns in fabric are sometimes of questionable taste.

      (2) Large patterns add size to the figure.

      (3) Busy patterns in fabric are generally distracting from the stage.

      (4) See yourself from a distance comparable to the length of hall in order to judge efficiently.

      (5) Crosswise stripes add weight and subtract height.

   d. Color

      (1) Above all, the color must be becoming from near and far.

      (2) Be sure to coordinate color of dress with accessories.

6. Shoes

   a. Coordinate with costume as to color and style.

   b. Avoid excesses; try for fashion versus staginess.

   c. Consider the occasion carefully when opting for boots, sandals, or sport shoes.

7. Jewelry

   a. Try for the same good taste as in real life. (A wise fashion coordinator once said, "When in doubt, take off one piece.")

   b. Make sure that any dangling pieces do not distract the audience from your eyes or face or call undue attention to breathing mechanism.

   c. Be very sure no pieces interfere with singing.

8. Hair

   a. Check both full face and profile for becomingness and rear view for neatness.

   b. Make sure style is neat and reveals the eyes. Throwing your hair about to get it out of your eyes gives an undignified impression and distracts the audience from the musical experience.

B. Male attire

1. Suit versus jacket and trousers ensemble

   a. Sports jackets are to be avoided, but a dark blazer is acceptable.

      (1) A blazer and pants ensemble cuts height and adds weight.
      (2) Coat and pants of same color and fabric add height and achieve a slimming effect.

   b. A solid-color suit is always good.

   c. A vested suit is elegant.

   d. Make sure pants are long enough to hide socks completely.

   e. The fit must be comfortable so that no tugging down of jacket or sleeves is necessary.

2. Tie

   a. A conservative one is best.

   b. Make sure your tie is not so tight that singing is made uncomfortable.

3. Shoes

   a. Coordinate shoe color with suit.

   b. Dark shoes are best.

   c. Be sure shoes are well-shined.

4. Shirt

   a. White is no longer necessary, but it remains the most elegant.

   b. White is not good on television; pale blue is better.

   c. Cuffs should be one-half inch below jacket sleeves.

   d. Check to see that the sleeves return to position after an arm movement.

   e. Make sure the collar is comfortable when singing.

5. Socks

   a. Always wear dark socks!

   b. They must be high enough to hide leg skin when you are sitting on stage.

   c. Socks must be tight or secured by garters so that there are no wrinkles.

6. Vest

   a. Be sure its length is adequate to avoid an unsightly gap between your trousers and vest.

   b. Suspenders are recommended; they are safe and comfortable.

7. Hair

   a. Choose a neat and becoming style.

   b. Avoid outlandish styles.

   c. Keep your hair away from your eyes and face so that your eyes can be easily seen by the audience.

III. Formal appearances

   A. Female

   1. General

      a. If your accompanist is female, coodinate your dress color and style with hers.

      b. Check both front and back for fit and becomingness.

      c. A good rule is: not too decolleté.

      d. Raise your arms and walk in your gown when checking the fit.

      e. Create a visual effect by coordinating color and style of gown to reflect to some degree the recital theme, careful as always to use good taste.

   2. Gown

      a. Style

         (1) Consider the size of auditorium when choosing the style.

         (2) Generally, one chooses a style that is slimming, but since distance is slimming in a very large auditorium, you can risk a bit of fullness in the skirt, sheen of the fabric, etc.

         (3) The fit must not be so tight as to call attention to abdominal breathing movements.

         (4) Princess lines are more slimming than belted or waistline-seamed styles.

         (5) Trains are elegant and graceful (as well as a bit mature) but they can get tangled; practice beforehand in such a gown.

         (6) A skirt can tangle too; make it a bit shorter in front.

         (7) A tightly fitting skirt means that you cannot sit during intermission; a bit of fullness is more manageable.

         (8) The use of a stole or cape depends upon your ability to wear them without their becoming a distraction and your ease in handling them. Properly used, either one becomes a useful prop.

b. Fabric

(1) Dull fabrics subract weight.

(2) Shiny fabrics (satin, sequins, rhinestones) add weight.

(3) Taffeta and brocade give a subtle sheen.

(4) Velvet is rich, elegant, possibly a bit mature (but good for early music, when it borders on being a costume).

(5) Chiffon is feminine and graceful and becoming to most figures.

c. Color

(1) Color should carry well in the auditorium but not at the expense of being unbecoming.

(2) Personal coloring should be set off by the color of the gown.

(3) Test the color under the lights; what gel makes a good or bad effect? Lavenders, blues, and greens are especially hard to light.

(4) Pale colors are less stimulating than bright colors.

(5) Bright colors add weight; dark colors subtract weight.

(6) An audience wants to see something special; the formal occasion and the esthetic of your musical message demand more than drabness, however dignified.

d. Wear shields: those lights are very hot!

3. Shoes

   a. Test the color under the lights, as you do your gown.

   b. Color of shoes should match or coordinate well with gown.

   c. Be sure shoes are comfortable and broken in.

4. Jewelry

   a. Earrings must not distract by sparkling or shining too much in the light or swaying or dangling to distract excessively.

   b. If in doubt, remove one more piece of jewelry.

B. Male attire

1. General

   a. Formerly, tuxedos or tails were obtained from custom tailors. Now they are frequently rented. Custom tailors are not necessary if you wish to own your own, because good-fitting evening clothes, especially tuxedos, are now readily available off the rack at lower prices than many suits. (Most reputable rental establishments will keep your measurements on file so that you need only telephone for convenient pickup.)

   b. When renting or buying, be sure to take with you a person knowledgeable about tailoring and fit.

   c. Tails remain classic but tuxedos have changed in style and tailoring details toward a less subtle, a more "peacock" look.

    d. In choosing tails or tuxedo and accessories, play it safe and err on the side of conservatism; the conservative look generally projects elegance, whereas too stylish a choice may be offensive to the conservative members of the audience.

2. Jacket

    a. An Edwardian cut to a tuxedo is flattering only to tall, fairly slender men.

    b. A short or thick-set body is better off in a traditional, looser cut.

    c. Check such tailoring details as piping, brocade lapels, etc. to make sure the effect is flattering to figure and face.

3. Pants

    a. The length of pants must be on the long side, but not so long that they bag at the bottom near the break.

4. Shirts

    a. A white turtleneck shirt is acceptable only when you are sure that it will not be offensive to your audience on a particular occasion.

    b. Make sure that your body-build can carry off the turtleneck style; long slender necks fare better in a turtleneck than short, thick necks.

    c. Ruffled shirts should be used only when they are flattering to your build and age.

    d. Colored shirts with a tuxedo are now in style; the effect is less formal and less serious.

    e. Two shirts (one for the second half) will help to assure personal freshness.

5. Vests and cummerbunds

    a. Tuxedo vests and cummerbunds (velvet, brocade, colored, etc.) can be very fancy.

    b. A contrasting color does call attention to such figure faults as a protruding stomach or, excessive shortness.

    c. Shiny fabrics add weight to portly figures; dull fabrics tend to slenderize.

    d. Make sure that a tail waistcoat does not ride up when your arms are raised, thus making your shirt poke out messily.

6. Protect your investment in tails or a tuxedo. Remember the hot lights and use a strong deodorant or have shields sewn into the jacket. (You should also be pleasant to be near after the concert!)

Should I rehearse in my recital gown before the recital?

You certainly should. Let's say a particular gown has a small train. You need to rehearse the skill of handling it gracefully. Experienced singers do not underestimate the necessity of practicing such things. A feeling of naturalness and physical comfort in your recital attire is not a frivolous concern. Any discomfort that interferes with your concentration, especially one so easily disposed of, should be dealt with. A personal rule, learned through experience, is to practice in your gown until you feel as natural in it as you do in your bathrobe.

Exactly what should I eat and what should I do on the day of the recital?

Only deductive logic and common sense can provide the answer. Each singer has a personal solution, arrived at by trial and error. For most, eating a full meal too near the time of the performance results in lethargy, which makes them sing at a disadvantage. On the other hand, a light dinner after four o'clock in the afternoon will usually ensure the needed energy. As to what to eat, some find carbohydrates anathema to be avoided at all costs. For some, toast and a small quantity of fruit eaten close to concert time serves as a pick-me-up. Some must eat only bland foods, some only protein. Tea or coffee is another personal choice, again learned from experience. In short, there are as many answers as there are metabolisms. Learn which is yours.

Traveling on the day of a concert, though at times unavoidable, can be a serious handicap for the singer and accompanist. The lulling drone of car wheels and motors causes lassitude and inertia for some time after the trip. By far the best activities on the day of a recital are rest, quiet, light eating, a short walk, and time for a calm review of the music and texts from the program.

One of the advantages of the recital as opposed to other media of vocal performance is that you may schedule your own rehearsal times for greatest convenience and productivity. You are usually limited only by the presence on your program of accompanying artists other than your pianist. Under these conditions, rehearsal time must be chosen at the convenience of all concerned. In any case, scheduling a dress rehearsal on the same day as the recital ought to be avoided at all costs. Should the rehearsal be the least bit strenuous, it may tire you and most likely will take the bloom off your voice. In planning the ensemble rehearsal a day or two earlier you gain the valuable time with which to rethink and assess your work and behavior.

What's so important about rehearsing in the recital hall?

Our impulsive response is to say, "When you have done your first recital without a rehearsal in the hall, you will understand." Here is a representative check-list of things that must be done at the hall:

1. Check the tuning and action of the piano. This includes the entire condition of the piano. Lest you think that we exaggerate, permit us to illustrate. In a certain tropical country, pressed for time and harassed by the heat and humidity, we neglected to check the piano thoroughly. Imagine Mr. Sonntag's surprise on the first chord of the concert when his

foot, searching for the pedal, encountered nothingness. How does one tactfully ask the music committee to supply piano pedals?

2. Check the acoustics and balance of the hall, and place the piano in the proper position. At first you may experience a disorientation. For some reason it does not sound or feel as it did in the studio. This anxiety can be dispelled in short order. Take measures to find the best location for the piano and to eliminate or minimize all possible curtains or back-drops that absorb sound. Having done this, sing again and acquaint yourself with the new sensation. It is quite possible that some halls will never give you the comfortable acoustic sensations you were accustomed to elsewhere. Practice coping with the disquieting sensations until they interfere minimally with your technical control.

3. Give all instructions to the backstage personnel. Check out the geography of the stage and backstage. By this we mean: From where do I enter? Will there be a curtain? Where is my dressing room? Perhaps we should have said, *Is* there a dressing room? At an afternoon rehearsal in another town, discovering to our horror that there was no dressing room at all, no off-stage area, and that we had to enter from the open air, we spent the rest of the afternoon searching out a black umbrella large enough to cover both of us in case of rain between song groups.

4. If you do not want your eyes to be described as pools of sepulchral darkness and if you do not wish the audience to sacrifice half of its pleasure by being deprived of your eyes, check the lighting very carefully![4] When you do your rehearsal in the hall ask a friend to view you from mid-audience and criticize your overall appearance. Awareness of the effect of lights on one's bone structure is part of the craft of a recitalist. It either enhances the visual appreciation of the audience or mars it. Most singers profit from using an amber or pink gel, due to its soft and warm effect on the face and figure.

By doing these chores assiduously before the concert you will have escaped numberless possible harassments and you will have given yourself the pleasure of total concentration on what you are going to do.

I'm all right once I'm in front of the audience, but what can I do to alleviate my suffering in that dreadful green room?

First, recognize that what you have done *before* you arrived in the green room can affect what happens *in* the green room. Stagefright, that inexplicable misery that makes cowards of us all, is not truly irradicable. You can, however, ameliorate the condition by not cramming or superficially skimming over your preparation work. By thorough, deliberate, *slowed-down* learning techniques it is possible to replace stagefright with

4. Jennifer Tipton, famed lighting designer, says that ninety-nine and nine-tenths percent of the audience is not conscious of the lighting, but one hundred percent of the audience is moved by it.

cognizance of your competence. This in turn allows you to concentrate on what you are going to do and drives out fears of catastrophe that might befall you on stage. (See Chapter 10.)

It is more difficult to give advice about what you ought to do in the green room, because one must work out one's own method, but the following is a list of what *not* to do.

1. Do not allow visitors backstage before the concert or during the intermission.

2. Do not waste your energies by talking.

3. Do not fret about letting down your voice teacher.

4. Do not try to be "great." Just try to use well the skills you have spent so much time acquiring—vocal, musical, dramatic.

5. Do not chastise yourself about your responsibility toward family or friends.

6. Do not arrive at the hall so early that you become psychologically drained before performing nor so late that, through anxiety, you will lose composure.

Here are a few representative "dos":

1. Quiet concentrated reviewing of musical and technical points from the recital is helpful.

2. Sing full voice before going out, if it has (during the rehearsals and rehearsal-concerts) been judged to be useful or necessary.

3. In short, keep your mind on what you are going to *do* and not on what *might* happen.

Our personal recommendation is as follows:

1. The accompanist, having most often the responsibility of the introduction, keeps his mind on what he is going to do, by this method. He places the music to the first song in front of him, on a table if necessary, and concentrates so intensely that he is literally playing page one in his mind (or on the piano, should there be one backstage).

2. The singer, with the further responsibilities of text and language, of facing the audience plastically, of sheer memorization, finds the following method of pre-concert concentration useful, especially for new programs. For every song on the program she has written (after rehearsals and practice-concerts) a list of important dos and don'ts. In the green room, before the recital and between groups, she maintains concentrated attention to this list, again keeping her mind forcibly on what she will *do*. As Stanislavski says, "To find public solitude is to conquer nervousness."

Why did my friends all say they were extremely nervous for me when I first walked out to the piano?

Because you walked in awkwardly and arrived center stage with visible relief, clutching the piano with your right hand as if it were your only safe haven, your audience felt apprehensive for you.

Since the interpretation of text in addition to music demands a certain amount of personal communication, a singer is accustomed to dealing with the fact of personality in entering and bowing. He knows that there must be immediate rapport as he enters. It would behoove instrumentalists to take this ability seriously, because, to quote stage director Robert Ackart, "if the artist's entrance is ill-timed, ungainly, too remote or too eager, his audience is put off and it is no easy job to win back its allegiance once this reaction has set in!" Moreover, even real dignity of spirit can be diminished or even concealed from the audience by a posture slouch. However unfair it may be, a drooping posture conveys only lack of assurance or composure.

One method to assure that the singer's attitude toward the people in the audience will produce a sincere yet dignified communication is for him to hold the thought while entering that he is, quite simply, glad that they came and complimented by their presence. When entering the stage, the experienced singer knows that taking in the entire audience with his glances subtly flatters his public into an initial warm mood of acceptance.

One must be aware that the artist is himself on the stage only when he is entering, leaving, or bowing. While singing, he is what the work demands. When, indeed, he is himself, to quote Mr. Ackart again, "he communicates directly; it is important that this communication be effected warmly, assuredly, and in the proper tempo to make the audience feel comfortable in the artist's presence."

An accompanist who walks on the stage on the heels of the vocalist displays at once his inexperience. If indeed he wishes to be considered an artist in his own right and responsible for his share of the evening's success, he must not trail after the singer in a puppy-dog fashion. A useful device is to count four or five seconds after the entrance of the singer, then, while observing the audience, walk neatly to the piano, assemble the music, and prepare to begin. At the conclusion of a group he should remain seated, gather the music, and finally leave the platform only after the vocalist has walked some distance toward the wings. If the singer wishes the accompanist to bow after a group, the accompanist should do so with a cheerful attitude and with no show of humility, lest he put to a lie his singer's original gesture. His bow should be sincere, straight to the audience, performed at the right of the piano bench, and, above all, unencumbered by music.

Incidentally, should a singer at the time of a recital suffer from a cold or any other vocal indisposition, he should never inform his audience of the condition. What you may think of as bravado will only condition the public to be suspiciously watchful of your vocal problems or errors, and hence less appreciative of your artistry.

Are there occasions when the bad temper of the audience impinges upon one's concentration?

With the focus of your mind centered where it ought to be, you will probably not give heed to the audience's disposition for a while. When it finally permeates your consciousness, it will be because they show warmth, indifference, or animosity. When the audience is affectionate, bask in their general approval without losing sight of your goals. When they are indifferent, try harder. When they are hostile, you must choose between battle and defeat. You may also infrequently encounter hecklers who are actually disruptive. At this point, you must deal with the situation either by ignoring it or with reciprocal severity.

Why do I fall apart and forget everything when I get in front of people?

There can be several reasons. First, analyze your methods of study to see if they are producing maximum security. (See Chapter 10 for guidance.) Second, immediately after you have the memorizing done and the ensemble fairly well coordinated, invite friends (enemies are even more effective!) to each and every rehearsal. Performing before very few people in a smallish room puts the pressure severely and prematurely upon yourself and is much more demanding and pressured than the same performance before a large audience in a large hall. Furthermore, putting this pressure upon yourself in advance clearly indicates to you *where* you will lose concentration if your nerves get the better of you. After each rehearsal you can then take the necessary steps to correct or make more secure those places indicated. Under such a regime, facing the larger audience, will, by contrast, seem less stressful and, by giving you an actual feeling of relief, will make it possible for you to enjoy giving your recital.

Third, test the control of your skills in a larger audience situation. Try out your program at home with invited audiences. Remember that the recital was originally a salon entertainment. Offer your program to your church or synagogue. This practice will provide you with the very real benefits of performing your songs in the program order. You will learn the feeling of uninterrupted continuity and gain confidence accordingly.

After each rehearsal-concert reevaluate where you lost control and why. Discuss with your coach and your voice teacher ways and means of improving your ability to think and operate on more than one level during performance.

In performance, attention to one skill often robs attention from another, thus resulting in a domino-like collapse of them all. It is the interaction of your skills that must be placed under control in order to increase security in performance. For those who still suffer horribly before the concert and so badly during it that a good performance is impossible, help may be on the way from the medical profession. Experiments with stage-fright sufferers are underway; they involve a "beta-blocker" drug, a compound that lowers adrenalin. Until results are in, the only alternative is to be as secure technically as possible.

I was so embarrassed when I applauded and no one else did!

Do not be embarrassed. All applause is welcome. If an artist has programmed a group of songs or a cycle during which he would prefer no applause, he should have printed on the program a note to that effect.

Occasionally an overly enthusiastic member of an audience will suddenly applaud midway in a song. Unwittingly he points up the singer's inability to sustain mood properly. (See Chapter 6.) The singer in this instance is the real culprit. Therefore he should not quiet his audience with an imperious hand gesture that may well be offensive. Instead, let him earnestly continue to sing, redoubling the effort to sustain a stronger mood, secure in the knowledge that his audience will shortly quiet down, having recognized its blunder.

Is there a rule for acknowledging the accompanist?

So far as we know, there is no rule, precisely because it is a personal matter. The acknowledgment of applause, like entering and bowing, is a moment that reflects not only each of the two artists as individuals but also the relationship between them. Consequently, after each group, I prefer to acknowledge the applause of the audience alone at first, then together with my accompanist. In addition, I personally enjoy acknowledging my accompanist at the end of an individual song when I feel his playing has been in some way unusually contributory. At the conclusion of a recital it gives me great pleasure to take most of the bows with him at my side.

How long should the intermission be?

Fifteen minutes is the usual time for an intermission. But where is it written that there cannot be two intermissions? Your program may well benefit from two shorter intermissions. Do not be afraid to be different.

When I did my last recital I made silly mistakes at the beginning of the second half. Why?

The second half of the program usually contains slightly easier music; this presents a particular hazard. The first half has gone well in spite of its difficulty. During the intermission one has a feeling of justifiable satisfaction and a consequent natural relaxation of tensions. Stealthily, relaxation turns into carelessness. You start the first song a bit unconcentrated; one careless mistake breeds a second and panic ensues. To avert such a scenario, after a well-deserved rest at the beginning of the intermission, reestablish your concentration as you did before the first half.

Does a singer ever receive adverse criticism about speaking during a recital?

Some people are dogmatically opposed to any speaking from the platform. Others may feel that explaining a song is a condescension on the part of the singer. There can hardly be a rule governing such matters. It resolves to a matter of taste. A few guidelines suggest themselves. In general, you will find that speaking proves more effective during a light-hearted group of songs; when the written word cannot explain the song as well as the personal spoken word, speaking is for me advisable, especially since it also establishes rapport with the audience.

An otherwise complimentary review by a Miami critic contained criticism of my speaking before some Brazilian songs sung in Portuguese. The Brazilian songs, however, lent themselves to spoken explanations for several reasons. They are humorous, and we know that humor is usually best at the immediate moment rather than when it is diluted by the printed word. Also, these songs contain allusions to local color and folklore that are not clarified by the words of the song.

You will probably not open yourself up to criticism if you confine spoken remarks, even those done expressly to dilute the formality of the occasion, to the kind of information that could properly be termed an oral program note. (See above, page 152.)[5]

Because American audiences generally favor informality, speaking from the platform offers advantages, provided that the speaking is ingeniously "rehearsed." An unrehearsed speech is too apt to fail in its total effect, if only because the rest of the program is so well planned and studied. Naturally, your speaking must *seem* spontaneous. (In the rare case of singers who are both experienced and gifted at informal public speaking, it can be truly spontaneous.) If you have done your preparation well, each of your different audiences will believe that you have made up your words at that moment, in spite of the fact that you have said essentially the same words at each recital.

5. The conservative New York Times on a Sunday in May, 1978, reported that "If —— had managed to play the guitar with as much easygoing charm as he revealed when chatting with the audience at Carnegie Recital Hall. . . , his recital would have been a complete delight. . . . he talked about the music, pondered the listening habits of his four-year old son, and described how Manuel Ponce's dog would howl when Andrès Segovia played the eight repeated E's that introduce the wonderful molto adagio section of Villa Lobos's Prelude in A minor." The Times' approval of the "casual eloquence with which Mr. —— told his stories. . " suggests that there is more than one critical point of view with regard to speaking by the performing artist. Almost certainly, most professional recitalists would insist that the *audience* is delighted to experience the personality and charm of the artist that is revealed through the spoken word.

What do I tell the usher about the flowers?

Tell him or her to bring flowers to the stage without hesitation exactly upon your first reappearance after having completed the program. If possible to arrange, a male usher for a female singer and female usher for a male singer makes a nice picture. The vocalist must be on guard not to prolong the acceptance of these tokens lest the audience feel constrained to extend the applause—no matter how well deserved—past the point of spontaneity.

Could I sing "Annie Laurie" for an encore?

By all means. An encore, that extra gift that artists bestow upon the audience in gratitude for its appreciation, becomes a fine opportunity to display at a relaxed moment their favorite musical inclinations, their humor, or a skill for which they are justifiably known. Therefore, this moment is traditionally served best by old favorites, humorous songs, or famous operatic arias which have no place on the program itself. One must learn to judge the disposition of the audience during these final moments in order to make on-the-spot decisions as to the number of encores.

Contingent upon the fervor of the audience, an artist may be assured of at least two encores. In this case, the first planned encore might well be in quiet contrast to the final song of the recital, the second a brighter or more colorful one.

Only rarely does a singer sing an encore after a cycle or a program of song cycles. The structure of a cycle makes an encore somewhat inadvisable. However, an encore after a recital of, say, all Spanish music is certainly seemly. In such a case, another song from this repertoire is à propos.

Before planning to do a "bis," which is a repeat of a song already sung during the program, consider whether this type of encore really satisfies the audience as much as it does on first hearing.

I once spoke to a celebrated singer who felt that it was not necessary to attend the after-recital party because, as she said, "When I finish singing, my work is done." Was she right?

She was wrong. A recital is an intimate form of musical communication. One must accept the assertion that any audience has the right to meet the artist and thank him or her. In the case of a recital, a short time assigned for social meeting is beneficial for all concerned. The party fulfills this need. An artist who wishes to pursue a career as a recitalist must try to attract a public following. A body of followers usually assures reengagements. The public loves to touch in some way the personal life of an artist. It is in this sense that the recital party becomes part of the artist's duty. (Obviously, illness or unfeigned fatigue are valid excuses for missing it.) At the party the artist must be himself. He should not stay too long, but he must show interest by remembering names![6] The audience must be trained and nurtured until it feels the desire to become devotees of the song recital.

Do you have a philosophy about critics?

Many famous artists have openly declared that they do only one thing about critiques: ignore them totally. A powerful argument in favor of this attitude is best described in the playwright Edward Albee's words: "In the theater, an author has got to be grateful quite often for good reviews for the wrong reason. It's enormously fortunate that an author can receive good reviews for exactly the reason that he intended." It is surely as infuriating and frustrating for an artist to receive a good review for the wrong reasons as it is to receive a bad review for whatever reasons.

Yet one can mount a strong argument in favor of reading and weighing all reviews. The positive benefit that a considered and competent judgment can exert on an artist's work is of immeasurable value in that artist's growth. It is hard for a performer to remember that a critic is not a superman. He does not exist on a higher level than other musical professionals, he is just an ordinary audience member (as he hastens to point out to anyone who registers a complaint) who happens to write as well as any other reporter hired by his newspaper. As he often reiterates in his own defense, he writes only what he sees and hears. He is ignorant of the personal problems and the artistic and technical growth of the performer. He sees and hears only what the performer does at the moment of performance. (It is precisely because the critic really *is* just a single human being that he tends to write more sympathetically of a singer whose background he knows, a fact that impels a competent artist's manager to supply the critic with details of his client's credentials in advance of a debut performance.) Therefore, whether this man with a pencil in his hand gives a good or bad review, his words *do* reflect how you appear to an unexceptional audience member. It follows that if his perception of your greatest strengths (or weaknesses) does not agree with your own self-evaluation, then whether or not you agree it is wise to reappraise what you are doing.

Nevertheless, an ill-considered or incompetent judgment can be devastating, and permanent in its effect. This fact has prompted many scandalous and scurrilous remarks against critics, some of the most amusing of which were written by Eric Satie:

> There are three kinds of critics: the important ones, the less important ones, and the unimportant ones. The last two kinds do not exist. All critics are important.

6. A certain renowned artist makes it a special point to send thank-you notes to his host while waiting for the departing plane. He also sends Christmas cards. He is also reengaged.

There is no such thing as mediocrity or incompetence among critics. A critic who is mediocre or incompetent would be the laughing stock of his fellow critics and it would be impossible for him to exercise his profession—I mean his priestly calling.

Only the critic can impose discipline. . . . Anyone who disobeys is to be pitied. . . . But we must not obey our evil passion. How can we tell which are our evil passions? By the pleasure we take in giving way to them and the pain they cause the critics. They have no evil passions, poor fellows. They have no passions of any kind—not at all.[7]

Schoenberg, too, was driven to lash out against the critics. Castigating the Viennese press for repeating a popular canard about Mahler in Mahler's obituary, Schoenberg retorted sarcastically that this seeming injustice probably equalizes in the long run: the composer will be rewarded with posthumous honor in recompense for the persecution he suffered while alive, whereas the esteem enjoyed by the living critic will be offset by the disdain of future generations.

Richard Dyer, in his excellent article "Singing: Does It Ever Make Sense?"[8] states that talking about (and criticizing) of singing is very difficult. Agreement is unlikely, owing to many interwoven factors. These factors are mingled with myth, metaphor, and inconsistencies, partly due to the critic, who often originates them. The noble but embattled field of voice pedagogy has contributed its quota of confusion as to terminology. Skills that Mr. Dyer believes should be evaluated by the critic include:

1. note accuracy
2. pitch
3. knowledge of instructions from the composer
4. enunciation
5. dynamics
6. dramatic understanding

Generally accepted is the fact that much sarcasm has been penned by critics who fall into the trap of writing cleverly instead of truthfully. (Much of Claude Debussy's ribald attacks on works of his contempories was omitted from *Monsieur Croche, The Dilettante Hater*,[9] a book devoted to the French composer's critical writings. The conjecture is that he regretted having written them and held them back from the early publication.)

7. Myers, Rollo H., *Eric Satie*, Dover Books, 1968.
8. The New York Times, March 17, 1974.
9. Claude Debussy, *Monsieur Croche, The Dilettante Hater* (New York: Viking Press, 1957).

Unfortunately, at the time of its publication, literary sarcasm can do considerable harm to a performer's status and to his ego. Until sarcasm is no longer employed, a singer who is unfairly attacked in such a manner has no option save to attempt to ignore the review.

The following observations are drawn from a survey we made of recital reviews in *The New York Times* in 1976 and 1977.

1. Critics generally did not discuss the program per se *if* they liked the artist. But when they found the performance poor the choice of songs was questioned, though infrequently. In this way, certain songs were deemed unsuitable for a particular voice by virtue of a lack of technique or natural vocal endowment. Also infrequently, it was observed that a particularly dull program was composed predominantly of a single type of song. Little more than this was discussed about programming.

2. Favorite terms in constant use were: finesse, intelligence, interpretive ability, dynamic level, musicality, phrasing, vocal color,[10] expressive shadings, articulation, "white" or "dry" voice, flair, forcing the voice, nuance, and "floating" the voice. Pitch seemed to be paramount in the average critic's mind. Accuracy of trills and coloratura were also very much on the line to be judged. Vocal monotony was mentioned often.

3. Critics occasionally disagreed on certain points. Once in a great while, a recital was heralded by one and doomed by another. This serves to remind us that it is futile to expect criticism of today or any day to be wholly objective.

4. Critics rarely described audience reactions unless the singer was an established artist whom they happened to like. One questions why the incontrovertible fact of public reaction seemed to be comfortably included only when the artist was known. Audience reaction must be a valid indication of a singer's ability whether or not he is famous.

5. Finally, we observed that extra-artistic standards often played a far too important role in many critics' reviews. Such standards included nationality (European versus American); the singer's association with a leading American or European opera company (certainly not in itself a guarantee of recital ability); and the availability of opera recordings of the singer (also of questionable worth in a review).

---

10. The very question of vocal coloring is highly subjective, whether it be discussed by singers, critics, or voice teachers, who often consider it fraught with possible dangers technically. In actuality, it is probably an automatic and largely uncontrived effect occuring when a singer thoroughly understands and is involved with the text. As such, it is properly within the purvue of the critic in his review.

9 Research

A PLEA FOR THE NECESSITY OF DOING MUSICAL AND LITERARY RESEARCH

Just as no opera singer worth her salt would dream of going on the stage as Carmen ignorant of the original novel, of the elements of Spanish dance, of the history and psychology of Spanish gypsies, and of castanet playing, so a recital singer must take care to leave not the smallest detail of the literary or musicological background of the songs unexplored. To gifted artists, the music means more than an aggregation of enjoyable, pleasure-giving sounds. Gifted artists make every effort to know something about a composer, his proper position in history, the relationship of one composition to the rest of his oeuvre, the compositional techniques he employed, and the performance techniques involved.

Each artist has his personal method of research. This is how Vladimir Horowitz describes his method.

> This year I play two pieces of Fauré. First of all, I studied the whole composer. I play everything he wrote. Ensemble music, everything. I play myself—not listen to recordings. Records are not the truth. They are like postcards of a beautiful landscape. You bring the postcards home so when you look at them you will remember how beautiful is the truth. So I play. . . . The texture of the music talks to me, the style. I feel the music, the spiritual content of his compositions. I know also

everything about the composer. I always believe the composer and not what the others write about him. I read the letters of Fauré, what he was thinking. They gave me the character of the composer. What he liked in music, what he didn't like.[1]

A singer cannot consider scholarship an end in itself, although knowledge does result from such work. Rather, the reason for this activity is a totally pragmatic one: a singer's primary goal is to "get inside the song" and "make it his own." Margaret Rae, in a speech before the New York Singing Teachers' Association, pointed out that "empathy is a word borrowed from modern psychology. It means a 'feeling into' and is defined as 'the imaginal and mental projection of oneself into the elements of a work of art.' When a person projects himself into a piece of music or literature, he responds emotionally to its contents *in addition to comprehending it logically* [italics ours]." We suggest that the artist can never truly make the song "his own" until he understands every aspect of the music and the poem.

Singers cannot, however, be held responsible for the kind of painstaking research that trained musicologists do. A source book written by a singer/musicologist is rare indeed. Yet there is no excuse for singers being unacquainted, for example, with the form in which the song is set, or the era and style in which the song was written. Such knowledge is not an empty gesture of scholarly vanity but influences directly the quality of interpretation and performance. Singers performing a Berlioz song who are unenlightened on the history of mélodie versus romance limit their interpretive abilities. Singers doing Baroque music who are utterly unconversant with ornamentation significantly reduce the quality of their performance.

"I read literature, psychology, sociology—everything except economics," Claudio Arrau has said. Regrettably but understandably, most singers are far more likely to have acquired musical rather than literary backgrounds, since musical subjects are required in conservatories and music schools. Generally speaking, the literary dimensions of songs go unexplored, often regarded by them as unnecessary or too time-consuming. Literary research supplies singers with a rich source of interpretive ideas. As the poetry chosen by composers for their songs increases in quality and complexity, so does the music written to these texts.

The goal of producing a performance as faithful to the composer's intentions as possible requires more than literal fidelity to notation; it means somehow fathoming the depth, breadth, and complexity of the

1. Helen Epstein, "The Grand Eccentric of the Concert Hall," *The New York Times Magazine*, January 8, 1978, p. 46.

most imaginative impulses of men, many of whom lived hundreds of years ago. To approach this goal . . . [one] must steep himself in a number of other things—as much of that composer's output as possible, as well as language, culture, human experience, psychology, performance practices of the period.

If indeed you are the kind of musician whose goal is described above by James Levine, then it is imperative for you to acquaint yourself with the life and times of a composer. To do this you must be willing to research the background of your songs. Far from being a disagreeable task, this work often becomes so enjoyable and compelling that devoted and diligent exploration sometimes develops into a positive mania for collecting related memorabilia.

Unfortunately, singers seldom take pains to look up the poem of a song in its original form. (Do you know that there are four lines missing from Samuel Barber's "Nocturne"? Between "All my aching flows away" and "Even the human pyramids" there were originally these lines: "Condorus of the future rise through the stupor overhead and a million shaking sighs spring from the insulted dead." Can it be inconsequential to your understanding of Samuel Barber's purposes and creative methods that he chose to delete these lines? Surely, consideration of why he felt impelled to excise them from his setting of the poem would be a revealing and rewarding exercise for you.)

Singers seldom insist upon reading the larger work from which a fragment was taken. (Have you read far enough in *Wilhelm Meister* to find the fragment used by Hugo Wolf in "Kennst du das Land"? Mignon's memories of "das Land" are very real, even though she cannot identify them as memories of Italy. Ours can be real only if we know, from reading the novel, that the land *is* Italy. For example, the "Marmorbilde" are, as one who reads the novel knows, most likely Italian statuary from Mignon's home.)

Singers seldom check out exactly who that obscure person named in the title was. (Are you really sure who Suleika and Bilitis were? And incidentally, what *is* a Knaben Wunderhorn? Not having perused Pierre Louÿs's *Songs of Bilitis*, one would be ignorant of who Bilitis is, where she is, and her age and personality. Surely it is central to your interpretation of these songs to know that Debussy chose one song from each of three periods of her life—youth, adulthood, and maturity. Indeed, the third song means absolutely nothing unless it is understood to be a symbolical description of the end of youthful fantasy.)

When you are singing the *Ludions* cycle by Satie are you aware that Léon-Paul Fargue was describing sights and scenes experienced during his notorious and incessant taxi-riding about Paris? (Making sense out of these poems is impossible if one has not studied Fargue and his life, his compulsions, and his writing methods. Satie certainly knew that Fargue wrote sometimes in baby-talk, that Fargue described unrelated impressions flashing by his taxi-window, that Fargue was credited by Parisians with knowing the city better than anyone, that a list of Fargue's favorite things included cats, ears, courtyards, chimneys, grazing deer, blind alleys, frogs, railroad men, taxis, washing of streets, the hours from midnight to 6:00 A.M., pretty women, and Paris itself, all of which are included in his poems. Shouldn't you know what Satie knew?)

When you were singing "The Dying Nightingale" by Norman dello Joio did you make sure that you knew what an actual nightingale sounded like? (Once you make it your business to search out the call of the nightingale, we think you will discover both strict and fanciful musical allusions to the nightingale's song within piano and voice parts.)

When your attempt at research has been thwarted after your first efforts, do you stop there? (Many allusions that appear classical are not to be found in the usual sources because they are imaginary. Had you pursued your subject to a final solution, you would have brought to light the facts that Orplid in Hugo Wolf's "Gesang Weylas" and Silpelit in Wolf's "Elfenlied" are both figments of the poet's imagination.)

When you are singing Debussy's "Fantôches" or "Le Faun," do you realize that the poems are from a set inspired by the life-styles pictured in the paintings of Watteau and Fragonard? (In these paintings one always finds depicted sculpture placed in gardens where formality is typified by manicured trees and shrubs and elegantly dressed women and men. The gardens are peopled by *commedia dell 'arte* characters as well as the nobility. Upon looking at these paintings, a person with a knowledge of the poems cannot but realize that the poet intended to breathe life into the pictures with his poetry.)

When you are singing Hindemith's *Marienleben* cycle, are you aware that Rilke's goal was to describe the Virgin Mary in terms of the Greek ideal? (The thoughts and words voiced by Mary in some of the poems are a bit puzzling. In the Annunciation song, Rilke says (in paraphrase): "It was not that an angel entered which frightened her, but that he had the face of a young man." In "Vor der Passion" Mary says to Jesus upon the cross, "If you had wished, you could have been born *not* of a woman. A savior should properly be found in the mountains or some strong place. A rock could bear this grief better than a woman." In "Pietà" she says, "The last time I felt your weight upon me, you were in my womb." All of these slightly unexpected reactions are understandable when one realizes that Rilke, as explained in the foreward to his poems, is serving the Greek ideal—Mary as a woman, not as a divinity.)

When you sang the "Serenade," did you realize not only that Britten tailored it to Peter Pears's voice, but that throughout the years of their artistic collaboration Mr. Pears influenced and broadened Britten's literary interests? (Knowing that the aesthetic vocal requirements of "Serenade" are conditioned by the vocal style and gifts of Peter Pears, interpretive and musical decisions can be made with greater authority.)

When you are struggling with the non sequiturs of Malipiero's *Quattro Sonnetti di Burchiello,* do you realize how clear they become when you have researched the poet Burchiello? (Not even your word-for-word translation could have helped you to make sense of the poems. Only discovering Burchiello's identity as Italy's first nonsense poet could solve the utter incomprehensibility of these songs.)

Consider once again Mr. Levine's words: "It means somehow fathoming the depth, breadth, and complexity of the most imaginative impulses of men, many of whom lived hundreds of years ago."

SUGGESTED TITLES FOR RECITAL SINGERS AND ACCOMPANISTS

Music History and Theory

English Song, Dowland to Purcell, Ian Spink; Scribner.

Music of Spain, Gilbert Chase; Dover Publications.

Twentieth Century Music, Peter Yates; Minerva Press.

The New Music, Aaron Copland; W. W. Norton and Co.

A History of Modern Music, Paul Collaer; Grosset and Dunlap.

Musical Form and Musical Performance, Edward T. Cone; W. W. Norton and Co.

Music from Inside Out, Ned Rorem; G. Braziller.

Music and People, Ned Rorem; G. Braziller.

American Music since 1910, Virgil Thomson; Holt, Rinehart, and Winston.

Ideas and Music, Martin Cooper; Chilton Books.

The Interpretation of Early Music, Robert Donington; St. Martin's Press.

The Performer's Guide to Baroque Music, Robert Donington; Scribner.

The Music of Black Americans, Eileen Southern; W. W. Norton and Co.

Music and Some Highly Musical People, James Trotter; Johnson Reprint Co.

French Song from Berlioz to Duparc, Frits Noske; Dover Publications.

French Songs, Charles Panzerà; Schott.

The Theories of Claude Debussy, Leon Vallas; Dover Publications.

French Music from Berlioz to the Death of Fauré, Martin Cooper; Oxford.

A History of Song, Dennis Stevens; W. W. Norton and Co.

Approach to New Music, Wolfgang Rebner; C. F. Peters.

Biography

The Singer and His Art, Aksel Schiøtz; Harper and Row.

Debussy: Man and Artist, Oscar Thompson; Tudor Publications.

Journal de mes Mélodies, Francis Poulenc; Grasset (Paris).

Recollections and Reflections: Richard Strauss; Boosey and Hawkes.

Schumann, Andre Boucourechliev; Grove Press.

Hugo Wolf, Frank Walker; Knopf.

Gustav Mahler, Bruno Walter; Schocken Books.

The Great Singers, Henry Pleasants; Simon and Schuster.

Interpretation

Interpretation in Song, Harry Plunket Greene; Macmillan.

Interpretation of French Song, Pierre Bernac; Praeger.

The Art Song, James Hurst Hall; University of Oklahoma Press.

Schubert Songs, Richard Capell; Macmillan.

The History of Music in Performance, Fredrick Dorian; W. W. Norton and Co.

Mind Your Musical Manners, Claudette Sorel; Marks Music Corp.

Audition, Michael Shurtleff; Walker & Co.

Catalogues

Music for the Voice, Sergius Kagen; Indiana University Press.

Repertoire for the Solo Voice, Noni Espina; Scarecrow Press.

Classical Vocal Music in Print, ad. Thomas Nardone; Musicdata.

Word by Word Translations of Songs and Arias (Vols. 1 and 2), Berton Coffin, Werner Singer, Pierre Delattre; Scarecrow Press.

The Ring of Words; An Anthology of Song Texts, Philip Miller; W. W. Norton and Co.

Handbook of Johann Sebastian Bach's Cantatas, Werner Neumann; Breitkopf & Härtel, Leipzig.

Directory of American Women Composers, Julia Smith, ed.; National Federation of Music Clubs.

The Singer's Repertoire, Berton Coffin. Vol. 1: Coloratura, Lyric, and Dramatic Soprano; Vol. 2: Mezzo Soprano and Contralto; Vol. 3: Lyric and Dramatic Tenor; Vol. 4: Baritone and Bass. Pruett Publishing.

Diction

Singers' Manual of English Diction, Madeleine Marshall; Schirmer Books.

An Outline of Italian, French, and German Diction for the American Singer, John Moriarty; E. C. Schirmer.

Singers' Manual of Latin Diction and Phonetics, Robert S. Hines; Schirmer Books.

Singers' Manual of German and French Diction, Richard Cox; Schirmer Books.

Singers' Italian, Evalina Colorni; Schirmer Books.

Phonetic Readings of Songs and Arias, Berton Coffin *et al.*; Pruett Publishing.

Acting

My Life in Art, Constantin Stanislavski; Theater Arts Books.

Stanislavski on Opera, Constantin Stanislavski and Pavel Rumyantsev; Theater Arts Books.

Acting; The First Six Lessons, Richard Boleslavsky; Theater Arts Books.

Acting, Toby Cole; Crown Publishers.

The Dramatic Imagination, Robert Edmond Jones; Theater Arts Books.

The Resurrection of the Body, Edward Maisell; Delta Books.

Accompanying

The Unashamed Accompanist, Gerald Moore; Macmillan.

Singer and Accompanist, Gerald Moore; Macmillan.

The Well-Tempered Accompanist, Coenraad V. Bos; Presser.

The Art of Accompanying and Coaching, Kurt Adler; University of Minnesota Press.

GUIDELINES FOR PRACTICE

1. In order to mount a studio recital with a theme (one song by each student), research songs with texts from plays or novels, such as Honegger's *Petit cours de Morale* from Giraudoux's *Suzanne et le Pacifique*; Schubert's "Hark, Hark the Lark" from Shakespeare's *The Tempest*; or "Hotel," one of the songs from Samuel Barber's cycle *Despite and Still*, the text of which is from James Joyce's *Ulysses*.

2. You are a baritone who wishes to perform Poulenc's *Le Travail du Peintre*. Research information about the various paintings and the painters' styles alluded to in this work in order to prepare yourself sufficiently.

3. Find a variety of early music by British composers from which a program for one or two male voices could be built.

4. Research the specific qualities of, and the differences between, the two French song forms—mélodie and romance. Find a number of appealing and worthy romances from which a group could be selected.

5. Search out compositions by black composers, giving special attention to those before the twentieth century (such as Samuel Coleridge-Taylor), with the view to preparing a program drawn entirely from the works of black composers throughout the ages.

6. In Poulenc's song "Violon," taken from his cycle *Fiançailles du Rire*, set to poems of Louise de Vilmorin, there is a reference in the first line to "couple amoureux." Seek the exact meaning of this allusion (it does not refer to a flesh and blood couple).

7. Given the subject "Christmas Legends in Four Countries," find enough songs for a program with two or three singers.

8. Find materials from which you could make a part of a program or a group of songs related to Hallowe'en—mysticism, elves, sprites, mermen and maids, witchcraft and witches, nixes, goblins, trolls, sorcery—in both America and Europe.

9. From Garcia's traveling zarzuela troupe to Albeniz and Falla's arrival in Paris, Spanish rhythms and melodies had a striking influence upon composers of many non-Spanish nationalities. Find enough from which to devise a program.

10. The following references appear in major song literature. Find out exactly who and what each one is.

Ganymede	Coeur-Bub
Gruppe aus Tartarus	Goyescas
Hidalgo	Maja, majo
Walpurgisnacht	Der Feuerreiter

11. How many major composers can you find who made settings of folk music of the British Isles?

12. You are a baritone who has been assigned by your voice teacher Purcell's "Let the Dreadful Engines." Your task is to find the play from which this is taken, the character who sings it, and his motivation.

13. Because an understanding of the poet's life is essential to your performance of *Les Illuminations* by Britten, do an in-depth study of this part of Rimbaud's life.

14. Research the chronology of Virginia Woolf's psychological states corresponding to her diary entries that are dated in the title of each song in *From the Diary of Virginia Woolf* by Dominick Argento.

15. Put together a group of songs with texts by James Joyce. Write program notes for this group, stressing all details that relate to Joyce's love for music and singing. Joyce was given to making geographical references—imaginary and real. Do not neglect to ferret out the location and/or significance of each such reference.

10 Methods of Study and Memorization

How do *you* begin to study a song? Do you jump into it singing full voice, cosseting yourself emotionally? We strongly believe that in this way you do yourself and the music a disservice. Instead, *listen* to the entire song, responding to its esthetic appeal. Any decision as to whether you like it or not cannot be taken while indulging in what would certainly be fairly inept vocalizing. Listen to a record or let your coach play it through. Speak the words. Try to understand the overall meaning. Only then, and only if you like it (don't sing it if you don't like it!) are you ready to tackle it.

LEARNING THE MUSIC, THE FIRST STEP

The first step is an irksome one, to learn the notes. The phrase "learning the notes" does not mean simply learning *pitches*. Matters of rhythm and tempo are far more important than the pitches at this stage. True musical security cannot be achieved if the command of the rhythmic elements is in any way weak. Except in the most contemporary music, once the rhythms are sorted out with absolute accuracy, pitch problems are minimal. Even in extremely avant-garde music, basing your study of the pitches on a rhythmic command of less than one-hundred percent accuracy is asking for trouble somewhere down the line.

Silence is musical. Silence plus one note is musical, but one note is not musical. Even at the most primitive level, music must consist of two sounds in a rhythmic relationship. This is why rhythm is the basic element of music and, accordingly, the element that provides stability. Consequently, we recommend that the goal of musical security will be served far better by first learning the rhythms; second, the rhythms plus the words; third, the pitches without the words; and, finally, pitches, rhythms, and words together. In short, rest all other disciplines on the bedrock of correct rhythms. This, then, should be your system of study:

1. Speak the rhythms alone, without pitches or words. Using "la" or some such syllable, study small segments at a time, gradually increasing the speed from very slow to a faster tempo than that marked in the music. When you can sing all the rhythms easily and consistently correct at the too-fast tempo, proceed to step 2.

2. Speak the rhythms with the words, without pitches. Again, study small segments at a time before attempting long segments. Again, increase the tempo from slow to faster than the proper tempo until words and rhythms are consistently and easily accurate at the fastest tempo. When reciting the words in rhythm, it is most efficient to practice them with most of the intended diction skills operative.[1]

3. Sing the pitches alone. (Do not worry if, when searching for accurate intervals, you distort tempo or rhythm temporarily.) Using only "la," work on the same small segments; use the same sequence of tempos as a test of accuracy.

4. Sing the pitches to "la," concentrating on demanding correct rhythms. Proceed from a slow to a fast tempo, as before.

5. Sing pitches, rhythms, and words at tempos from slower to faster than necessary.

6. Take great care not to learn anything wrong! Unlearning is a tortuous process.

7. Only now is it time to learn to *sing* your song!

Although such a system might seem to be very time-consuming, it is actually extremely efficient in the long run (much faster than correcting wrong habits later). For either the beginning or advanced singer, it results in an infinitely more secure musicianship, thus freeing the singer to attend to vocal and interpretive problems.

Do not sing one note more than necessary during this early stage. Instead, use the piano, croon lightly, sing falsetto, sing softly down an octave—any method—but do not allow the initial period of learning the

---

1. See below for more on diction.

notes to freeze the voice accidentally into awkward or harmful patterns which will have to be unlearned later.

STUDYING THE SONG

Form

At this point, take a few minutes to study the musical form of your song. The song will ultimately be easier to memorize if the formal arrangement is clear in your mind. More important, understanding the form of a musical piece is a great interpretive aid. The musical structure used by the composer was, after all, not a gratuitous choice; the form *is* in a sense the meaning. (A three-part form must by its very nature express a contemplative or lyric moment, whereas the durchkomponiert form may be used for poetry that sets forth a dramatic sequence of moods.)

A sensitive, musical person will find that the emotional meaning of a three-part form[2] is different from, let us say, a variation form.[3] In the three-part form, what does it mean to you to return to the A section (A[1]) after the B section? Is A[1] a reaffirmation of the text? Is A[1] emotionally stronger or weaker than A? Has the composer made some slight changes the second time around? Would you gain interpretively and stylistically by ornamenting A[1]? Is the B section in strong conflict with A or is it simply a reflection on the same idea? From the answers to these questions, or ones like them, you will determine for yourself what is the significance of this form.

How does a rondo form[4] with the returning A section illuminate the words? What effect does a two-part form leave?[5] Again, why do you think the composer did that? Why did he evade the cadence? Why did he write in 12/8 time instead of using triplets in 4/4? The form and the notation on the printed page represent the only real message the composer can convey to you. It is up to you to scrutinize what is there and to be aware of its meaning to you personally. This meaning, it goes without saying, may be something entirely different for another singer.

Ever delightfully unabashed at sharing his personal musical feelings when conductor of the Collegiate Chorale in New York City, the eminent Robert Shaw wrote, "I believe that form in music is a symbol of relations

---

2. E.g., "Piangerò la sorte mia," Handel.
3. E.g., Part II of "Busslied," Beethoven.
4. E.g., "Gretchen am Spinnrade," Schubert.
5. E.g., "Der Tod und das Mädchen," Schubert.

of values, not merely a blueprint of construction technique."[6] He also felt that

> the spiritual and emotional implications of form in music are not to be taken glibly. Pattern is not simply two plus two. Or perhaps two plus two is a far more significant thing than our childish memorizations testify. Certainly two plus two has not the meaning of two times two, nor yet of four times one. The new whole is greater here, also than the sum of its parts. The elements of pattern possess an inexplicable significance beyond their patent arithmetic.
>
> Form in music is a symbol, and it symbolizes something to which we can only give the name of spirit. When we have recognized the devices and tabulated the relationships, we will not have explained it away. It exists in spite of our understanding. At some point deep in human consciousness pattern will answer pattern, and that will be no crisp intellectual gymnastics, but a warm and moving awareness. What we call emotion is surely a part of it. Tears, laughter, and a tensing spiritual temper are well within the beckon of Form.[7]

Nevertheless, one cannot describe the objective of form as beauty. Eight measures is not more beautiful than ten. Most of us agree that music is meant to be enjoyed. To understand gives pleasure. So does form, in organizing ideas to give comprehensibility, also give us beauty.

According to Edward Cone, the comprehension and communication of musical style can be considered the final responsibility of performance. Cone defines totally satisfying musical composition as one that is capable of both immediate and synoptic comprehension. While most practical performance instruction is aimed toward heightening immediate apprehension, his essays *Musical Form and Musical Performance*[8] present an approach that emphasizes the "performance of form." Cone conceives musical form as being basically rhythmic: "It is not, as conventional analysis would have it, thematic, nor, *pace* Schenker, harmonic. Both of these aspects are important, but rhythm is basic."[9] Therefore, valid performance depends "on the perception and communication of the rhythmic life of a composition."[10] Thus, the comprehension of the rhythmic structure of a composition becomes the basis for understanding its form and style and for successfully communicating this to an audience. Finally, the structure of the whole must be presented at the expense of more superficial details important only in the surface structure: "Every

6. Robert Shaw, personal letter.
7. Robert Shaw, personal letter.
8. Edward T. Cone, *Musical Form and Musical Performance*. New York: W. W. Norton and Co., Inc., 1968.
9. Ibid., p. 25.
10. Ibid., p. 35.

valid interpretation thus represents not an approximation of some ideal, but a choice: which of the relationships implicit in this piece are to be emphasized, to be made explicit?"[11]

Accompaniment and Structure

You should next examine the accompaniment. Let the study of the piano part give you not only musical security but a further understanding of what the composer was trying to express. On the pragmatic level, ask yourself: When am I supported by the accompaniment[12] and when am I not?[13] How do the introductions and interludes bring me in rhythmically?[14] If some difficulty is experienced melodically in the early stages of learning, sing aloud the piano note or notes to which your first note has a relationship.[15] Later you can simply think these notes. Is the accompaniment intended to be an equal voice[16] or a literal "accompaniment?"[17] If the voices are equal, who is the soloist at which moments? The proper tempo is set not just by what suits the voice part and what the words dictate, but by the figures in the accompaniment.[18] Will it not sound rushed when the speed of your quarter notes makes the pianist's thirty-second notes so fast as to be almost unplayable?

Language and Diction

Before taking up methods of studying the text per se, let us consider the requirements of the various languages in which your song might be written.

11. Ibid., p. 38.
12. In Aaron Copland's "Ching-a-Ring-Chaw" the piano provides an uninterrupted and inflexible support to the singer.
13. In David Diamond's "On Death" the piano actually enters several lines after the voice.
14. In Falla's "Polo" (*Siete Canciones*) there is virtually no way to find your entrance correctly time after time without memorizing the rhythmic lead-ins of the accompaniment. The tune is minimally helpful.
15. In Randall Thompson's "Velvet Shoes" (bars 67–69) the tune (formed by the phrase ending with the piano's sustained E sharp and the singer's F) brings him in easily. In Fauré's "Clair de Lune" the piano's well-defined melody leads in bar 12 directly to the singer's entering note, in effect fabricating for one minute a new composite melody.
16. In Wolf's "Auf dem grünen Balcon" the piano plays a melody that is completely independent of the voice's melody.
17. In Obradors' "Dos Cantares Populares" the piano is literally an accompaniment of strumming arpeggios.
18. In Brahms' "Meine Liebe ist grün" the piano's alternating eighth notes, not the vocal line, indicate the correct tempo.

ENGLISH

We Americans somehow continue to be surprised that an English text does not guarantee an absence of problems. Certainly, French and German singers study how to sing in their native tongue. Italian coaches, aware of the probability of local and regional habits polluting the purity of their accent, keep a pronouncing dictionary handy on the piano to check *their own* language.

Why should we assume that speaking English is the same as singing English? The actual duration of sung vowels is longer than spoken vowels. That fact alone would necessitate a new command of English even if nothing else changed between spoken and sung language. But things do change demonstrably. Vowels must sometimes be modified, diphthongs clarified. No, it must be faced: English diction for singing requires a thorough study. To regard it as a foreign language is most productive. To sing in English is not *more* difficult than in other languages, but our careless treatment of it makes it seem so.

DICTION

Consider from a general point of view some of the ramifications of diction skills. Emile Renan, singer, voice teacher, and stage director par excellence, directs our attention to the existence of a second, often disregarded, meaning for the term diction. A classic definition of diction commonly accepted without question is "degree of distinctness of speech sounds." But the thesaurus gives also "manner of expression," "choice of words," "high level of word usage," and "eloquence." Mr. Renan believes that there is a need to "balance the demands of clarity as well as the (usually) unconscious responses that the librettist's choices of words evoke in the sensitive artist." He points out, as an example, that "Stanley Kowalski's given words cannot help eliciting a style of word utterance, and hence articulation, vastly different from Otello's or Melisande's."

As to the various schools of vocal thought regarding the restricted meaning of diction skills, no one would argue that proper enunciation and pronunciation of words does not guarantee vocal freedom, but bad diction skills can easily undermine vocal beauty. For these reasons, and also because of the vital importance of the word to meaningful singing, diction is not secondary to vocal technique. Moreover, diction always goes hand-in-hand with singing style and personality. Physical deportment plus facial and body indications are personality factors that, like diction, are communication aids.

Let us examine a few general principles. [For an exhaustive discussion of the subject, we suggest *The Singer's Manual of English Diction*, (Schirmer Books) by Madeleine Marshall, or *An Outline of Italian,*

French, and German Diction for the American Singer (E. C. Schirmer) by John Moriarty.] Although diction must be viewed technically as pronunciation, enunciation, and articulation, it is somehow irresistible to think of diction unilaterally as either a problem of intelligibility or a problem of vocal technique. The truth is that it is both, and the only viable solution is one that treads the delicate line between clarity and comfort.

The difficulties presented to the singer by the bare mechanistic control of consonants are caused by the fact that consonants have the capacity to destroy vocal stability, and thereby vocal beauty. They can close the mouth (the voice benefits from its being open); they can stop the air (the voice benefits from its constant flow); and they can give tension to the singing muscles (the voice benefits from their looseness). The solution is neither to stop pronouncing well (for vocal ease) nor to overpronounce (which leads to vocal misuse), but to find a way to give maximum intelligibility without sacrificing vocal beauty. Frequently, one technique provides both. Compromise is not always necessary.

Logically, one must acquire the muscular coordination that makes the consonants swift, crisp, and energetic, but loose. The ability to reduce them to the least physical movement without weakening them is perhaps the hardest part. It takes some application. The voiceless consonants are somewhat less conducive to tension than the voiced. Therefore, it is often advantageous to substitute voiceless for voiced, a practice that is almost undiscernible when done where most often needed—on the higher pitches. Moving them over to the right (that is, as close to the next vowel as possible) is more a matter of habituation to the legato connection principle advocated by almost all voice teachers. This makes possible the much valued "singing on the vowels." Then it is fairly simple to apply the specific rules from each language (e.g., the Italian double consonants, which are of necessity longer—but not more constricted!—and the sometimes obligatory glottal stop in German).

Using the *schwah* to separate consonant clusters is a good example of a technique that gives both vocal comfort and a high degree of clarity. Placing a vowel (the *schwah*, ə), however short, between consonants, effectively shortens the time spent on consonants and relieves the consequent tensions. This same separation highlights each consonant and prevents the composite twosome from being misunderstood. If the *schwah* is carefully sung on the pitch assigned to its word, the carrying power of the consonant is enormously increased. Just be wary that the added *schwah*, or the lack of it, does not inadvertently form another recognizable word.

There are many schools of thought about the vocal propriety and/or efficacy of the migration of vowels. But no one disputes that, when intelligibility is the primary concern, what the audience *perceives* as the vowel might as well *be* the vowel; that is, if changing an ill-placed I (sit) to an æ (sat) gives vocal ease and is perceived by the listener as I (sit), why not take advantage of the fact? Moreover, concepts of vowels irrefutably vary within languages and within nations.

Generally speaking, when vowels are modified, they are tilted one degree at a time toward more closed or more open. This is done for various reasons: comfort, a better-placed tone, etc. Spectography has proven that sung vowels and spoken vowels are not identical. Even within sung vowels, duration, pitch, and vocal strength prevent the sound from being the same.

In addition, those who espouse the cause of vowel modification sometimes answer critics who complain about integrity of pronunciation thus: if the listener *speaks* the language you are singing (while modifying certain vowels), then he will understand what you are singing in spite of your slight adjustments (as he does in the theater where he hears in context and fills in words that escape him, or as he does when he understands text in spite of a dialect or regional accent). If the listener does not speak the language being used, then he will not be offended that you have adjusted the vowels.

On the other hand, those who eschew anything less than absolutely pure vowels at all times usually base their stand upon vocal considerations. Yet, most singers are more than willing to accept the premise that, for example, high frequencies demand an adjusted-toward-open vowel. A strange detail becomes apparent when indulging in such migrations. If the singer during a rising melodic line "opens" his *i* (eat) vowel for comfort, the listener will still recognize *i*. If the singer, instead, actually moves wittingly to an *e* (slay), the listener will perceive *e*. In other words, the listener hears what the singer *intends* to sing. (Naturally, we presuppose sufficient diction skills for these purposes.) No matter how close to *e* (slay) his opened *i* (eat) is, if he still intends to sing *i*, we will hear *i*. Thus one could say that the pure vowel *i* is still acoustically present.

Diphthongs and triphthongs are best handled by means of rhythms; that is, the physical qualities of *ai* (my) include a pure *a* (palm) that moves to a pure *i* (eat). The decision as to when to move to the second vowel is governed mostly by conventions of the language being sung, and partially by vocal considerations of comfort and beauty. Often a ratio of 2/3 for the first vowel and 1/3 for the second is acceptable and intelligible. When the note is very long this proportion becomes 3/4 to 1/4 and when the note is very short the proportion becomes 1/2 to 1/2.[19] Again, a balance must be struck between the demands of clarity and

19. Ralph Appelman's *The Science of Vocal Pedagogy* (Bloomington: Indiana University Press, 1967) is possibly the most exhaustive treatise on the physiological and psychological ramifications of diction.

comfort in each instance. The comfort/clarity ratio generally works in this fashion: reserving the secondary vowel of a dipthong until the very end of the note gives maximum vocal ease, but pronouncing it earlier tends to accord it greater distinctness.

Even after learning and applying these mechanical skills, you have not completely plumbed the depths of diction problems. You may pronounce the words correctly, you may enunciate the text clearly, but you have not yet extracted the ultimate advantage from them. The expressive quality of the words needs more attention. When you sing in a language you speak, your easy sensitivity to text leads to automatic placement of stress and intensity through your articulation. The emotional content and meaning of each word is in this way revealed.

To touch on the most mechanical expressive possibilities of diction, let us use the word "sweet" as a point of comparison. When you say the Italian word "dolce" eloquently, you logically dwell on the liquid *l*, but when you say the French word "douce" meaningfully, the sibilant *c* is unconsciously extended, as it is with the German "süss." In English both the *w* and the *s* of "sweet" is inclined to be prolonged.

Returning to the discussion of the subtle influence of diction's broader aspects, we perceive that after organizing, assembling, and transforming all ideas, concepts, and images suggested to him by the music and text the singer must communicate all this to the audience partially through his diction skills—a considerable effort!

Mozart's setting of Italian librettos proves the proposition that he exploited all musical devices fully in order to extract maximum expressive impact from each word. You will find the double consonants actually notated and the prosodic accents represented by lower and higher pitches as well as by intricate rhythmic devices, *not excluding* rest values.

One suspects that the consonants differ from vowels in the nature of their expressive capacity. The vowels, being longer, tend to indicate emotions through the vocal colorations (bright, dark, etc.), whereas the expression supplied by the consonants is more connotive, declamatory, eloquent, sometimes even onomatopoeic. (And do not forget that the sound itself is used by each language for part of the meaning.) When they are properly unified and stressed, vowel and consonant together create a word that is alive and persuasive.

The aphorism "words are condensed but thoughts expand" leads us directly to the necessity for the expressive use of the words. They must paint pictures of the life created by the author and infect the audience with the desire to see those images. Thus the text enters into a rudimentary partnership with the composer and performer. And so we come full circle. To do this, you must initially possess the first-class diction skills we have described.

FOREIGN LANGUAGES

Now let us return to the subject of foreign languages for an American singer. It is clear that Italian, German, and French are the most essential. What exactly must a singer know about these languages? From a practical standpoint, it is necessary to have a good accent and to understand the basic tenets of grammar. The need for an authentic accent is self-evident, but why grammar? If you cannot find the infinitive in the dictionary because you do not know the verb forms, then you cannot do literal translation of a song text, which in our estimation is imperative. A big vocabulary is not necessary, just enough grammar to be able to look words up swiftly and accurately. Also, if the grammar is beyond you, how can you make sense of the text when you are singing?

What is not necessary but desirable is a conversational ability and a literary sense in that foreign language. With such skills comes a deeper understanding of nuance and the inflections of poetry or prose in another language. Hidden meanings are then made clearer; strange idioms and allusions then become an integral part of your personal interpretations.

Text and Subtext

When studying the various aspects of the text you must be prepared to spend a lot of time. Study the text separately. Why not write it on a piece of paper and carry it with you? This is what Hugo Wolf did, sometimes carrying the poem about for many years so that he might illuminate the words further with his music. Think of Verdi, sitting in his garden reciting aloud Shakespeare's words for three years before writing any music for *Otello*. Just as most composers began with the words, so must you. (For a full discussion of text-setting, see Interpretation, Chapter 11.) The great song composers can epitomize in a two-minute song what would take an entire novel or a whole play to set before us. You must determine the essential qualities of this complex and subtle experience for yourself. "Music may illuminate, ignore or betray the text. The artist must find his way to resolve any conflict."[20]

To make your own literal translation is unavoidable and absolutely essential. Pay close attention to the verb tenses and pronouns. Otherwise you might miss a moment of insight or a meaningful change in verb tense from, say, past to future. For example, in one of the *Marienleben* songs of Paul Hindemith, there is a shift from "Ihr" to "du." This moment signi-

20. William Gephart, chairman of the voice faculty, Hartford Conservatory.

fies a profound change in attitude from speaking to the world in general to addressing one person in the familiar form.

Question every word of the text (translated, when necessary), to be certain that you have discovered hidden meanings. Find some personal discipline that will force you to investigate the text's fullest depths. Here are some suggestions: (1) write out the poem in your own words; (2) prepare a synthesis of the poem, reduced to its main elements; (3) another remarkably simple method is to substitute a word of absolutely opposite meaning for each salient word as written. It is surprising how this strips away complacency, opens you to new thoughts, and makes you sensitive to the poem in its original form. An excellent example is the exquisite song "Memory" by Theodore Chanler.[21] Study this poem of William Blake:

> Memory, hither come,
> And tune your merry notes;
> And, while upon the wind
> Your music floats,
> I'll pore upon the stream,
> Where sighing lovers dream,
> And fish for fancies as they pass
> Within the wat'ry glass.
>
> I'll drink of the clear stream,
> And hear the linnet's song;
> And there I'll lie and dream
> The day along:
> And, when night comes, I'll go
> To places fit for woe,
> Walking along the darkened valley
> With silent Melancholy.

"Walking along the darkened valley with silent Melancholy"—why is the valley darkened and not light? (The picture of a darkened valley calls up further images—shadows, clouds obscuring the moon, etc.) Why a valley and not a mountain? (What things differentiate a darkened valley from a darkened mountain? Where would you walk in each? What would be your reactions to each?) Why is Melancholy silent and not talkative? (What would a talkative Melancholy say? How does a silent Melancholy affect you?) This trick, quite simply and efficiently, assures that you sharpen your senses to realize the full importance of each word, momentarily separate from the musical support.

---

21. Chanler was once described by Virgil Thomson as perhaps the only American composer who fit his criteria for a Lieder composer.

Do not neglect to research any obscure literary references. (See Chapter 9.) And do not let someone else do all this for you. Do not depend solely upon your teacher's taste and development. Your own effort in such work is not only most rewarding but integral to your interpretation. Claudio Arrau in an interview with Richard Dyer iterates his belief that putting himself into the world of the composer results in a creative flight of imagination, which in turn develops a type of interpretation that he properly and unashamedly calls Beethoven-Schnabel or Beethoven-Arrau, each different and both of value. No less an artist than Vladimir Horowitz agreed: "Once I sit down I transform myself. I see the composer. I *am* the composer."[22]

Recite aloud the words of the poem. Recite them aloud *daily*. Allow time for their full meaning to infiltrate your consciousness. Say them with meaning, plumbing the depths of the text. Speak them as a poetic recitation.

Avoid the pitfall of assuming that the search for textual inflection and nuance are confined to poems in a foreign language. Do not take for granted that an English text speaks for itself, leaving diction as the only problem to be confronted. John Duke, a superb composer of songs, says, "Speaking a poem so that its meanings become clear and its words, rhythms, and emphases are correctly reproduced is by no means an obvious and easy task. I suggest that a good recitation of the poem should be the first step in the study of a song in English, as in any other language."[23]

When you have come to a conclusion about what you think the words mean, return to the music. Question the significance of every mark, remembering that composers' notation practices vary widely. Mozart's style was to notate very little; Debussy marked everything meticulously. Does Debussy, through the music, its notation, and his prosodic arrangement of the words, show you that he concurs with your interpretation of the poem? What you are searching for is not what Verlaine meant by his poem, but *what Debussy thought Verlaine meant*. If his music does not jibe with your ideas about the poem and justify your conclusions, either revise your opinion or do not sing the song.

Test your comprehension of the interplay between the words and the music by the following method. Can you recite the poem aloud in tempo and in strictest rhythm with correct dynamic levels as dictated by the composer's markings without the dramatic content breaking down? Only when these two tasks go easily together have you solved the musical equation.

22. Helen Epstein, "The Grand Eccentric of the Concert Hall," *The New York Times Magazine*, January 8, 1978, p. 15.
23. John Duke, "Some Reflections on the Art Song in English," *The American Music Teacher*, February–March, 1976, p. 26.

The Recitative

A word here about the subject of recitative singing: the recitative adjusts its music to reflect every change of mood and action by avoiding melodic or harmonic commitments and their results.

Many singers like to begin work on a song (after it has been learned musically) by solving the technical vocal problems first. But even these "technique first" singers know that in learning recitative dramatic feeling of the text determines everything, including vocal considerations. Consequently, the process must be reversed. There are, of course, slight variations in performance practices from different historical periods that must be sought out and observed. Our discussion will confine itself to the preparation and learning techniques that will remain almost uniform, albeit colored by your knowledge of these various performance practices.

The bulk of recitatives sung by a recital singer will probably be found from early music repertoire. Therefore, such matters as:

1. the visible difference between Italian and French Baroque recitative time-signatures, and the proportion of one signature to another;

2. the exact meanings of early time-signatures and time-words, and especially their relationship to performance practice;

3. continuo accompaniment, its style as well as proper instrumental forces, for recitatives from the eighteenth-century repertoire, as contrasted to those of the seventeenth century;

4. whether the harpsichord should fill out the figured bass with counter-melodies or not;

5. whether the cadential or punctuational chords come on the last note of the vocal line or after it;

6. when unwritten appoggiaturas are standard practice;

7. the various musical situations requiring long or short appoggiaturas;

8. the proper dispersal of other types of ornaments;

9. the restrictions or precepts relating to the trill

are practical decisions best built into the recitative before the actual learning process begins so as to avoid any necessity for inefficient relearning later. For precise advice on performance practice of early music, especially those referring to differences between early practice customs and notation, we again refer you to Robert Donington's superb *The Performer's Guide to Baroque Music*.

Once your recitative has been rewritten a bit to reflect performance practices of the period, explore the rhythm and the tempo. Attack the rhythm first. Learn it as scrupulously as if no liberties were eventually to be taken. (In truth, the *rhythm* will change very little, if at all, whereas the *tempo* will certainly fluctuate.) Choose a tempo well on the slow side. Repeat the words in precise, accurate, even pedantic, rhythm until the speed can be vastly increased without mistakes. Add the pitches to the rhythm-plus-words combination at a slow tempo that increases until all is under easy control at an arbitrary fast tempo.

Now is the time to make interpretive decisions. Read the words over until their underlying meaning seems clear to you. Recite the words aloud, adding stress for emphasis, expressivity, or enrichment of the mood, idea, or drama. Do not rely exclusively on the music's rhythm for your eloquence; try to find it first from the words. Now examine the relationship between the sense of the words and the way the composer scanned the syllables. Together they help to reveal the implications of the music to you. That is to say that one set of clues as to the composer's dramatic intentions comes from the rhythmic proportions he assigned to various words. Pay very close attention to rhythmic combinations that you find different from what you personally would have done if you were to read the words aloud. This is likely to be a place where the composer will reveal certain hidden subtleties of his dramatic meaning. At the same time, extract all possible meaning from syllables that have been placed significantly higher or lower than other notes in that phrase or surrounding phrases. Pitch rises should indicate more importance. (When such accents are badly or mistakenly placed, it is very hard on the singer.) Remember that dramatic accents are achieved by pitches as well as durations. Try to fathom for what expressive purposes these things were done.

When you feel that you have unlocked the real meaning of the words, then practice the *communication* of this expression.

No matter how limited by the dictates of the historical period, the flexibility of the beat is virtually unchallenged as the fundamental device for communicating underlying import of the recitative text. Therefore, decisions of tempo should be made first, with due regard to pertinent performance practices of that period.

The latest research seems to indicate that a constant pulse was used in recitative from 1590 to 1625. The so-called reciting style of the seventeenth century was flexible but not unmeasured, the beat being guided by the feeling. Although the early Italian recitative does not require the beat to be so unmeasured as the later recitativo secco, they both require the singer to make interpretive decisions with more regard to expression than equality of beats. With Bach and Handel, recitatives were still more declamatory and less lyrical, but the French recitative of the same period remains, as in Lully's time, more of the cantabile and arioso type—that is, the enunciation is dramatic but the melodic line must, with rare exceptions, not lose all lyricism.

Look through the text and make note of the emotional changes—ranging from violent to gentle—between phrases. These are hardest to spot in very secco recitative, and easiest when pointed up by composed passages between vocal phrases. Make your decisions as to tempos that articulate the emotional changes (always dependent upon your musical freedom within the style). Be aware that your options include complete tempo changes, ritards and accelerandos leading to new tempos, as well as variations of them all. Try to use as many subtle tempo variations as possible, depending on how much speechlike freedom is permitted stylistically. Bear in mind that you learned the rhythms accurately at the very beginning of your study so that the eventual ritards and accelerandos would not disturb the true proportions set down by the composer. Dynamic levels are then fitted in, taking their cue, in the absence of any marks, from the feeling, just as the tempo does.

Check for musical phrases that, although separated by small rests, belong together because of the sense of the words or the underlying emotions. Contrast these rests with those that truly underwrite a major change of thought or mood. Exploit the length of the latter, waiting as long as the dramatic moment and the musical conventions allow, and minimize the former, clearly indicating where the thoughts begin and end. A clear mandate on the subject of rests in recitative comes from Stanislavski himself, who, when told that there was indeed a rest where he thought there was, said, "Then use it for all it's worth and in an artistic way."

As to the expressive quality of the words, take fullest advantage of the variety of articulations and great declamatory value of the consonants, as well as the many colors possible when singing the vowels. (See Chapter 7 for further ideas.) Note that idiosyncracies of the language are notated into the rhythm by such expert composers of recitative as Mozart. Watch for these indications.

Practice speaking the recitative text in the chosen tempos with the dynamics in the proper places, rhythms still in proportion, until the feeling and its musical means fuse into one communicative whole. Now and only now can you determine how to articulate all this vocally.

Accompaniment and Subtext

Moving back to your song study, consider what mood is prepared and sustained by the accompaniment. Does it always change at the same moment when the voice part does? (For example, in Schubert's "Frühlingstraum" the accompaniment at measure 15 concomitantly with the voice changes the mood decisively.) Or does the accompaniment change the mood first, anticipating the voice entrance with words that describe the new condition? (In Mahler's "In diesem Wetter" from *Kindertotenlieder*, 91–100 of the piano interlude transport us, very gradually, from stress and storm to peaceful acceptance at the voice's entrance.) Or perhaps the accompaniment figure (e.g., the leaping fish figure in "Die Forelle" by Franz Schubert) indicates a description of some constant factor in the words. When the accompaniment figure is unchanging throughout the song, how does it support the mood of the vocal line? (Schubert's songs abound with samples of the accompaniment figure subtly changing from major to minor in order to underwrite the mood.)

Examine the interplay of line between your part and the accompaniment. What part of the inner life of the song is expressed by the accompaniment? One of the most compelling of a vast list of special insights that Dietrich Fischer-Dieskau invariably gives to his audiences is his insistence upon listening intensely to the accompaniment and drawing forth the vocal line from the instrumental line. In searching for your personal sense of the song's shape, it is often helpful to draw a color graph of its emotional hills and valleys from the first note to the last.

Let us look again at Theodore Chanler's setting of William Blake's poem "Memory." Underlying this poem is an uneasiness, not an overriding sadness, just a lack of happiness. (Refer to the text of the poem on page 191.) An explanation of the musical devices as they appear to one singer should prove helpful to the interpretation.

Chanler chooses a 4/8 time signature, but writes constant triplets in the right hand. (Why did he not use 12/16?) Initially, these right hand triplets are coupled with single eighth notes in the left hand, giving a kind of stability. The voice part delineates the prosody of the words beautifully and with infinite subtlety by alternating between two sixteenths and a triplet sixteenth figure as necessary. Then, as the "sighing lovers" appear, the left hand as well begins to do some groups of two against the triplet figure. Tap with two hands the rhythmic skeleton of the accompaniment:

This demonstration evokes enough unease to convince one that the feeling given by the words was shared by Chanler. The uninterrupted right hand triplets brilliantly yet subtly manage to suggest the water, the walking, and the false serenity that overlay the unease—all in one figure. (For a further discussion of the accompanist/singer interplay see Chapter 7.) A final caution: at each practice session work a little at each ingredient—voice, music, text. Do not frustrate yourself by trying to accomplish all three at once. Allow sufficient time for comprehension to come to you. Solutions that seem intuitive actually come from slow and orderly consideration of the three ingredients.

In the less usual role of vocal accompanist, the great Rudolf Serkin has been quoted by Benita Valente as saying that "the word is always the vehicle in singing. The music comes second." Perhaps we would not choose to go that far. It should become clear, however, that in your endeavor to find your own convincing individual understanding of a song—to "make it your own"—you are most of all a musical detective, seeking to unlock the mystery of why the composer did what he did.

In a New York Times interview with Peter Heyworth, Fischer-Dieskau says that you have to find out what [the composer] was really moved by, what was the mood that brought him to compose that text, what was the first step. Only then should a singer move on to the music. That is what the composer did when he wrote the song.

MEMORIZING

And now you are ready to memorize. Is it not apparent that, having studied well, the memorizing is practically done?

As in the studying process (see above), we wish to proselytize for memorizing the words first. Learn them away from the music. You must be able to say the words aloud with meaning and without resorting to singing the tune as a crutch. If you cannot, you do not really know them. Your responsibility is greater when the words are in a foreign language in which you are not very proficient. In this case, you must be able to recite the words aloud with expression and without recourse to the music, while *thinking* the literal translation!

Walter Taussig, assistant conductor at the Metropolitan Opera and an experienced vocal coach, once said that memorizing is harder for the musically gifted than for weak musicians. A strong musician can make up several musical ways out of any lapse of memory; he finds it so easy to read music that he has trouble buckling down and learning the specifics. Therefore, one's only recourse, unless blessed with a photographic memory, is to learn by rote, as less gifted musicians do instinctively and of necessity.

Rote learning is in the long run most efficient, because for best results during performance the material that is memorized must reside in the subconscious. A singer who has memorized intellectually is put into a position during performance where he must sacrifice part of his valuable concentration in order to assure the correct notes and words. This is not only a waste of his resources, it may well prevent his memory from functioning at all. It is far better that the music and words should be lodged in the subconscious, programmed to reissue at certain stimuli; memory must *allow* itself to be revived during performance.

A marvelous discussion of the brain as a sort of computer, the rote-learning process as the computer-programmer, the music and words as the input, and the act of performance from memory as the final print-out retrieved from the computer can be found in a small pamphlet, called *On Memorizing*, by Tobias Matthay, published by the Music Department of the Oxford Press. One finds it hard to believe that it was first published in 1926!

To paraphrase Mr. Matthay, people may be placed in three categories with regard to memory:

1. those who memorize swiftly and forget swiftly;
2. those who memorize slowly and surely, and never forget;
3. those who memorize slowly and laboriously and forget at once!

(Those falling into the third category Mr. Matthay advises to avoid a public career as a performer.) Whichever category is yours by nature, your work will be better for understanding that memorizing means making associations, constructing a sequence of suggestion-connection channels. All three forms of memory (musical, visual, muscular) in music imply analysis first, in order better to construct your associations. "Playing from memory" means activating the sequence of suggestion-connection channels and not interfering with what is required by thinking "What comes next?" Says Mr. Matthay, one must realize the "whence" for each musical thing, so that when the preceding note is sung the connection to the next will automatically be called forth.

Although Mr. Matthay disdains to discuss a routine for implementing this kind of knowledge when committing to memory, preferring to leave that to the individual, we will offer a few suggestions based on experience. Learn the words separately, making connections prompted by the logic of the text. If you are singing in a language you do not speak, it is wise to require of yourself both the literal translation in the order written[24] and the foreign text while simultaneously thinking the translation. Having already analyzed the melodic, harmonic, rhythmic and moodal structure during the earlier study, you will do best (after learning the words separately) by taking small natural divisions of the music and repeating them, paying strict attention to the printed page. When the small

---

24. German word order always seems slightly strange to Americans. ("He to the river in the spring went.") Poetic text disposition in any language may well be awkward to foreign ears. The order must, through familiarity, become unexceptional.

sections have established their interior associations, repeat two small sections together, and so on until large segments go together.

There is no doubt that persisting for too long a time or with too long a section of music is counterproductive. Mr. Matthay wisely counsels us to strengthen our memory as we do our muscles by frequent and short exercise. As psychologists have proven, spaced learning is better than unspaced. Thus, small sections repeated daily at first, getting longer as the memory permits, are best. Above all, do not cram! Cramming is difficult and pressured. It cancels the advantage of effortless learning which would otherwise have accrued to you by osmosis *between* regular practices. Most important, it renders the musical experience unenjoyable.

Do not leave the score too early, especially if you are a good musician! On the other hand, we urge you to memorize as soon as feasible so that you can begin to understand your song on a different level. A rule of thumb might be to repeat the song daily with scrupulous accuracy until you find yourself singing the tune and words away from practice. This is a good sign that you are ready to leave the music.

A small word here about using the accompaniment as a major memory aid. Having studied it well earlier, you will find it easy to use the tunes or the rhythmic devices of the accompaniment to bring you in at your entrances. Sing the accompaniment aloud in your daily repeating practice, using salient features to set up your suggestion-connection channels. One goal is never to count unless it is absolutely necessary! (Three bars of plain quarter notes in the piano part might qualify as necessary counting places.)[25] Let the accompaniment bring you in on time and effortlessly.[26] You should not be involved with counting during performance except in certain super-tricky places, so your concentration can be where it belongs.

Songs with multiple verses (strophic) set to lyric poetry often present the greatest memorization problems. One frequently finds it a great chore to distinguish between the various verses, either because the words of a lyric song are so very similar from verse to verse or because the fact of same music for each verse means there are no differentiating features to help orient you. The use of mnemonics is germane to our discussion at this point because these devices are one last-ditch method for providing the relationships and associations that make the process of memorizing such problem spots easily surmountable.

In Schubert's "Ungeduld" the problem of strophic verses is com-

25. In the introduction to Schumann's "Stille Tränen" there are two bars containing twelve quarter notes. Here one must count. In the introduction to Bizet's "Adieu de l'hôtesse arabe" one does not count notes but rhythmic patterns.
26. In Fauré's "Clair de Lune" the piano's well-defined melody leads in measure 12 directly to the singer's entering note, in effect fabricating for one minute a new composite melody.

pounded by the repetitive "Dein ist mein Herz!" that completely obliterates any distinguishing characteristics for each verse just prior to the most problematic spot—the very first words of the next verse. Furthermore, three of the four verses begin with the word "ich," making it even more ticklish to keep track of which verse you are about to embark upon.

One solution (where normal methods fail) would be to tie the three "ich" verses together with one mnemonic device. Having memorized each line by the usual method of logical progression of meanings, you will usually find it simple to make it through the verse without error, provided that you have begun correctly. As a rule, therefore, the primary function of the mnemonic device is to get you started properly, either at the beginning of a verse or a phrase.

In the case of "Ungeduld," just memorize the order of the letters S–M(ö)–M(ei), noting that they are in reverse alphabetical order. (Let the verse that does not commence with "ich" shift for itself for the time being.) Now connect the letters S–M(ö)–M(ei) in your mind with "ich schnitt'," "ich möcht'," and "ich meint'." Now you have reduced the problem to manageable proportions. Each time you finish "Dein ist mein Herz und soll es ewig bleiben" just remember where you are in the mnemonic scheme, and where the one non-S–M–M verse is located.

Not only at the beginning but even *within* the verses of some strophic songs there are such subtle similarities, so close in meaning that more than one mnemonic "spot" is required in each verse. Verse 1 of "Ungeduld" begins with three similar phrases sung at breakneck speed, all starting with "ich"—"ich schnitt'," "ich grüb'," "ich möcht'." Further complicating the mental processes is the fact that "ich möcht'" is also the opening phrase of verse 2. Verse 2 continues with two phrases beginning with "bis"—"bis dass" and "bis er." As if this were not enough, the second phrase of verse 3 has yet another repetition of "ich möcht'"! Verse 4, one is happy to note, has a fairly simple scheme.

One now sees that a larger pattern is necessary in order to solve these complications and prevent straying into the wrong verse either at the opening measures or in the middle of the verse.

Verse 1: ich s chnitt'
          ich grüb'
          ich möcht' es sä'n
Verse 2: ich m öcht'
            bis dass
              bis e r
Verse 3: Den Morgenwinden
          ich möcht' es säuseln
Verse 4: ich m eint'

The big S–M(ö)–M(ei) scheme remains the same and most important. In verse 1 the order of the three "ich" phrases must be remembered with special attention to the placement of the ever-present "ich möcht'," since it occurs in all three verses. The two "bis" phrases are alphabetical in order, *d* before *e*. In verse 3 one must remember that the second phrase begins with "ich möcht' es säuseln." Obviously these devices cover only that part of the memorizing of the song where they are most helpful, or indeed when they are the only way to achieve security.

The solutions presented for "Ungeduld" exemplify the use of mnemonic devices for those places where normal memorizing procedures do not give dependable results. Such devices can, of course, be adopted for problem spots in songs that are not strophic.

Remember that a singer has considerably more responsibility than an instrumental musician. Among other things, you are responsible for language, with all of its attendant complications and you have the psychological distraction of facing an audience straight on, without an instrument between. One study shows that any singer in a stage production with costumes, props, sets, a conductor, and other singers is at each moment balancing *forty* psychological processes. In a recital, without any of these things, a singer is responsible for at least twenty psychological processes. To prove this for yourself, start counting the interrelated musical, vocal, linguistic, and dramatic processes in a recital.

What does this mean to the process of memorizing? It is exceedingly important that the things that *can* be made automatic be made so. Surely the pronunciation and enunciation of the text can be programmed to be automatic by proper practice. Surely the command of the musical duties can be made automatic, or nearly so. The conscious mind has to be free to grapple with vocal technical skills, dramatic sincerity, and those musical ensemble questions that cannot be automatic.

GUIDELINES FOR PRACTICE

The following songs are accompanied by questions and directions meant to spark your imagination as you study the song for purposes of expressivity. By organizing, assembling, and transforming all ideas, concepts, and images suggested to you by your analysis of the music and text, shape your personal concept for each song.

1. "San Basilio" by Ildebrando Pizzetti (popular Greek poetry, trans. Tommaséo), a narrative-lyric song.

   a. There are three people in this song. Who are they? How do the verb forms help you to infer the age of the first person who speaks (in quotes)? What do the words "scarpe di bronzo e ferree vesti" tell you about the second person to speak (in quotes)?

b. There are two very important *doubles entendres* in the sixth line of music. Solve their meanings. Carefully distinguish between the meanings of "donde" and "ove." Where did Saint Basil live and what made him famous? Does this relate to the subtext of this song?

c. Does the original "andante mosso" marking suggest more than a tempo? The words and the vocal line will help you to decide. How does this tempo change and why? Near the end of the song justify dramatically the ♩ ♩ ♩ and the 𝅘𝅥𝅯𝅘𝅥𝅯𝅘𝅥𝅯 figures in the vocal line. What is the significance to you of the ♪♩ ♩ ♩ pattern in the piano?

d. At what exact musical moment does the miracle happen? How do you deduce this?

e. At the end of the song, what does it signify to you that the vocal line, after two single patterns of 𝅘𝅥𝅯𝅘𝅥𝅯𝅘𝅥𝅯 , suddenly bursts into a series of three such patterns before ending on the same high note? How do you interpret the final *trattenuto* of the piano part?

2. Here is a list of elements that are typical of Charles Ives's writing:

use of:
hymn tunes
popular melodies
topical political references
minstrel tunes
parlor piano music melodies
ragtime
written explanatory notes
Stephen Collins Foster tunes
impressionistic visual and sound images
Civil War tunes
parody
remembrances and reflections of country life
quotations from other serious composers
polyphony
wrong notes added for their own sake
sudden resolving of dissonance into complete consonance

references to:
transcendentalism
revival meetings
timbres achieved by echoes

beauty of nature
the Puritan civilization of New England

In these four songs,

"General Booth Enters into Heaven" (1914)
"Tom Sails Away" (1917)
"Feldeinsamkeit" (1898)
"On the Counter" (1920)

locate the places where Ives has used the above devices. (Note the date for each song; it is significant.) In what way does this influence your interpretation?

3. "The Junk Man" by Howard Swanson (Sandburg), a lyric song.

   a. What kind of a person is speaking these words? In what physical condition is he? How important is this condition to his inner feelings? How do you know whether or not he is really convinced of his words?

   b. List the ways in which a clock is analogous to the speaker.

   c. Can you find three programmatic references in the accompaniment and one in the vocal part?

   d. In what ways (similar to an overture) does the introduction set forth the basic musico-dramatic elements of the song?

   e. Are Swanson's dissonances integral to this specific text or part of his usual writing style?

4. "Nuvoletta" by Samuel Barber (Joyce), a fun song.

   a. Is this song totally nonsense? What factors give you the answer?

   b. There are at least sixteen literary allusions in this prose text. Can you explain them? Why are so many of them related to the Italian language?

   c. In what way, if at all, does the music underline these allusions in the vocal and piano lines?

   d. Why did Barber choose three beats to the bar ($\frac{6}{8}$ and $\frac{3}{4}$) as his basic pattern? What function do the few $\frac{2}{4}$ and $\frac{4}{4}$ bars serve? Of what importance are the rhythmic irregularities and syncopations to the interpretation?

   e. What does the added sixth in the final chord mean to you?

5. "David Weeps for Absalom" by David Diamond (the Second Book of Samuel 18:33), a narrative-lyric song.

   a. This song is utterly compelling because of Diamond's choice of apt and telling musical means of expression. Find them. (For example, look at the syncopations, the musical translation of word accents, the choice of durational values in the vocal line, and the single bar of ⅜.)

b. Find a threefold rationale for Diamond's use of open chords (only octaves and fifths).

c. By what musical means does Diamond achieve the extra-ordinary drive in this song?

d. Where is the climax of this song? Is there more than one?

e. Can you find a reason for the indication "maestoso" which is dramatically serviceable?

6. "Song of Perfect Propriety" by Seymour Barab (Parker), a character song.

a. Who was Dorothy Parker? In what way did her life-style color her writing style and content? How does this aid your interpretation of the song?

b. What is there about the accompaniment figures that express the full subtext of the poem?

c. The verbs in this poem directly contribute to setting up the joke and giving the punchline. How?

d. How do Barab's extravagant musical markings give you a key to the dramatic understanding of this song?

e. What can you do plastically to exploit the piano's final musical comment?

7. "Loveliest of Trees" by Celius Dougherty (Housman), a lyric song.

a. What is the form of this song? How does the meaning of the words suggest the musical form adopted by Dougherty?

b. In what way do the musical means of the piano postlude underline the evident mood changes of the text?

c. Do you feel that Doughtery's chromatic harmonies enhance the prevailing spirit of the poem? If so, in what way?

d. Does the final piano chord have a specific meaning for you? What is it?

e. At what specific bar does the song really begin, emotionally and musically? What specific bars really comprise the prelude? How does Dougherty achieve this?

8. "The Blessed Virgin's Expostulation" by Henry Purcell, realized by Benjamin Britten (Luke 2:42), a solo cantata (outgrowth of a character song).

a. Explore the human condition of a mother and her departed child and relate this to the Divine Family. Read the complete Biblical passage from which the text is taken in order to answer such questions as: How long has Jesus been gone? Does Mary know where He is? What are their ages at this time? Trace the significance in Mary's life of the allusions to Herod, Gabriel, and Judah's daughters.

b. The traditional form of the cantata contains recitative and aria, in which the recitative furthers the plot and the aria crystallizes a lyric moment. In what way does Purcell's cantata live up to this format, and how do the verb tenses contribute to your understanding of it?

c. There are two sets (four each) of calls to Gabriel. One set is marked < and the other, >. Discover whether these marks are Purcell's or Britten's and justify them dramatically.

d. The meaning of the following single words is expressed coloristically in the accompaniment. How?

quickly	footsteps
pity	farewell
tiger's	motions
doubt and lab'ring.	

Justify Purcell's reasons for his metric spacing of notes and rests in these sections of the text:

where does my Soul	why, fairest object
was it a waking Dream	no, no, no vision
I call, Gabriel	of Mothers, most distress'd

e. Purcell uses a ♫. figure for the word "little." Find a reason for his use of this text-setting device. Discover an additional reason for his use of this device on the word "quickly." By extending this rhythmic pattern, Purcell achieves a third kind of effect on the word "sweet." What is it?

9. "Jazz dans la Nuit" by Albert Roussel (Dommange), a lyric song.

a. Find in the introduction three jazz elements which fulfill a second duty as expressions of dramatic moods to come.

b. Write a movie scenario complete with camera angles (distant as well as close-up shots) for this song. This will clarify the locale and the action of each of the four or five small scenes within the poem.

c. In this song there is more than the usual amount of words that can be exploited for vocal expressivity. Watch particularly nasals and consonants. Here is a partial list:

flambent	étouffent le frolement
s'évanouissent	en sanglotant
plaintes	cache
inconnue	

 d. What is the common element among the various accompaniment figures? Compare the way Roussel's use of the accompaniment serves to underline the mood changes of the text with the way Schubert's does.

 e. Search out the programmatic devices used by Roussel in the vocal and piano lines.

10. "On the Beach at Fontana" by Roger Sessions (Joyce), a lyric song.

 a. When was this poem written? Where? What is an "epiphany" as it relates to Joyce's writings? How do these facts contribute to your understanding of this song?

 b. What are the twin themes of the poem and how are they reflected in the musical themes?

 c. Study all piano interludes. Decide whether each one advances the mood *before* the voice or reflects what the voice has *previously* articulated. When is the voice or the piano paramount and why?

 d. There are faintly programmatic references in the music which relate to:

slime-silvered stones	regularity (of the sea)
menace and foreboding	fragility
tenderness	

Find them.

 e. Note the rhythmic devices of both piano and voice parts, such as: the three changes of the ♫♫♫ pattern, the repetition of the ♫♩ ♫♩ ♫♩ left-hand pattern, the various methods of displacing the § time in the vocal line, the change to ¾ in the piano part while the voice stays in §, (in the postlude) the changing of the sixteenth-note pattern into eighth notes. What is the relationship of these changes to the poem? Why is the last chord an exact repetition (position, too) of the chord that begins the song?

11. ¡"Vade Retro!" by Joaquín Turina (Marín), a character song.

 a. Who might be called the *real* protagonist of this song? Who is speaking? Find three reasons in the text which suggest why "Don(na) Giovann(a)" might serve as a title for this song.

b. What purpose do the two allegretto dance sections serve? In order to make use of the fact that only the piano plays this music, find two physical ways to interpret these interludes.

c. In what ways is this girl an archetypal fictional girl from a Latin country? How does "Pablo" figure in this story? Why does the episode with "Pancho" seem to be the most insulting to her?

d. Why does Turina use so many rests before the names? Why does he stop when he does? Why a fermata before the first allegretto section and not the second?

e. Why does Turina ask for speech rather than singing on the last two words of the song?

12. "Wild Swans" by John Duke (Millay), a lyric song.

a. How old was Edna St. Vincent Millay when she wrote this poem? Where was she? What was her physical condition? Connect these facts with the poem and your interpretation of the song.

b. Note the exact rhythmic and melodic patterns of the introduction. When are they used in the body of the song and when are they abandoned? When the voice enters, what rhythmic patterns are paramount? Why do you believe Duke has done it this way? Where does he indicate ritards and where are there none? Why?

c. How do the variations among $\frac{2}{4}$, $\frac{3}{4}$, $\frac{5}{8}$, and $\frac{6}{8}$ bars serve the prosody as well as the mood of the text?

d. Where is the melodic or musical climax of this song? Is it at the same moment as the poetic climax? Why is this so?

e. What is the significance to you of the minor third which appears with the jagged rhythmic pattern in the piano part, especially at the end of the song? Why is the last chord unresolved?

11 New Music

What is New Music?
Evidently it must be music which, though it is still
music, differs in all essentials from previously composed music. Evidently it must express something which
has not yet been expressed in music.

ARNOLD SCHOENBERG[1]

OVERVIEW

The term New Music was chosen as the title of this
chapter in preference to the more common expressions contemporary
music, modern music, twentieth-century music, and avant-garde music.
"Avant-garde" and "contemporary" necessarily raise the questions:
avant-*what*? and contemporary *with whom*?[2] Can "modern" really be
said to characterize music written before World War I? If Charles Ives is
judged to have anticipated many or most twentieth-century innovations
and developments, then "twentieth-century" is not an entirely accurate
term with which to describe music written before 1900. Therefore, we
avoided these terms.

1. *Style and Idea* (New York: Philosophical Library, 1950), p. 39.
2. Cathy Berberian, noted practitioner of New Music, says that words like avant-garde are
   dated. They imply shock, but no one is shocked any longer.

A large proportion of singers is reluctant to learn or program works by twentieth-century composers. Yet it would seem appropriate that singers of this century feel some sense of commitment to the music of their time and of their peers. We remind them that twentieth-century vocal music is not *all* in the very front of the avant-garde. At the outset, a major purpose of this chapter is to quell the unjustifiable apprehension with which many singers regard the New Music repertoire. We intend to reassure such singers that the mysteries of new vocal techniques, new notation systems, new ensemble responsibilities, new pitch and rhythm skills, are not so arcane as they might imagine. By having the history of New Music put into a useful perspective, they will be encouraged to see the virtues of New Music and/or the exciting challenges engendered by it. They will be given a practical and helping hand in organizing specific ideas for programming New Music and some convincing reasons why it is in their best interest to perform twentieth-century music.

Twentieth-century music written for the voice has tended to be less revolutionary than music written for instruments. While it is very difficult to categorize New Music, it can be broadly divided into three compositional groups. There are those composers who cling to an expansion of what was done in the nineteenth century, those who combine tradition with new traditions, and those who adopt new means toward new ends. Most New Music written for the voice is not indeterminate, multi-media, or of another *outré* style. It is not even twelve-tonal, even though this is a style in which music has been composed all over the world since the end of World War I.

Partly because of the nature of the human voice, song literature tends to persist in a continuous tradition despite periodic dislocations. Even innovative twentieth-century composers had their roots in the past. Conversely, the works of some traditionalists were seen as "new" at the time. From our present vantage point we can view both types of efforts as offshoots of a mainstream of vocal writing.

Mainstream twentieth-century composers like Busoni, Carpenter, Delius, d'Indy, Dukas, Falla, Gretchaninov, Hahn, Janáček, Loeffler, Mahler, Medtner, Nielsen, Rachmaninoff, Ravel, Reger, Respighi, Roussel, Satie, Sibelius, and Strauss were contemporaries of Debussy. They helped to create a background that produced Schoenberg, Bartók, and Stravinsky. Some twentieth-century composers had a partiality for old habits of harmony and rhythm, which they combined and blended into all manner of new styles. Their music has given immense enjoyment to performers and listeners alike: Bliss, Bloch, Copland, Koechlin, Poulenc, Schoeck, Still, Vaughan Williams, and Weill.

So the recital singer should see that he need not feel compelled to perform works in the forefront of the avant-garde. A list of twentieth-century song composers whose names should elicit only admiration and eager enthusiasm includes Auric, Barber, Castelnuovo-Tedesco, Chanler, Copland, Diamond, Espla, Françaix, Gideon, Griffes, Guarnieri, Hindemith, Honegger, Hovhaness, Ibert, Jolivet, Kodály, Malipiero, Medtner, Milhaud, Pizzetti, Poulenc, Prokofiev, Respighi, Rorem, Satie, Sauguet, Shostakovich, Szymanowski, Thomson, Villa Lobos, Walton, and Weber. These composers, for the most part, gave only part of their attention to instrumental music, preferring the human voice and having a predilection for words.

Another list is comprised of composers whose names have been known to strike terror into the hearts of impressionable and overly cautious recital singers. All of the following composers have written some songs that are well within the capabilities of trained musicians: Bartók, Beeson, Berg, Cage, Carter, Crumb, Dallapiccola, Druckman, Fine, Ginastera, Messiaen, Rochberg, Schoenberg, Stravinsky, and Webern.

The work of those composers of the true advance guard admittedly necessitate more labor. This does not automatically signify that their requirements are impossible to surmount. In any case, you will never know unless you try, and it will be well worth the venture.

Students sometimes ask how to begin such a venture. First of all, do not assume that Barber, Britten, Copland, Messiaen, Prokofiev, Rorem, and Szymanowski have nothing new to teach you about new musical and vocal techniques. Spend considerable time with their music. When this music has in a sense been digested, move on to Bartók, Berg, Schoenberg, Stravinsky, and Webern. If you wish to go further, remember that your privilege of instinctive kinship with any music can be triggered by immersing yourself in performances of that musical style, rather than just picking at random a composer to study. Allow yourself plenty of time and persevere in your listening efforts until you can make a reasonable judgment whether or not to pursue this direction. A few well-known names of the avant-garde are Babbitt, Badings, Berio, Boulez, Feldman, Henze, Ligeti, Maxwell Davies, Stockhausen, Subotnick, and Ussachevsky.

In no way are we qualified to write a scholarly dissertation on New Music, nor do we wish to break our rule of "practicality above all" invoked throughout this book. We do, however, understand the needs of the average singer and accompanist. Therefore, in lieu of a written history describing the evolution of New Music, we offer three tables that we are confident you will find more efficient for easy reference.

It has been said that it is impossible even for a real scholar to write a proper and specific history of all New Music. Although we agree, we feel that the chronology in Table I (Chronology of Activities in Nonharmonic Composing since 1900) though necessarily succinct, delineates for the inquiring singer the general and explicit developments of New Music.

It is, however, largely limited to placing chronologically the works of those composers who are in the forefront of new experiments of the day, rather than those composers whose works are familiar to many singers.

Table II (Definitions of New Music Terms) defines briefly the major twentieth-century stylistic genres and mentions some of the most renowned composers of each.

When one examines how and when the first repudiations of nineteenth-century Romanticism began, it is fairly simple to pinpoint such composers as Debussy and Ives, who were breaking the rules before 1900. They were succeeded (in Europe) by Schoenberg, Bartók, and Stravinsky and (in America) by Carl Ruggles and Henry Cowell—each followed in great measure by his disciples. Therefore, Table III (New Music Composer/Teachers and Their Students) charts the lineage of composer-teachers and their students. This chart will be found as an appendix at the end of this chapter. We believe that these tables will enable you to orient yourself with ease as to where each composer fits into the collective history of the New Music.

Must special considerations be given to the programming of New Music? Often this repertoire is reserved for specialist performers singing specialist programs. Such a separation that effectively puts a program out of the main stream is yet another way of contributing to the museum-piece image of the song recital, exactly what we are trying to avoid.

Frequently, exaggerated awe for the formidable task of learning and understanding the compositions of this century leads to an avoidance of this repertoire. Even those who are good at programming have preconceived notions as to its worthiness. Referring to such problems, Bethany Beardslee, the respected performer of Webern and Schoenberg, says, "It is just like any other music; it simply takes more work." Ms. Beardslee eschews the use of terms such as "serial" or "aleatory." "The most important consideration," she says, "is that one perform a good piece of music regardless of its place in music history."

The twentieth-century singer of New Music must decide what is worthy in the absence of a helpful tradition of works labeled by authority as good or bad. The performer must be a critic of the newest repertoire.

REJECTION OR ACCEPTANCE
OF NEW MUSIC

Audiences today are as divided in their attitudes toward the New Music as they were in the nineteenth century. They regard new music as either all good or all bad. The following discussion treats various ramifications of these attitudes and prejudices in an attempt to aid the singer who must eventually make programming choices based upon reactions of audiences, critics, and the music profession to the New Music.

Choosing between good and bad is no easier for the performer than for the critic or audience. The most common temptation is to confuse pleasure with beauty. Imitative and bad works can "please" a listener because he recognizes that a type of artistic workmanship with which he has learned to agree gives immediate pleasure, while the originality of a new work throws him off and makes him uneasy. Genuinely new musical experiences must be admitted to our attention. They may not at first, nor ever, afford us pleasure. But, inevitably, a work of art does exist, regardless of our approval or disapproval.

As a medical doctor recently reminded us, there may very well be as-yet-unknown chemical or physiological bases for the satisfaction given us by those harmonies to which we have grown accustomed.[3] He also suggests that there may be something yet to be uncovered about the difference between acquired and natural sensory reactions, whether they be visual, olfactory, gustatory or auditory. He contends that science has, for example, yet to define red or green, or how we distinguish between sound and noise. Since there is no adequate scientific distinction between sound and noise, the doctor argues, is it not then possible that the body considers certain vibrations to be noise and therefore rejects them as music?[4] Furthermore, the mysteries of body rhythms, which are only beginning to be fathomed, exemplify our lack of scientific knowledge. Almost everyone has experienced jet-lag produced by upsetting the accustomed proportion between sleeping and waking hours. Consequently, the doctor reasons, perhaps some aversions to rhythmic devices of the New Music do not represent habituation but honest physical reaction.

We must all work toward being cultivated receivers, at developing the capacity to listen without presumptions. The repertoire of the last two hundred years has taught us to expect certain satisfying harmonic relationships within a given key. The performers and listeners should teach themselves to hear each composer's speech, idiom, and syntax without falling into the trap of asking, "What is his music all about?" His music is not *about* anything but what he *does* with it.

In examining various viewpoints regarding the New Music a question arises. Can everyone wholeheartedly endorse what many people call elitist composing, the "great art" that Schoenberg himself refers to as requiring "the alert mind of an educated listener," whose presence renders the composer able to write for "upper-class minds"? One would concur

3. So much do different sounds produce different effects and different moods that experts on meditational techniques are wary of using the most famous and reputedly very powerful mantra, *om*.
4. Not only the human body but plants as well. According to Tomkins and Bird's *Secret Life of Plants* (Avon, 1974.), plants react favorably to classical music and tend to grow in the direction of the speaker, but subjected to hard rock, they die.

with his statement that popularity is achieved by "illiterate" composers (Schoenberg's term) who still write regular and repetitive phrases of two, four, and eight bars, whereas density of structure, a hallmark of new music, is an "obstacle to popularity." Yet, would not those of this decade who crusade against elitist art object to his self-congratulatory stance against the presumable "lower-class" minds of the twentieth-century mass audience?

At this point there should be a healthy chorus of dissenters proclaiming, "It is, nonetheless, dangerous at the box office to program the works of avant-garde composers." True, the present-day audience does identify with what was popular in its time: eloquent melodies, regularity and symmetry of form, chromatic harmonies, specific personal allusions, Romanticism, individual bias, traditional harmonic progressions, programmatic imagery, recurring melodic themes, careful illustration of poetic subtext. Protected by their resistance to change and their insistence on regarding a proper recital as a Lieder recital only, they defend themselves against new experiences. Feeling understandably that the regimented tensions of Beethoven's music are a crowning achievement of art, it is natural that they suffer disorientation when confronting Schoenberg's seeming lack of control and when attempting to hear the master design behind total serialism. In addition, without denying the enormous importance of recorded music as an audible library, the record album has nevertheless become to many concert-goers the venerated pattern against which all other music must be compared. Particularly does this audience then resist the uncomfortable demands that new works make upon them. Their view of the contemporary composer as an intruder in their comfortable musical museum perhaps explains the current wave of nostalgia that may be but a surface manifestation of a deeper commitment to cultural conservatism.

But it is important not to defend the "incapacities" of the popular audience. Rather it is far more important to awaken in them the desire for new opportunities to hear music. A very strong influence upon the audience's habituation are the reports of critics, historians, and reviewers. Too often they report publicly their own incapacity to comprehend the unexpected as if their failure in some way proves the work of art (which they have not understood) to be inferior. The net result of critics' judgment against new works or in favor of one type above all others is restricted programming. (Even Schoenberg did not envisage twelve-tone music as the end of new compositional roads.) In answer to the critics' query, "But is it art?" Peter Yates says that whatever is musically to be done is required to be done as the composer decrees "and whatever he offers as direction *is* his art."[5]

5. *Twentieth Century Music: Music after the Harmonic Era* (New York: Minerva Press, 1968), p. 189.

Ad nauseam one hears, "We must give the public what it wants." This is a defensive statement of current habituation. It is not the audience we must fear, but those who dictate the musical "opportunities." (This most often means established repertoire done once again by performers of established name only.) When someone who believes in discrimination is in a position sufficiently influential to enforce his biases, then the threat is very real. The powerful critic can publicly run down and/or punish. The powerful impresario, program-maker, or concert-director can exclude. To forbid pleasing or enjoyable music of whatever style is dangerous. To encourage the performance of all kinds of music is the only way to separate the short-lived from the lasting. A listener who sheds tears over Schumann is not necessarily incapable of listening appreciatively to Schoenberg.

PROGRAMMING

In truth, a good case can sometimes be made for the prerequisite of bravery when programming works of modern composers. There are several ways to present New Music to good advantage:

1. Simply program it as any other repertoire, with scrupulous regard to a juxtaposition providing variety. On a traditional recital (see Chapter 2) the New Music group would come at or near the end. Take time to re-examine this cliché premise. When too many new compositions are sung successively, the effect is diluted. Better to create a frame for the contemporary piece. Surround it with two others that are easier fare. Do not put the audience on the defensive. Cosset them a bit.[6]

2. Take advantage of any opportunities to coordinate your twentieth-century music with local art exhibits. If there were, for example, an exhibition of Miró works in the community or university art museum, then surely Poulenc or Satie would be à propos and would create audience appeal. Or, venturing further into the avant-garde of this century, you might program the kinds of music that relate to the work of such artists as Louise Nevelson or Kenneth Noland. Intriguingly, René Leibowitz[7] actually wrote some vocal music on texts by Picasso. Some other attractive combinations that might be exploited are the following:

a. impressionist painters: Monet, Pisarro, Renoir, and impressionist composers: Debussy, Ravel, Roussel

6. Cathy Berberian describes this as her method.
7. Twentieth-century composer, teacher of Pierre Boulez.

b. video art (usually accompanied with soundtracks by modern composers), typical artists: Nam June Paik, Stan van der Beek, and soundtrack composer, or others who work with electronic techniques, typical composers: Berio, Mayazumi, Mumma, Pousseur, Subotnick

c. superrealist or photorealist painters: Cottingham, Estes, Rusché, and composers with synthesized or electronic techniques: Davidovsky, Gerhard, Hiller, Penderecki, Schaeffer, Stockhausen, Ussachevsky

d. expressionist graphic artists and painters (Die blaue Reiter): Jawlensky, Kandinsky, Klee, Kokoschka, Marc, and expressionist composers: Ruggles, Schoenberg, Webern

e. surreal painters: Dali, Magritte, and music by John Cage

3. Time your recital to coincide with a performing arts event such as a play whose author is represented on your program, or a ballet or a play whose incidental music was written by a twentieth-century composer highlighted on your program.

a. Shakespeare the playwright, coordinated with Shakespeare the poet (who can be represented by any of the following composers: Amram, Argento, Arne, Blacher, Britten, Castelnuovo-Tedesco, Chausson, Diamond, Franco, Fortner, Hoiby, Honegger, Lessard, Rieti, Stravinsky, Thomson, Uhlela).

b. The playwright García Lorca whose poetry has been set by Arizaga, Caamaño, Crumb, Pittaluga, Poulenc.

c. Schiller's poetry appears in Henri Sauguet's *Quatre Mélodies sur des Poèmes de Schiller.*

d. Honegger has used prose from a Giraudoux novel in his cycle *Petit cours de morale.*

e. Jean-Paul Sartre's *No Exit* (music by Ussachevsky) could be coordinated with a performance of one or more of Ussachevsky's vocal pieces on your program.

f. As for ballet, Falla, Satie and Stravinsky have all collaborated with other professionals such as Diaghilev in ballet productions as well as writing vocal music.

g. John Cage and David Tudor have associated closely with Merce Cunningham and his ballet company.

h. The Alvin Ailey Company dances *Feast of Ashes*, with a score by Carlos Surinach, who has written much vocal music, and *Ariadne*, written by André Jolivet, who has written such vocal cycles as *Les Trois Complaintes du Soldat, Poèmes Intimes, Trois Poèmes Galants.*

i. The ballet *Episodes*, choreographed by Margery Mussman, has a score by Leos Janáček, who wrote the cycle *Diary of One Who Vanished*.

j. Twyla Tharp has choreographed two ballets by contemporary composers under the influence of jazz and ragtime: *The Bix Pieces* with music by Bix Beiderbecke and *The Raggedy Dances*, with music composed by Scott Joplin. Some imaginative combinations could come from these sources.

k. Eliot Feld's company has in its repertoire *Harbinger*, with music by Prokofiev and *Pagan Spring*, with music by Bartók. Let such combinations suggest possibilities to you.

4. Let the New Music work be the "happening" on your program, whether it be completely a surprise event or just off-beat, multi-media, or indeterminate music.

5. Arrange your program so that it peaks with a first performance by a composer who consents to be present for his traditional bow. Or, the author of the text might be found nearby. Exploit the fact of either presence in the advance publicity.[8]

6. Build your program around a poet (or group of poets stylistically linked) whose works have been set by composers of various eras including the twentieth century.

a. Cocteau can be represented in compositions by Auric, Honegger, Milhaud, and Poulenc.

b. Rilke's poetry has been set in German and French as well as translations in English and Spanish by Aitken, Badings, Barber, Beck, Bernstein, Engelbrecht, Horvath, Krenek, Ott, Steffan, Ussachevsky, and Voormolen.

c. Elizabethan poets might be represented by composers from Dunstable to Quilter and Thomson.

d. Medieval texts have been set in Spanish, French, and English by Barber, Bush, Crosse, Edmunds, Lamaña, Rodrigo, Stevens, and Trimble, among many other twentieth-century composers.

e. Dylan Thomas presents a special case: not only are readings of his poetry very popular but frequently his one play, *Under Milkwood*, is performed as a reading; his works have been set to music by Milton Babbitt, Robin Holloway, Netty Simon, and Igor Stravinsky.

---

8. Singers should investigate partial funding for such occasions, available through state councils for the arts and other foundations.

7. Devise a program, a sizable portion of which is devoted to music for voice and a single instrument, spanning many eras, including various compositional styles of the twentieth century. An example of a combination offering rich possibilities might be voice and flute, for which the following, among others, have written: J. C. Bach, J. S. Bach, Bantock, BenZion, Bliss, Caccini, Caldara, Chaminade, Cowell, Crumb, Diamond, Feldman, Flanagan, Handel, Head, Hovhaness, Ibert, Luening, Mamlock, Marx, McBride, Meyerbeer, Musgrave, Pepusch, Pinkham, Pollock, Riegger, and probably others as well.

8. Should the occasion of an art show featuring the works of twentieth-century women arise, plan a coordinated recital using the compositions of twentieth-century women composers, such as Martha Alter, Grazyna Bacewica, Johanna Beyer, Margaret Bonds, Radie Britain, Roslyn Brogue, Rebecca Clarke, Gloria Coates, Jean Coulthard, Blanche Gerstman, Miriam Gideon, Peggy Glanville-Hicks, Elizabeth Gould, Miriam Stewart Greene, Augusta Holmes, Jean Ichelberger Ivey, Eunice Kettering, Barbara Kolb, Elizabeth Lutyens, Elizabeth Maconchy, Ursula Mamlock, Joyce Mekeel, Dorothy Rudd Moore, Julia Morrison, Thea Musgrave, Alice Parker, Pauline Oliveros, Barbara Peutland, Priaulx Rainier, Shulamit Ran, Ruth Crawford Seeger, Louise Talma, Phyllis Tate, Ludmila Ulelha, Nancy Van de Vate, Joan Franks Williams. Be sure to plan the publicity to coordinate well with the art exhibit.

9. For audiences who are known to be aficionados, or where the climate is one of approval (such as universities or associations dedicated to twentieth-century music), try programs limited to the New Music repertoire. Questioned as to their opinions on the subject of all-New Music programs, three great ladies of this repertoire, Bethany Beardslee, Cathy Berberian, and Jan DeGaetani, agreed that an all-contemporary recital is a mistake, since it isolates such music as a specialist endeavor, besides deadening the audience's perception by saturation. Nevertheless, there is a demonstrated audience for such programs. Therefore, some suggestions:

a. a New Music program shared among several vocalists

b. a New Music program using instrument with voice

c. a New Music program, one half for one or more instruments with voice, and the other half for voice with piano only

d. a retrospective program of the works of one composer only, using any forces called for

e. a New Music program of two contemporary composers (half and half) whose works differ greatly

f. a New Music program of works drawn from one country

g. a New Music program utilizing works in one language

h. a program of contempory song cycles only

In all of these programs care must be taken to work out a maximum variety of styles and languages according to the principles of Chapter 2.

10. There are many possibilities for interplay between the arts—a practice highly representative of this century—that can help you to get an audience for New Music repertoire. When you have arrived at a multi-art concept of which your recital is one portion, why not suggest to the director of the film festival, for example a composite audience experience like *Beauty and the Beast* (*La Belle et la Bête*), a French film directed by Cocteau with score by Georges Auric, together with your recital featuring the poetry of Cocteau and the music of Auric in various combinations? Or, why not suggest to the college or university museum director that an exhibition of Michelangelo reproductions could be effectively combined with vocal works by Britten, Pizzetti, Liszt, and Wolf that are set to Michelangelo's poetry or that illustrations by William Blake be combined in some way with his own poetry as set by Antheil, Britten, Citkowitz, Thomson, or Vaughan Williams? Or that works by Black contemporary painters (such as Jacob Lawrence, Romare Bearden, and Alma W. Thomas), works by Black primitive painters (such as David Butler, William Edmundson, and Horace Pippin), and works by Black abstract sculptor Richard Hunt be combined with poetry readings from the works of Langston Hughes, Mari Evans, and Paul Lawrence Dunbar and music composed by David Baker, T. J. Anderson, Wendell Logan, Mark Fax, Hale Smith, Noel da Costa, Olly Wilson, and Howard Swanson. Any of these ideas or others like them could produce a mini-festival. Or how about two consecutive evenings, the first a basically theatrical event in which audience and actors interreact (as in the Living Theater performances, or a recent revival of *Candide*), the second evening a basically musical event in which the lines of demarcation between the arts are blurred, such as one of Henry Brant's theatrical-musical extravagances. Perhaps at the same time even an exhibition of Rauschenberg with his typical allusions to other art works?

Three final cautions: (1) Do not feel constrained to do any new compositions to which you are less than committed. As in any music, it simply does not pay to perform out of duty. An inner conviction of its worthiness is still a necessary guideline. (2) Do not plunge in when you are unsure. Work your way up. Start with earlier composers like Bartók, Stravinsky, Webern, and Berg, whose styles are well known. Next time, perhaps, move to Cage, Ligeti, or Berio. Use as your guide recordings of performers who are known to manage the style well. (3) Whereas younger audiences are more than ready to go willingly wherever avant-garde music leads, older, more conventional audiences must be gentled into appreciating the New Music event. Exercise taste. Place the modern piece very carefully to achieve maximum interest. Try with all the means at your disposal to extract the most advantageous hearing for it.

As to intellectual reasons for your choice, there is virtually no difference between a concert containing modern music and one without it. One can plan a recital to please the audience. Or one can assume that the audience arrives expecting the performer to exercise taste and looks forward to experiencing what he has chosen. Certainly, the worth of some compositions one can guarantee, but for others some risks must be taken in order that the recital form be kept alive and viable in this area.

A problem arises when the idiom or content of a modern piece is somewhat beyond what the audience expected. Certainly procedures which are moderately inscrutable need some clarification. All listeners find it hard to grasp certain complicated twentieth-century designs that are not readily comprehensible. Yet the music must stand on its own. An explanation of what is being done, either orally or in program notes, is not a substitute for the actual music. Nevertheless, it is not uncommon to encounter explanations as long as or longer than the compositions themselves. This dilemma is not easily resolved by the singer; each case must be decided on its own merit and in the light of the singer's experience.

PERFORMANCE RESPONSIBILITIES

The twentieth century has a wider range of performance standards than any previous era. Premieres are probably the worst performances because the work and its concept are unfamiliar to the performers. Standards are the highest in urban centers, and at universities where composer/performers[9] often make the difference. Nevertheless, wherever we choose to program new music, our performance responsibilities to this repertoire involve accuracy; knowledge of styles, concepts, and composers; and interpretation.

9. The composer as performer is not so new. Since World War II there have been some new reasons for the phenomenon, however. Composers have always sought a performance which comes closest to what they have in mind. The invention of magnetic tape and its recorder during the war coincided with the new directions taken by music. Some of this New Music made enormous demands upon the individual and ensemble performers. Some music was so difficult that the musical establishment could not, even when the performers were up to the technical requirements, support the expense of the long rehearsals, the immense complement of performers, etc. When the composers turned to tape, and eventually to computer composing, there was suddenly no further difficulty and the composer was where he wished to be—in full control of the elements.

Accuracy

The performance of New Music repertoire demands, first and fore-most, accuracy. The singer/accompanist team must search out a com-plete realization of the composer's intentions by means of a literal trans-lation of his notation.

NEW NOTATION

Leading the parade of duties to be completed before performing a piece of modern music is the task of deciphering the notation.[10] Other duties such as learning the correct notes and rhythms, overcoming en-semble problems, mastering new vocal and textual techniques, must be secondary. Often the notational system used by the composer is the most time-consuming obstacle for the performer. A propos is Schoenberg's reference to "my musical picture-puzzles."

Not until the first half of the twentieth century were any attempts made to revise a system[11] that had served for centuries. By the twentieth century, Schoenberg was concerned with two problems directly relating to notation: (1) that the effect of a musical composition changes with each hearing and (2) that only his own will and design should prevail.

After World War II the notational changes were many and serious. Of necessity, new systems were devised to parallel the new composition-al techniques. Total serialization required the greatest possible specific-ity; indeterminacy, on the contrary, required complete freedom of inter-pretation. Entirely new systems appeared, as well as adaptations of exist-ing methods. As a result, no longer could the performer rely upon his easy and clear understanding of the composer's intentions, formerly fur-nished by the comfortable old system.

The "utter correctness" so desired by the composer opens up another field for conjecture. Hampered by our honest respect for unerring accu-racy, we usually give no thought to certain paradoxes. On the subject of correct pitch, Mozart's written A, played at today's commonly agreed-upon pitch standards, would surely be "incorrect" to Mozart's ears. Eighteenth-century just intonation music played today on an instrument

10. Busoni called notation "an ingenious expedient for catching an inspiration." Whether or not the means are, in some cases, more ingenious than the inspiration remains to be seen. Are the new notational systems too complex to be practical, too specialized to be broadly applied? The obligatory presence of the composer to instruct at rehearsals would seem to support this view partially.

11. The Medieval and Renaissance periods used a notational system which we now read but do not correctly interpret. In the eighteenth century musicianship meant the skill of the performer—his ability to read notes and often to embellish them guided by prin-ciples of good taste and learning. During the nineteenth century musicianship for a so-loist meant the ability to interpret notation in his own way.

tuned to equal temperament would certainly convince an eighteenth-century musician that we cared only for notation, not "correct" sound. Would not the harmonic relationship of such a performance be "out of tune" to Bach? Tuning our instruments to a higher mean pitch as we do, would not the vocal tessitura of the Ninth Symphony seem unnatural and "wrong" to Beethoven hearing it today? When a harpsichordist and organist trying to provide the same dynamic shaping of a rhythmic phrase as is possible on a piano distort that rhythm, we have another situation in which the "correct" notation is not followed. Amplifying a harpsichord on records accustoms us to a distorted tone quality that results in an incorrect intonation.

Our new composers are spurred on by such considerations as the above to search for notational systems which will convey their exact instructions with utmost clarity. Yet notation, its translation into sound, and what the listener hears are all variables at best. Even an electronic composition will vary with equipment and acoustics.

Achieving independence of sounds causes notational problems—free pitch alteration in time; differing and changing tempo references for each voice; differing decay times for various instruments playing together. Changes in the writing of pitch indications center around the demise of diatonic relationships in the works of some twentieth-century composers. Under certain circumstances, all twelve pitches are now regarded by some composers as if they were equal. (The tempering of the piano has assured this equality, but the singer's pitches and certain instruments' pitches must vary according to use.) When the twelve tones are used as equal, then the old rules governing sharp and flat alterations are not so germane.

Many innovative schemes have been proposed: give the staff more lines; make the notes black and white to show keys; widen the staff lines so that the notes can sit closer to a line or exactly equidistant between the two lines. Adding accidentals to all notes has been the favored solution for some composers. In a fully chromatic, atonal, or twelve-tone style, accidentals apply only to the note in front of which they stand. At times this practice is carried to extremes such as insisting upon a natural before a long series of identical notes even though the very absence of any accidental would have indicated a natural. This results in an overly marked page that is confusing.

Two additional areas of complication are microtones and tone clusters. Microtonal notation generally solves the problem by the use of very logical alterations upon conventional accidentals (such as ♯, ♭, and ♭, designating in turn a little lower than the sharped note, a little flatter than the flat, and just the regular flatted note.) For tone clusters, various symbols are adopted to indicate that all notes between two specific pitches should be played. Henry Cowell's original scheme has been widely adopted. In his system, ♯♯▤ would indicate that all the notes between the two F's be played with the two durations; ♯♯▤ designates all black notes; and ♭♯▤ means to depress all notes silently, holding with the pedal. Other variations are:♩, ♩, ♩, and Ⅱ.

Some composers dealing with the newest techniques regarded conventional notation of rhythm as almost totally ineffectual for their purposes. In New Music, any two single lines that must move at different tempos are difficult to coordinate by familiar metric indicators, especially when precisely graded ritard or accelerando passages are required. Problems of ensemble may be vexing. The disjunct and/or irregular rhythms common to much twentieth-century music may conceal coordinating pulses. Therefore, in compositions where a common pulse does exist, a new way of grouping separate notes together helps the performer to visualize the beat, as in ♪♪♩ ♪♪♩ ♪   , now notated as: ♫♫ ♫♫ . This seemingly intricate new notational manoeuvre is not so different from the old one. Composers (among them one of the great song writers of the twentieth century, Benjamin Britten) simply recognized what all singers know: insistence upon notating separate syllables with separate noteheads and flags makes for difficulty in reading, whereas beaming together short durational values helps the eye sort out accurately and quickly the messy and confused appearance of such a rhythm. Moreover, new time signatures, such as 3♩. or $\frac{3}{♩.}$, designed to occupy negligent gaps in the former system, are simply our old friend, $\frac{9}{8}$ time, in a new guise. It calls your attention to a fact you already knew: $\frac{9}{8}$ does not really mean that there are 9 beats to a bar. Lacking a single digit with which to indicate a dotted quarter note, composers had always written $\frac{9}{8}$, denoting the divisions of the beats rather than the three beats that were executed. Another example, Bartók's $\frac{3+3+2}{8}$ signature is simply a logical way of indicating how to divide the eight beats in $\frac{9}{8}$ or the four beats in $\frac{4}{4}$. Although many of the innovations solve some old difficulties, one wonders why it is necessary to write $\frac{4}{4}$ as 7:4 or $\frac{3}{3}$ as 3:2.

For the problems posed by polymetrics the solutions are numerous: (1) constantly changing metronomic marks; (2) dotted arrows to show accelerando or ritard; (3) + and − marks showing speed deviations; and (4) proportionate notation. In most proportionate notation schemes all notes are black, spaced to show duration, and beamed to show phrasing, as in this example of an accelerando: ♩ ♩ ♩ ♩♩♩♫ Again, it is a system logical to the mind and efficient to the eye.

Only a few ideas for notating articulation, timbre, dynamics, etc. are standard for singers. Sprechgesang is the most notable among them. In *Pierrot Lunaire* the Sprechstimme is notated on a regular five-line staff. Actual pitches are indicated by percussion symbols using an x with a flag (♪). Since *Pierrot Lunaire* a three-line staff has sometimes been used with approximate pitches of high, middle, and low.

John Cage has referred to the difficulty of putting indefiniteness into words. To this end, aleatory or indeterminate compositions use a notational method sometimes called "frame notation." It allows an elastic interpretation within a restraining framework, which depends upon the kind of freedom desired. For example, the pitches and the total duration of the piece might be specified, but not the details as to the combination and sequence of pitches, rhythms, tempos, dynamics, etc.

Another method of notating indeterminate or multi-media compositions is to use graphic analogs that indicate musical textures and attitudes by means of a free and unlimited choice of shapes that defy systematization. For example, crowded or vacant spaces on the page can be used to imply activity and silence, or darker and lighter noteheads can be employed to show dynamics. The range of possibilities is literally limitless. This example uses smaller and larger noteheads as well as empty and filled-in ones:

Electronic music has crystallized its notation into two main types of scores: (1) realization scores, which contain all the technical data essential to produce a piece, and (2) representational scores, which are to be followed by a reader. Realization scores cannot be "read" by the performers, and representational scores are usually tape plus a live performer. Encoding systems transmit data of two types: technical information (e.g., frequencies and intensities) or descriptive information (e.g., verbal characterizations of various sound types).

Since many composers put together their own notational systems, each composer's scheme must first be learned by the performer before tackling the score. Frequently, many pages of instructions are necessary to explain the new devices, and just as frequently, confusion is caused by two composers who use the same symbol to indicate two different musical ideas. A practical note: if the notation of your composition is not clear, contact the composer or books by a reputable authority. Remember that all recordings are not authoritative; some are obsolete, due to a shift in criteria.

New Musical and Vocal Skills

Composition for the voice in the avant-garde repertoire has changed to the point where the human voice is now considered just another instrument. Thus, as with any other instrument, the voice has been given more and more nonconventional (some critics would have said "unnatural") technical skills to master.

Bethany Beardslee reminds us that many twentieth-century vocal effects are not really new—glissandos and wide leaps, for example. Other "new" vocal effects used with and without other instruments include "tonlos" whispers and half-whispers, shouts; percussive noises such as tongue clicks; voiced or unvoiced plosives; sustained consonants such as *sh, zh,* or *s*; popping lips and cheeks; squeaks by teeth, lips, or tongue; whistles of various kinds; falsetto; vocal double-stops; and nonvocal effects such as stamping, hand-clasps, or finger-snaps, formerly used only by pop singers. Upon examination, most of these vocal and nonvocal effects have been used on occasion from Mozart's day to Ella Fitzgerald's.

Sprechstimme, however, stands out as a genuine innovation. Whether it is called contoured speech, or an elocutionary use of the voice, it raises both notational and technical problems. It is important for the neophyte singer of *Sprechstimme* to realize that she has encountered it before in other forms: the slight exaggerations of great recitative singers who achieve a result more in the direction of speech than singing; the "dirty" intonations of jazz singing; the sound nonsinging conductors and instrumentalists create when they try to indicate rapid musical passages with their voices; and the *Sprechstimme* produced by young children, fluent as imitators of speech intonations but not yet proficient at real musical scales or intervals. Thus, for a singer who is master of recitative singing, *Sprechstimme* is simply a more methodical and less instinctive matter of learning to sing the line, break it into speech, and finally to sing/speak by hitting the pitch and leaving it. Nonsingers like Rex Harrison do the opposite. If he can manage, so can you.

On the other hand, here is a case in which the composer *must* understand what the human voice can safely do. To push the technical frontiers forward is all very well and good, but to impair a vocal instrument is quite another matter. All variations on *Sprechstimme* are but *illusions* of speech. As any singer knows, he must really sing if he is not to harm his voice in the process of pretending to speak. The primary reason for this is a physiological difference between speaking and singing that limits the range at which even the *illusion* of speaking can safely be achieved. Even Rex Harrison is not so foolish as to try to speak above this "cut-off pitch!" Singers and voice teachers know this instinctively, if not intellectually, because at a certain point it is actually painful. There are well-documented instances in which the composer's demand for *Sprechstimme* upwards from high G in the treble staff has done physical damage to a soprano's voice. Here is a case in which it does not pay to refrain shyly from speaking out.

What is written down runs the gamut from awkward, through difficult, to impossible. A singer is not always being of assistance to a living composer with whom she is working by not confessing to where and why the exigencies of the music seem impossible. Although composers would no doubt refute this claim, singers *do* have an exaggerated respect for the sanctity of the written music and *do* keep silent about technical matters. They know full well that gentlemen's agreement among composers attributes singers' complaints to laziness, lack of musicianship, or other reprehensible qualities. The singer should be encouraged to speak up when he feels qualified to say that a vocal principle is being violated to such a degree that accuracy is impossible. In the end we all want what the composer wants—that his notation will be *clearly* indicative of his intentions.

Learning to sing with tapes demands that the singer acquire a different sense of rhythm. Where he formerly felt beats, he must now learn to sense time spatially. His live notes are the only variable in an otherwise absolutely reliable musical situation.

Something must be said here as to the sharpened sense of microtonal pitch acquired by any performers or listeners of electronic music. Following the nervous agony and/or boredom of first experiences in dealing with arbitrary sound patterns, one begins to become aware of the relationships that succeed and those that fail. One also becomes painfully aware of the confused tonality that seems to satisfy most contemporary orchestras, of the distortion caused by poorly designed concert halls, and of the pedestrian quality of much so-called musicianship masked as "correct" notes.

Singers contemplating the difficulties of microtones need not fear for their ability to master them. In point of fact, today's pitches *are* arbitrary. Voices often alter pitch from that of their piano accompaniment by degrees which are not indicated by our present notation, as for example, when they "bend" notes for inflection or when then unwittingly sing minimally sharp and flat. These variations are particularly noticeable when that voice tries to tune to an orchestra rather than a keyboard instrument, as, for example, when a coloratura cadenza previously learned at the piano must be sung with an orchestra.

Using the voice as an instrument of color with phonemes rather than poetic texts gives rise to some slight memorizing difficulties, since most singers are text-oriented. To exploit the fact that the voice is the only instrument capable of changing a sound without reattacking, nonsense syllables are widely used in twentieth-century compositions, especially those experimenting with Asian techniques.

It is understandable that many singers feel that new composers write, with a reckless indifference to the practicalities of the singing instrument, what is singable only by a handful of specialists. Yet the number of young singers who earnestly labor to master the New Music increases daily. It may no longer be necessary to be a specialist in order to sing this music, but being a virtuoso is a great help. Unless one sings extremely well at the outset bad vocal health can be a consequence of performing this repertoire. To be scrupulously fair, not all vocal demises can be blamed on contemporary repertoire—witness several well-known divas of the 1960s and 1970s. Cathy Berberian, the brilliant singer of the New Music repertoire, believes that a refresher course in bel canto between twentieth-century musical engagements might aid many a singer. If a singer goes into New Music without a classical background the voice will have a hard time holding up. As Charles Ives' father cautioned him during his student days at Yale, "You must learn the rules before you break them."

Clearly, many avant-garde composers find singers and the human voice generally a nuisance, and, as did Schoenberg, look forward to a day when mechanical methods will render it obsolete. Electronics experts have succeeded in producing the sound of a clarinet. The human voice has recently been synthesized as well.

Mastering the New Skills

Singers who are committed to programming the New Music must acquire the requisite skills. Cathy Berberian insists that, after you have shed your "cultural baggage," there is no difficulty in shifting between the various styles of the New Music. Simply work at the basics so that eventually you will be technically free. Your vocal and musical reflexes must be very fast. She gives her students exercises in shifting styles (folk, pop, jazz, Baroque) and encourages them to experiment with their voices in such unorthodox ways as vocal imitations of people and things (a child, a foghorn). She reports that the eminent composer Luciano Berio aptly named these new vocal techniques "La Nuova Vocalitá." Still, not every singer will be able to manage well all styles of the New Music as well as previous historical styles. They should be stimulated by their teachers to develop their own potential and originality, wherever that may lead professionally.

Some of the techniques New Music demands of singers are accuracy and flexibility with the complex rhythms, speed of execution between registers, highly varied dynamic levels, and modes of articulation.

One must be able to handle easily and accurately metrical rhythm with accompanying contradictions in various combinations at various levels. One must become skilled at perceiving measurement even when it is obscured by those irrational divisions that are spawned by nonmetrical rhythms—closely related to jazz improvisational techniques. It is very difficult for most Western performers to measure more than a one-minute duration; this ability can be extended (and must be for twentieth-century repertoire) with practice, as Asian musicians attest. A conscientious use of the metronome is probably indicated for practicing. Singers should remember that they have already had experience with practicing these rhythmic problems although they have not labeled them as such. Singing with an organ or a harpsichord, as compared to a piano, requires attention to the differentiation in the time span of their intervals.

As for pitch considerations, precision and total dependability at singing the characteristic wide leaps, dissonant pitches, microtones, and *Sprechstimme* are absolutely essential.

Jan DeGaetani, specialist in modern music and brilliant at many other styles, describes her method for practicing *Sprechstimme* thus: first speak the text in rhythm. When this is under control, sing the lines with all the accoutrements of normal singing (pitch, vibrato, legato, etc.). Next learn to attack each note on pitch and immmediately leave the pitch, keeping it in flux as you approach the following note, where you do the same things. The end result is a legato line with approximate pitches.

The following is a practical, though admittedly personal procedure for solving musical problems excluding microtones, microrhythms, and *Sprechstimme* in New Music for the benefit of singers who have not yet formulated their own methods.

We must again emphasize that unless the notation system must be deciphered the first task in tackling a difficult new piece is to study the rhythm. On the occasion of the first stage rehearsal of *Wozzeck* at a world-renowned opera house, the internationally acclaimed conductor, a superb musician respected for his stringent musical demands, informed the assembled cast, "When the difficulties of this score force you to choose between the right notes or the right rhythms, I want you, at all costs, to be *on time!*"

Rapid shifts between compound and simple time signatures, between metric values, between beat divisions of two, three, four, five, six, and seven are the hallmarks of such music. Time spent practicing for control of these elements is well spent indeed, since more traditional music in your repertoire will also benefit from this upgrading of your musicianship. Learn, too, to mark your score with your own clarifying symbols, e.g., if ♫♩ in ⁶⁄₈ time confuses your eye, change it to ♩·♩ .

Without the pitches, learn the rhythm of your own part, disregarding the accompanying lines at first. Then, when your rhythms are reliable, check the other parts or accompaniment for rhythmic patterns that may put you off. If possible, tap those rhythms while speaking your own, or in some other way deal with such spots. Do not ignore them.

When the rhythms are mastered, add the words. When you can speak the words and rhythms of your own fragments accurately and in tempo, add the rhythms of the interludes. Do not bother to play the notes, just tapping the rhythms will do for now. Practice entering correctly and in tempo after the interludes. When you are confident of your accuracy, you are ready for the pitches.

While learning the pitches, mark permanently in the score your pitch strategies, which facilitates speed of execution; e.g., a circle around your beginning note and a line connecting it to the circled note from which you get this first pitch. You will soon acquire the experience to evolve a personal system. Do not insist upon the correct rhythm or words during this part of the process, except possibly for the instrumental interludes (when it is convenient to do it so).

A small volume could be written on the subject of how to get your first note of the phrase. Here we will try to treat the most important variations of the issue. A seemingly simple strategy is to find the same note somewhere in the preceding instrumental or vocal interlude. Whether you find the same note, a note an octave above or below your note, or a note from which you can sing up or down a smallish interval, the pitfall is the same. To serve your purposes, the chosen note must be audible. That is, *seeing* it on the page does not signify that you will *hear* it when the other instruments are playing. Here are several illustrations of other factors that sometimes interfere:

1. The tempo at which the salient note goes past may be so fast that your pitch is inaudible.

2. The octave in which it appears may be too high above or too far below your singing range for you to perceive the pitch successfully.

3. The chosen note may be present and strongly so, but contradicted by equally strong neighboring dissonances.

4. Your pitch may be in the middle or on the very bottom of a tone cluster where it cannot be separated from the pile (the top note of a cluster is usually safest).

You must expect to decide by trial and error which note is dependable. Also, as your experience grows, you will be able to choose better and more swiftly, and your hearing will improve as well. You will learn that instrumental indications in the score are of great help. To illustrate, if the note you must hear is played by a trombone among many notes of lighter texture, then it will be very distinct to your ear, whereas a pitch played by one string instrument among other strings will not be reliably discernible. If the instrumental interlude before your entrance is long, a note that is reinforced by several isolated repetitions of that pitch will be of more help than a note you hear only once. Arbitrarily assigning leading tone function to a salient note that is one-half step lower than your entering note is a very useful device.

It is most efficient to practice these connections aloud initially rather than trying to *think* silently the connection. For example, your note is an

A and a strong G-sharp appears one and one-half bars before your entrance. Play on the piano a few haphazard tone clusters (no attempt at correct notes) surrounding a clearly played G-sharp in the proper octave. Catch the G-sharp. Sing it aloud while the tone clusters continue for the one and one-half bars. One beat or so before your entrance go up to your A. Enter on time with the A. The reason for prolonging the instrumental note, G-sharp, rather than going immediately to the A and prolonging *it* is this: when the process eventually becomes a silent one, the G-sharp is real but the A is mental, imagined, and can be forgotten more easily. In any case, remember that singing the helping note aloud does wonders for securing it in your memory, because memory of pitches is partly physical.

Be reassured that you do not have to choose strategies correctly the first time. Simply revamp your tactics after the first rehearsal when you discover what does not work. Once a note, infallible in its ability to trigger your starting note has proven to bring you in correctly, begin to play the capriciously selected tone clusters in the rhythm of the bars leading to each of your entrances, putting the signal note in its proper place. Then practice entering in tempo.

When the beginning note of each phrase is easier to find, proceed to the remaining notes of the phrases. The following procedure works very efficiently. For the first few days of learning pitches, invent chords that will encompass as many melody notes as possible, disregarding the actual harmonies or lack of them. Learn the pitches as they sound when buttressed by these chords. Remember, however, that not all notes need be chord tones. Some can be treated as appoggiaturas or upper and lower neighbors. For example, if the first five notes of a phrase are B-sharp, C^1-sharp, G^1, E^2-flat, F^1, then a chord that could encompass these would be an E-flat dominant seventh (the C-sharp becomes an enharmonic D-flat). Using the B-sharp as a leading tone to the C-sharp makes for a simple and efficient way of learning all five notes. (Even those who are capable of singing accurate intervals regardless of the underlying harmonic scheme will find the chord helpful. Those with perfect pitch have, of course, a swifter alternative.)

Here is a system for learning those troublesome large skips, suggested by Carol Knell of the University of Wisconsin at Stevens Point. During the learning process, invert all intervals over a fifth. This way the singer practices nothing larger than a fourth while routining the pitches. When confident, she returns to the wider skips. Wide leaps present the singer with two obstacles—the pitches themselves and the actual width of the skip. Bethany Beardslee counsels the singer faced with difficulties due to wide leaps to "learn to feel them in your larynx"; in other words, muscular memory reinforces pitch memory. Jan DeGaetani does with twentieth-century wide leaps the exact opposite to what she would do in other literature, that is, she does not strive for the normal blending into one quality. Instead, she works at speedy shifts between registers.

Adding the responsibility of the proper rhythm, practice with the chords until you can manage the melodic line accurately (in tempo) and with the correct rhythms. Now begin gradually to leave out the prop chords until you are secure and faultless when singing in tempo without them. In this manner, one first becomes confident of the pitches and eventually finds the real logic of their proper place in the composer's plan.

At this juncture you must challenge your command by adding those arbitrary piano tone clusters under your melodic line, deliberately trying to throw off your concentration. This is the time to check in the accompanying instrumental lines or other voices for minor seconds that are juxtaposed so closely to your notes as to threaten your security and accuracy. As with the rhythms, do not close your ears to them, attempting to ignore their influence; admit the sounds to your consciousness by pounding them out on the piano while singing, the better to learn how *not* to succumb.

Now, having assured your command of such segments, go back to tempo. Go through each medium-length section of music without stopping, playing the intervals (in the form of tone clusters with correct rhythm and tempo, but with no attempt at correct notes, except for those required in order to enter correctly or to withstand the pitch temptations) to indicate the other parts. This method may well be criticized. The singer does indeed spend some time within a harmonic design other than that which the composer intended. Nevertheless, nothing, including time, is lost. The end result is security, plus an easy sense of belonging to the proper scheme before the first rehearsal with the ensemble. Besides, by this time you will certainly have become a better musician.

Unfortunately it is often necessary to remind non-singers of the facts of the vocal instruments: dissonant pitches are infinitely harder for a singer to achieve with precision (even muscular fatigue or respiratory illness can add to his pitch difficulties). He has absoutely no geographical reference points, no black keys to the left of which lies an invariable F, no valves, no frets, nothing to measure by. All, not part, must rest on the quality of his ear-training.

Surely the microtones of Asian-influenced music call for an eartraining of a superior sort. Here again, the lack of a spatial point of reference hampers the singer more than an instrumentalist. He has learned to relate his hearing to mean tuning and it must be retrained to accomplish these microtone just tunings. Jan DeGaetani advises that this training is best done away from the piano.

Perfect pitch is consequently an immense plus for a singer of this repertoire since it cuts his learning time at least by half. Yet it must be admitted that a singer with perfect pitch cannot tune or listen harmonically as well as one without it. At times it is actually annoying to have perfect pitch because each person's A is different and older instruments, too, are pitched differently. To quote Cathy Berberian, "Perfect pitch is ideal but not indispensable."

Knowledge of Styles, Concepts, and Composers

The second large responsibility assigned to the performer of modern music is conceptual awareness. He must be aware of the historical, conceptual, and systematic framework of the piece he is performing. Tables I, II, and III were devised to assist you in orienting yourself to the framework of any composition you are studying.

In a sense we are philosophically opposed to the classification of music by the terms defined in Table II. Such identification tags have the effect of stopping our healthy investigations into the true nature of the new compositional styles. Composers of the twentieth century do not differ so thoroughly as these labels would make us believe. There is, for example, a humor and a rationality in Schoenberg's music that the word "expressionism" hides. There is a tender passion in Stravinsky's music that is belied by the term "neo-Classicist." These "isms" we shall examine in Table II all came about in succession due to the strenuous efforts of composers to break loose from the tedious rules and traditions of the nineteenth century. Take care, therefore, to use Table II for general orientation only, not as a substitute for your own explorations.

TABLE I   CHRONOLOGY OF ACTIVITIES IN NONHARMONIC COMPOSING SINCE 1900

General Trends before World War I
Composers begin to invent various ways of separating themselves from Romantic music. First few attempts concentrate on trying to extend the tonal system as far as possible. Romanticism is anathema.

Debussy, diverging radically from his predecessors' practices, begins with his works to herald the end of the harmonic era; with what he learns from gamelan music heard at the 1889 Paris Exposition, begins to loosen European conventions.

Schoenberg's expressionism, as in *Pierrot Lunaire*, is gradually breaking down tonality as the organizing force in music. Some attempts at what will be called mixed-media to be found in *Pierrot Lunaire*.

Stravinsky, in awe of endless possibilities, imposes stringent restraints upon his composing; gives European music what amounts to a rhythmic injection; uses harmonies that are polytonal; puts Russian folk melodies to great use, saying, "Great composers do not imitate; they steal." Called a sophisticated primitive, he innovates in the area of orchestral timbres. Influenced by his teacher, Rimsky-Korsakov, who was an orientalist, Stravinsky becomes interested in Asian musical techniques.

Busoni, pursuing what would later be called "neo-Classicism," disdains the mass audience, asking for freedom from conventions of rhythm and form, from excessive respect for notation, from our system of scales, from performance-technique limitations.

Bartók, best of the folklorists (Arabian, Turkish, Hungarian), uses rhythmic intricacies, sharp harmonic dissonances, chords in other than thirds, polyharmonies, pentatonic scales, to expand the tonal system.

Ives, in America, working entirely alone, realizes that he must violate "nice" harmony. He liberates it, frees consonance and dissonance, uses vertical and overlay harmonies, makes use of Cowell's new tone clusters, with breadth and versatility anticipates many twentieth-century developments and innovations, develops a style from free chromaticism to twelve-tone. (In a note to a pianist attempting a piece of his, he writes, "All the wrong notes are right.")

Carpenter and Griffes, much taken with Asian and Eastern music, follow impressionistic leads.

During World War I
All work in comparative, if not complete, isolation.

General Trends between the Wars
An end to musical structure based on the tonal system has been partially effected by some composers. There follows a period of bold, straightforward originality, healthy investigations into atonal systems, the ironic, the grotesque, jazz, quarter-tone music, etc. In Europe there are post-Impressionists, anti-Impressionists, dodecaphonists, atonalists, serialists, neo-Classicists.

Europeans in America are: Bloch, Stravinsky, Schoenberg, Weill, Toch, Hindemith, Krenek, Wolpe, Milhaud.

American composers, led by Varèse, learn in the twenties to band together in the League of Composers and the International Composers Guild. Many American composers interested in folk (influenced by Copland), primitive, Asian and extra-tonal elements. Cage and Cowell investigate the use of tone clusters, fist and elbow chords, Oriental scales and instruments, indeterminacy, and mixed-media. Some electronic inclusions, compositions for motors and amplifiers.

The most fundamental change is wrought by the discovery of the atonal/serial compositional technique that discards once and for all any distinction between consonance and dissonance. Schoenberg, after 8-year silence, wanting complete freedom but also coherence, conceives of 12-tone, equal-tempered scale, a device for limiting choice but allowing flow of intuition; objecting to term "atonality," calls his new language an "emancipation of dissonance."

In the 1930s, after forty years of revolutionary crises, many rules of harmony, rhythm, and melody have been broken down, while Stravinsky abandons primitivism and realism, adopts and adapts musical ideals of 18th-century, followed by other composers.

A mass audience is ready. How to approach it? The invention of sound for films offers new vistas for composers. Hollywood uses German- and Russian-trained Romantic composers primarily, but French and Russian films dare to use contempory composers such as Prokofiev.

Many Americans study with Nadia Boulanger in Paris. Electronic sounds beginning with the Theremin, lead to invention of Ondes Martenot.

Twelve-tonists remain aloof from experiments with jazz due to its tonal basis.

During World War II
The invention of high-fidelity equipment and magnetic tape recorders have immense influence on composers' methods as well as creating a mass music public.

General Trends after World War II
Between 1950–1965, conceptions of musical design come close to dispensing with contemporary limitations of notated sound.

In the chaos after the war, composers try to seek total control over music, to annihilate will of the composer in favor of predetermined systems. Serialism develops into total serialism (rhythm, too) and finally serialism plus computer or tape.

Musique concrète takes sound-objects (the equivalent of visual images) as its basis, thus altering compositional procedures. Music is prepared from recorded sounds. Affinity with theatrical forms is inevitable.

In the 1950s composers take the further step of denying the realistic sounds of musique concrète and using synthetic sounds. Eventually, to avoid monotony they begin exploiting tape and live performers.

Italy and France finally adopt serialism, which they had resisted heretofore. American school of composing absorbs something from Schoenberg while devising its own qualities. Because it is discovered that the same effect is available from a no-numbers system, that the logic of a numbers system does not guarantee a clarified impression to the listener, random or aleatory music begins to come to the fore. Some composers are intent upon abdicating artists' conscious power as chance challenges the intellect. With accidental determinants such as the toss of dice or a coin, aleatory composers try to bring the moment to heightened awareness. At first, performers are given limited freedom of choice; then performers are made to improvise their own notes. Thus fixed pitch and precise notation are no longer necessary.

Meanwhile, mass audience meets the classic repertoire for the first time, thanks to long-playing records, and rejects to a surprising degree the comparatively harder music of its contemporary composers.

A large segment of composers go in an Asian/Oriental direction with the use of Indian and Asian instruments, forms, scales and combinations of Oriental and Western instruments.

Eventually a determinate-indeterminate form of music evolves: the preparation is determinate but the reception is indeterminate. This opens the way to elaborations possible with electronic and/or computer music.

Mixed-media or "theatrical-performance" composers take the position that an action can replace a note, and a sound can do the work of an action; thus the drawing together of mixed arts in a multi-dimensional and multi-interpretable whole gives scope for the creative participation of an audience.

Aleatory music establishes a bond between pop and serious music; now jazz is influenced by serious music; since both jazz and indeterminate music are improvisatory, they can interchange.

Composed music is finally indeterminate, as Busoni predicted many years before.

TABLE II   DEFINITIONS OF NEW MUSIC TERMS

Expressionism
Expressionism is a term we are accustomed to hear in descriptions of certain German painters of the twentieth century. Their paintings were characterized by one or more of these tendencies: relationship with abnormal psychological conditions; avoidance of classical drawing techniques and/or representational shapes; and improvisation in colors (what Gunther Schuller calls Paul Klee's "orchestral repertoire"). Expressionism eventually referred to any art that distorted real images and avoided ideal norms of beauty for the sake of expressing the artist's feelings. A close connection can be made with the anti-Classical and anti-Romantic battles fought on the musical front by such composers as Schoenberg, Berg, and Webern in Europe and Carl Ruggles in America, typified in their compositions by intricate textures, atonal harmony, and non-Classic forms.

Dodecaphony, Twelve-tone, Atonality, Serialism, Total Serialism
In general, serialism refers to a manner of composition in which an order of sequence is set up for one or more elements of the musical procedure; these orders of sequence or variations of them are then repeated throughout the composition. The sequential order for pitch is called a tone-row; for units of time, a time-series; chords are accidental; keys are non-existent; hence the name atonality. Other elements include loudness and softness. The procedure was originally applied to pitch only and was called dodecaphonic or twelve-tone composition. Since 1950 composers have applied serial techniques to elements other than pitch, hence the designation total serialism. Among those composers writing with or adapting these procedures are (in alphabetical order): Babbitt, Berg, Richard Rodney Bennett, Berio, Boulez, Dallapiccola, Gerhard, Hamilton, Krenek, Lutyens, Martin, Maxwell Davies, Perle, Pousseur, Schoenberg, Searle, Webern and Wellesz.

Asian and Oriental Procedures
Until the twentieth century, Asian music was not an important influence on Western music. A kind of turning point came when Debussy, rejecting Wagner and drawn via the symbolist poets (Moréas, Mallarmé, Verlaine, Maeterlinck) to symbolism and impressionism, among other techniques, was exposed to the Indonesian gamelan. From that moment, music of the twentieth century shows an uninterrupted and continuously growing influence of Asian musical principles upon Western compositional techniques.

In China and India, serious attention has always been given to the transcendental and emotive power of music. A Chinese concept states that timbre and pitch are the two primary resources in music. Furthermore, fundamental to many Asian cultures is the poetic and mystic concept that each single tone is a musical entity in itself. A list of Asian musical elements differing from Western includes: the tuning system, instrumental characteristics, vocal qualities, performance techniques, pitch and rhythmic inflections, and perhaps most importantly, theory and philosophy.

The traditions of Asian music therefore include (1) the transformation of individual speech sounds into musical events, based upon their timbres as well as the dramatic meaning of the words; (2) constant subtle modifications in pitch, rhythm, and timbre; (3) an emphasis on the production and control of tones; and (4) a value placed on the varied functions of single tones. Other sources include the Zen tradition, Oriental calligraphy, Shakuhachi music, and Buddhist chanting.

It follows that such characteristic, yet diverse, twentieth-century compositional treatments as Scriabin's color spectrum/pitch experiments, Stravinsky's and Bartók's use of nonWestern melodic and rhythmic materials, Webern's concern with all the definable physical characteristics of single tones, Partch's 43-tone just intonation system, and the wide use of phonemics by such composers as Babbitt all spring from the rich source of Asian music.

Composers influenced in their procedures by Oriental and Asian techniques include, from Europe (in alphabetical order): Bartók, Blacher, Boulez, Debussy, Holst, Ligeti, Messiaen, Rimsky-Korsakov, Ruynemans, Scriabin, Skalkottas, Stockhausen, Stravinsky, Varèse, and Xenakis, and, from America: Cage, Carpenter, Coltrane, Cowell, Glass, Griffes, Harrison, Hovhaness, McPhee, Partch, and Young.

Electronic Music

The term electronic music originally referred only to sounds combined electronically, as contrasted with the name "musique concrète" (music assembled from a library of recorded sound "objects"). Electronic music now refers to a whole range of sound materials, musical styles, and esthetics. In the 50s composers began to combine concrete and synthesized sounds, prerecorded and live, and to apply serial techniques. The newest facet is the composer/performer.

The basic procedures for assembling an electronic composition require sound generation (oscillators or acoustic sounds introduced by microphones), sound modification (filters, modulators, reverberation, tape treatments, etc.) and sound reproduction and storage (tape, amplifiers and loudspeakers). In the future electronic music may be used to describe live performance and tape music may designate involved processes that require rehearsal.

Before 1950 experiments were made by Cage, Varèse, Hindemith, Toch, and Milhaud, among others. After 1950, led by the Paris studio of Schaeffer (where Boulez, Messiaen, and Stockhausen worked), Cologne (Pousseur and Stockhausen), Columbia University (Ussachevsky, Luening, Babbitt, Subotnick, Davidovsky, and others), other major studios that reconciled musique concrète and electronic music grew up in Milan (Berio), Tokyo (Mayazumi and Moroi), London (Gerhard), Warsaw (Penderecki), Brussels (Pousseur), Ann Arbor (Mumma and Ashley), University of Illinois (Hiller and Baker), and Toronto (Schaeffer).

Computer techniques are used to help precompose tonal calculations and to create electronic sound that will be used in ways that can now only be guessed at. Some new equipment can reproduce the sound of any instrument presently known, some never heard before, and a vocal range from bass to soprano.

Indeterminacy, Aleatory Music

Indeterminate compositional techniques are of two kinds: those that use means that are variable before performance and those that use means that are predictable before performance but put together through random practices. The designation aleatory (Boulez's term), now used mostly by journalists, has been supplanted by the term indeterminate.

The accepted aesthetic principles postulated by indeterminacy are:

1. Any sound or no sound is as valid as any other.
2. Each sound is a separate event, not related to any other sound by any rules or implications, important for itself but not for what it contributes to musical development.
3. Any assemblage of sounds is as good as any other.
4. Any means of forming an assemblage is as good as any other.
5. Any piece of music or composer is as good as any other.
6. Traditional judgments of value, expertise, and authority are meaningless.*

A composer may develop these principles in many ways. He may (1) make a synthesis of sound, action, and written word; (2) have notated instructions that nevertheless allow interpretational freedom; (3) employ graphic notation within fairly strict limits that allows improvisation with electronics; (4) organize theatrical happenings where attention is directed to simple elements repeated endlessly; or (5) indicate his intentions clearly but leave the realization up to the performer.

Composers who have worked within indeterminate procedures are (in alphabetical order): Ashley, Austin, Browne, Bussotti, Cage, Chiari, Cowell, Feldman, Grainger, Ichiyanagi, Ives, Ligeti, Maxwell Davies, Mumma, Nilsson, Oliveros, Satie, Sender, Subotnick, Swift, Tudor, Varèse, Wolff, and Xenakis.

Mixed-Media, Multi-Media, Intermedia
All three designations are applied freely to theatrical works or events that mix arts, forms, procedures, and electronic media. These works are directed at more than one sense and usually demand some measure of total environment (as distinguished from a proscenium stage only). Moreover, these occasions often aim to involve the audience and thus are influenced in some way by the spectators. One might summarize by saying that composers wrote for the ear until 1960 when they began to shift from sound to action. European composers have worked mostly within the proscenium theater limitations.

Composers who have used mixed-media procedures are (in alphabetical order): Ashley, Austin, Becker, Behrman, Berio, Bussotti, Cage, Finney, Glass, Hiller, Kagel, Martirano, Mumma, Nono, Partch, Oliveros, Pousseur, Reich, Riley, Schoenberg, Scriabin, Sender, Stockhausen, Stravinsky, Subotnick, Varèse, and Young.

Neo-Romanticism
Neo-Romanticism is a modern kind of Romanticism which has, in passing through a contemporary mind, emerged as something new. It ex-

* John Vinton, ed., *Dictionary of Contemporary Music* (New York: E.P. Dutton, 1967).

presses a romantic ideal in modern terms. Early in the twentieth century, after the shock value of such movements as Dadaism had been exhausted, a certain proportion of contemporary composers elected not to follow the path of serialism or electronic music. They chose to take advantage of the coloration techniques of Strauss and Sibelius and mix them with some more modern compositional techniques. Neo-Romanticism is a secondary phase of the modern stylistic upheaval paralleled by Stravinsky's move into neo-Classicism. Conspicuous by its use of recognizable melody even when such melody is consolidated with established avant-garde textures, neo-Romanticism has been both deplored by champions of modern music such as Henry Cowell who calls it "conscience-quieters" for composers who cannot find their own new direction, and welcomed by those identifying with Couperin, who reportedly preferred music that touched him to music that surprised him.

This apparent rebellion against severity and flimflam in the arts is most evident in architecture, although it has correlatives in painting and music. Neo-Romanticism's move toward a more conventional lyricism (paralleled by Philip Johnson's architectural directions) is not a retreat to the past but aimed at integrating historical forms into a new and complex whole.

Taking what they wish to use from the new techniques, and without condemning or abandoning older techniques, unthreatened by passion or melody, these composers—Argento, Barber, Britten, Chanler, Crumb, dello Joio, del Tredici, Diamond, Druckman, Griffes, Maxwell Davies, Nordoff, Respighi, Rochberg, Rorem—have all been referred to as neo-Romantic composers.

One must recognize in any discussion of stylistic genres that the notion of *style* is anathema to the twentieth-century avant-garde. They believe that structure and manner do not in fact have a separate existence—it just seems so. Previously, in other types of composition, performance was regarded as a competitive skill where excellence was achieved by conforming to standards set by the system. The new procedures of this era have now culminated in performances far less authoritarian. Indeterminate composers look for the possibilities of a more pliant approach to traditional literature as well as new attitudes toward performance.

Such goals led to the use of chance in compositions and improvisation in performance. The composer himself often assumes the role of interpreter and the performance might be described in the best parlance of the 1960s as a "happening." Highly integrated performances necessitated by the avant-garde compositions include skills at ensemble phrasing and improvisation. A great proportion of new music is, even as is early music, a matter of contributing to ensemble. The new indeterminate procedures must be distinguished from the old, jazz-derived improvisations, which are more conventional, tonal, and traditional. (Real jazz is communal improvising.) From one point of view, electronic compositions are seen to have reduced both performer and listener to a solitary state of imprisonment, whereas music was once regarded as bringing people together to share a common experience. With computer-aided electronics, *all* sounds are now at the disposal of composers. Some twentieth-century music is becoming a branch of technology—physics, logic, mathematics. The university music department often seems to take its tone not from the humanities but from the engineering sciences.

Interpretation

The third responsibility which must be assumed by the singer of New Music repertoire has to do with interpretation. As with any music, he endeavors first to make his views one with the composer's. He searches on ever deeper levels for a more penetrating grasp of the composition's structure, for this can give him the desired combination of control with liberation. With much modern music he must, in addition, take pains to become a somewhat bodiless conduit for the music.

It is evident that, for a singer, problems of interpretation and emotion hinge upon the expressive nature of his instrument and upon the existence of a text. Let us examine briefly the changes that have taken place in text setting over the past centuries.

Throughout the history of vocal music, the text and music have influenced each other in different ways. In recitative, the music has always been secondary to the text. In songs and arias, the text sometimes served as the actual impetus for the music; infrequently it was virtually inconsequential in relation to the music.

The traditional use of the voice was for singing, recitative, or melodrama. Composers were interested in illuminating or supplementing the various attributes of the text—its form, rhythms, melodic feasibilities, meanings, and some of its phonemic arrangements. Poets chose words for their sounds as well as their meanings and connotations.

In vocal music of the Middle Ages and Renaissance, the texts decreed the rhythms of the sung parts, the arrangements and length of phrases. Inflections of the text commanded directions taken by the melody. From the early Baroque on, the meaning of the texts were as important as their form, rhythm, and inflections. Changing dramatic situations and general expressive qualities of the text were paralleled by the music. To give insight into the inner life of the text by every possible musical means was the composer's objective. His tools were tempo, mode, key, phrasing, attack, singing styles, tessitura, vocal registers, rhythms, dissonance versus consonance, form, metric placement, word prosodies, leitmotifs, harmonies, and direct tone painting.

All these methods, except tonal factors such as key, mode, consonance, and dissonance, are still available to composers. Now, however, composers are exploring ways of using the voice other than singing—speech or speech sounds without morphemic substance, new organizations of rhythm, meter, timbre.

The search for new musical possibilities is combined with the desire to choose new ways of setting advanced contemporary writers. The late nineteenth- and twentieth-century poets (such as Hopkins and Mallarmé) chose words for phonemic substance, organized them into relationships more complex than rhyme schemes, onomatopoeia, internal rhymes, etc. For some twentieth-century composers, then, the meaning of the text does not help dictate the music's organization as much as its phonemic content, its nonmeaningful sound sources, its sensations, its naturalistic speech. Texts that are chosen by such composers may be structured or not to produce a result whose meaning is nonverbal.

Nevertheless, composers of this century have used traditional ways of incorporating the text into musical works. Both Ives and Schoenberg used direct tone-painting. Hindemith associated specific ideas with certain tonalities. Britten set words with normal word stresses, using variable meters. Schoenberg, while attentive to prosody, did not neglect the meaning of the text as a whole in his earlier vocal works, although he was sometimes admittedly inspired by just the first few lines of a poem. He went so far as to insist that his vocal works be done in the language of the country in which they were performed. This argues for the importance of verbal meanings to him at times.

Then Debussy, Schoenberg, Stravinsky, and Webern, reacting against the emotionalism of the late Romantics, began to invent new and nontraditional ways of treating texts. Stravinsky used such methods as chanting, percussive effects, one tessitura for extended periods, hypnotic repetition of single syllables. Ravel and Debussy treated the voice as one more instrumental timbre. Many began to reject literal meaning of texts, to experiment with matching vowel formants to electronic timbres, fragmenting musical line and space, linking speech sounds with pitches or registers, etc.

One hears frequently of composers "treating the voice as another instrument." Some of those who teach today's young composers have criticized this tactic as being, in many cases, an evasion of the problems of text-setting. Since self-enclosed musical systems tend to be disturbed by the entrance of a text, an easy solution is to break up the words into syllables so that the voice becomes "just another instrument." It is of course legitimate to treat the voice so, but to do it successfully the young composer must understand what "instrument" *is* the voice for which he writes. A long-standing complaint from singers (even those extremely sympathetic toward the aims of the newest music) is that some composers carefully study all the instruments for which they write except the *vocal* instrument. Not only do young composers often not comprehend the basic principles common to *all* human voices, but they just as often clearly do not begin to differentiate among the myriad vocal subdivisions and their attendant technical intricacies. A rather common practice (one which may well result in a composition that is virtually unperformable) is to know the range but then proceed to compose within, or *on*, the extremes with no regard for tessitura or vowel/pitch relationships.[12] The singer who is faced with a composition in which inefficient text-setting forces him to choose between enunciating well or making an acceptable tone can ask the composer to help reconcile the difficulty, or, if the composer is not available, make his own compromise.

Since the human voice expresses emotion much more directly than any instrument, its greatest gift has been more or less spurned by avant-garde composers of New Music even as they spurned Romanticism itself. This fact raises an interesting point: although fully intending to obey the injunction against "interpreting," is it really possible for the human voice to pronounce words and yet delete or suppress all morphemic meanings? At the very least, it would seem to require an immense effort. Music is so evocative that, if words coupled with music are performed often enough, surely a meaning followed by an unwanted "interpretation" will emerge in spite of the performer's wishes. Perhaps the widespread use of phonemes is more than an experiment in color. Perhaps it is the best method for excluding verbal meaning, and thus unwanted expressivity, from the human voice. Only the synthesizing of a totally electronic voice could do the job better. In order to follow the dictates and wishes of some composers in the forefront of the avant-garde, noninvolvement must be attempted, if not learned.

Two radically opposing viewpoints about interpretation are aptly epitomized in the following quotations. Ferruccio Busoni believed that

> the audible presentation, the "performance" of music, its emotional interpretation, derives from those free heights whence descended the art itself. . . . Great artists play their own works differently at each repetition, remodel them on the spur of the moment, accelerate and retard, in a way which they could not indicate by signs—and always according to the conditions of that "eternal harmony."[13]

But Igor Stravinsky counters with the argument that

12. Non-singers tend to take the singing instrument for granted as a piece of normal human equipment. Ideally, the vocally inexperienced composer should equip himself with such a detailed knowledge of voice, text, and music that it would be, for example, as inconceivable for him to write a vowel on an unsuitable pitch as it would be for him to write a low F for a violin.
13. Ferruccio Busoni, *A New Esthetic of Music* (New York: Dover Publications, 1962), p. 76–85.

music should be transmitted and not interpreted, because interpretation reveals the personality of the interpreter rather than that of the author, and who can guarantee that such an executant will reflect the author's vision without distortion?[14]

Yet this controversy is in some ways moot. Music cannot exist without the intermediary, the performer (a good reason why many modern composers have protectively become performers of their own music). Only the performer can with skill, creativity, and perception transform the notation into music. A note-perfect performance can also be sterile. A great performance is always inimitable. Even in totally controlled electronic music in which the performer is seemingly eliminated, speed and pitch may vary with the reproducing machinery. Music is an art of abstract messages—it can never be an exact communication or representation.

SUMMARY

Let us make a very pragmatic summation. You, the possessor of this emotion-expressing musical instrument, have three special tasks when working with this extra-ordinary repertoire:

1. You must command utter musical accuracy with a fair amount of ease, extending your technical skills into new territories far beyond singing, while being close to virtuosic at the traditional skills.

2. You must know how to expunge passion from your all-too-human instrument and you must understand when it is encumbent upon you to do so.

3. You must equip yourself with stylistic freedom and vocal flexibility, so that musical results can be unpredictable when so requested.

Nevertheless, the general capacities required of a singer of avant-garde music do not differ from those of the good recital singer: imagination, vocal ability, research capacity, cultural background, personal control, curiosity, and the ability to organize and control the raw materials.[15]

14. Igor Stravinsky, *An Autobiography* (New York: W. W. Norton, 1962), p. 75. Cathy Berberian reports that, from her personal knowledge, Stravinsky has suffered from that quote, having meant only to avoid the excessively "expressive" interpretations of the Romantic era still rampant during his formative period. Many of his opinions from that epoch changed radically later. With Stravinsky it was a question of the right dosage of "interpretation" (since none at all would be unthinkable and unbelievable). He wished to prevent the invention of things not in the score.
15. We are indebted to Cathy Berberian for the above criteria.

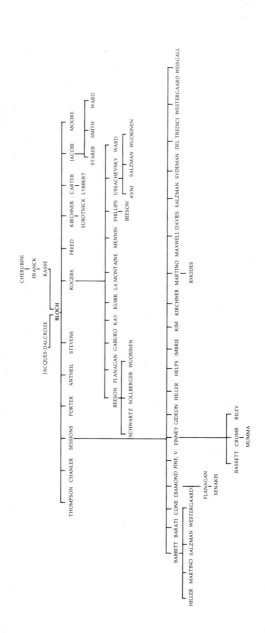

TABLE III NEW MUSIC COMPOSERS/TEACHERS AND THEIR STUDENTS

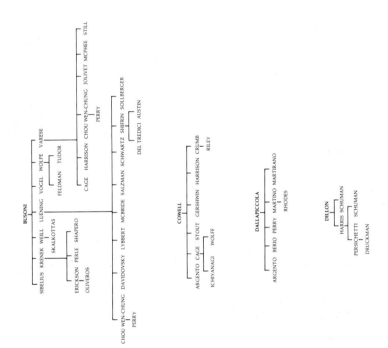

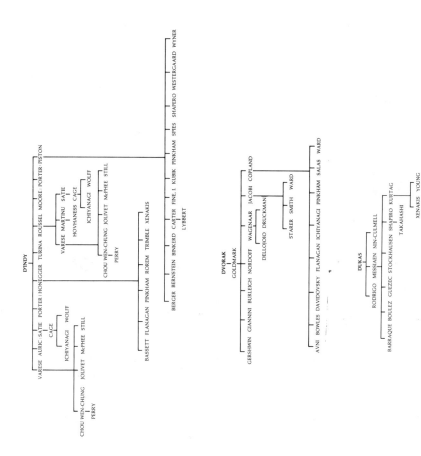

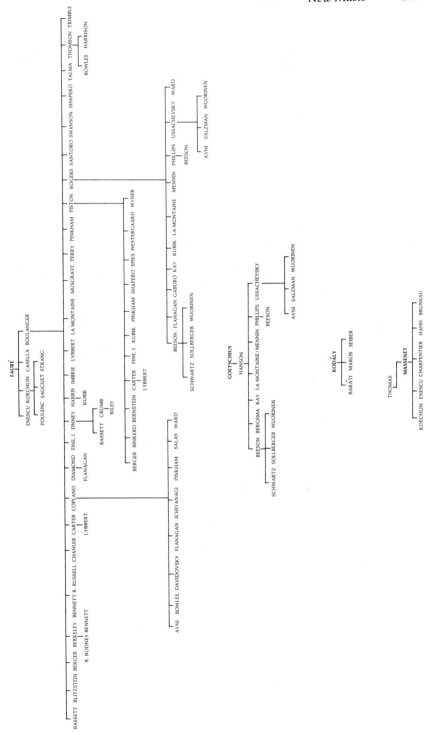

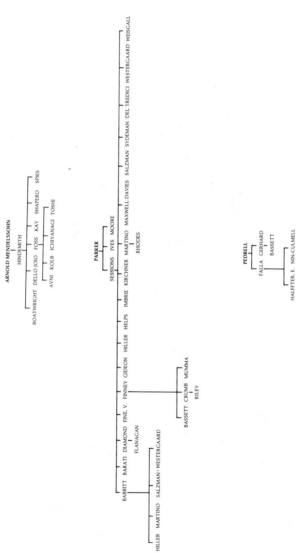

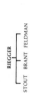

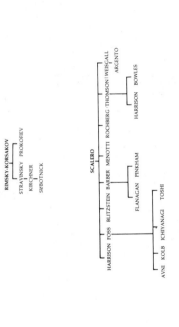

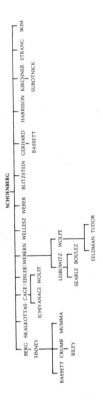

VAUGHAN

GUIDELINES FOR PRACTICE

1. Find a school of American painters whose style of painting would be historically and philosophically compatible with composers such as Copland, Thomson, Harris, Hanson, or Schuman. Construct a program of twentieth-century vocal music, suitable as a companion to an exhibit of the works of such painters.

2. Search out twentieth-century compositions set to Gertrude Stein texts that could be made into a group.

3. There are many composers of New Music who have set the texts of Brecht. Devise a program including some of these that could be used as a companion program to a dramatic work by Brecht.

4. From the many composers through the centuries who have set Shakespeare's poetry, put together an entire program, using as many varied compositional styles as you can neatly juxtapose.

5. Formulate a program, a large part of which has music for tenor and horn, utilizing the music from many eras, not omitting the twentieth century.

6. Many women composers of the twentieth century and earlier have set texts by poetesses. Block out a program that takes advantage of this fact.

7. Put together a program for a soprano voice, using the theme "Compositions with an Oriental Influence." Here are twelve composers from the nineteenth and twentieth centuries who have written such literature (there are many more):

Maurice Ravel	Harry Partch
Charles Griffes	John Cage
Albert Roussel	Francesco Santoliquido
Colin McPhee	Karel Szymanowski
LaMonte Young	Sir Arthur Bliss
Alan Hovhaness	Richard Strauss

8. Devise a program of vocal chamber music which is unified by a circumscribed group of instruments while it is varied by the unlimited choice of voice or voices. Find compositions which utilize various limited combinations from this stable instrumental pool with the addition of one or more voices. Try to draw your program from many musical styles in addition to contemporary music; e.g., limiting your instruments to strings, percussion, and one or two woodwinds would make possible a program which spans styles from early music through new music.

12 Vocal Ensemble Music

VOICE WITH INSTRUMENTS

A Historical Canvas

As an aid to repertoire selection, let us begin our discussion with a brief historical survey of available literature. Although it is probable that performances of vocal music with improvised accompaniment originated in primitive and ancient times, actual evidence of any composed accompanying lines appeared in the thirteenth century with such early polyphonic forms as the motet. The motet form was based upon a pre-existing tenor line, frequently set down in long note values or with repeated rhythmic patterns. This cantus firmus could be texted, untexted, or partially texted, and was usually performed by an instrument. Above the tenor there were either one or two newly composed melodic lines, both texted, sometimes with the same words, sometimes with different ones. Texts could be secular or sacred, in French or Latin; they ranged from extremely serious and pious to the most ribald and frivolous. When contemplating performance of these early works, it is helpful to remember that the lines above the cantus firmus are regarded as ornaments, not accompaniment.

Various other forms of vocal music (isorhythmic motets, lais, ballades notées, rondeaux, chansons balladées, madrigals, caccias) were invented in the fourteenth and fifteenth centuries with the advent of Ars Nova. As forms expanded, there was more emphasis on repeat schemes and secular texts. (Typical composers are Machaut, the fourteenth-century composer considered by authorities as the originator of the first artistically accompanied secular song, and such fifteenth century composers as Dunstable, Dufay, Ockeghem, Agricola, and Busnois.) Songs were now written with varying distributions of instruments and voices. The presence of the text usually indicated clearly which line was to be sung; in the remaining lines the instrumentation was up to the performers.

Today we are led to a viable modern performance philosophy by the following practices of the period: (1) great flexibility of choice precluded any actually *wrong* way of assigning the instrumental and vocal forces; (2) lines were kept intertwined yet separate by means of varying timbres, instruments, and voices. For example, a three-part composition might have been performed in any of the following forms:

a. instrumental tenor plus two voices

b. instrumental tenor, plucked, plus one voice, plus one melody instrument, bowed

c. three varied voices

d. three instruments, one bowed, the others plucked or blown

Common instruments of the era were the vielle, lute, recorder, sacbut, rebec, crumhorn, bagpipe, naker.

During the sixteenth century, Italians rejected the involved contrapuntal style of the Flemish and French foreign composers in favor of a simple four-part form, the frottola. (Bartolomeo Tromboncino, Marco Cara). In the frottola, also, any combination of forces was possible, from one voice and three instruments to four voices. The early Italian madrigal, simple and chordal in nature, is usually associated with several voices a cappella, although Monteverdi wrote both solo and accompanied madrigals.

Meanwhile England (Morley, Gibbons) took up the madrigal form, keeping it chordal and straightforward. In Italy (Gesualdo, Marenzio) a more involved chromatic and contrapuntal madrigal soon evolved. In due time the confusion caused by the excesses of contrapuntalism and chromaticism, sometimes involving six or seven parts, gave way to a new movement in vocal music that culminated in the aria proper. These composers, who sought to imitate the music of ancient Greece, were called the Camerata (Peri, Monteverdi, Caccini). The accompaniment to these vocal compositions was now more chordal and harmonic, and considerably simplified. In the late Renaissance (Dowland, Byrd, Milan, Narvaes) the popularity of the lute, guitar, and harpsichord decidedly advanced the quality of single instrument accompaniment.

The Baroque period, employing thoroughbass with concerted instruments, provides a very large repertoire for vocal chamber music. The solo vocal cantata in the Baroque was written to secular or sacred texts with continuo and obbligato instruments. The obbligato parts frequently assumed equal importance with the vocal parts. There is a wealth of material here (Bach, Buxtehude, Telemann, Schütz; Purcell and Handel; Marc-Antoine Charpentier, Campra, Clérambault, Rameau, Couperin; Scarlatti, Vivaldi, Cesti, Legrenzi, Tenaglia, Carissimi) for the singers who wish to use instruments in their programs.

A comparatively small amount of vocal chamber music was written during the eighteenth and nineteenth centuries. It was during this period that the solo cantata form gave way , due to the development of the orchestra, to the concert aria or scena. Composers like Arne, J.C.F. Bach, Blas de Laserna, Traetta, Mozart, Haydn, and Beethoven tried their hands at various combinations of voices and instruments, even making arrangements of folk songs. Art songs for voice and piano flowered, but relatively few composers wrote art songs with a solo instrumental obbligato. From the standpoint of quality, the range of these songs extends from Schubert's great "Der Hirt auf dem Felsen" to the (possibly less great) *romances dialoguées* during the early 1800s in France.

Twentieth-century composers, on the other hand, have produced considerable vocal chamber music, the significant features of which are a general equivalence of all parts, the employment of a wide variety of ranges and timbres, and the use of voice with instruments. Experiments with the New Music provide performers with a challenging and musically invaluable medium. (See Chapter 11.) Such experiments include: using the voice as other than the dominant part, *Sprechstimme*, nonverbal use of phonemes, percussive speech sounds, and voice with electronic tape.

Program Advantages

What are the advantages to the singer of including vocal chamber music in his recitals? Beginning a recital with, let us say, a Baroque solo cantata for voice and one or two instruments allows the singer to share the performing responsibility for a time. Including instruments in the program assures variety in more than one way: visually, in the literature, and in the very sound itself. Preparing music with an instrumental ensemble improves and strengthens the singer's musicality. From the point of view of audience appeal, chamber music is presently in its ascendancy, and the age of ensemble music, be it early music or contemporary, is upon us. Rational attention to the facts of the market place suggests that it is expedient for most career-minded vocal students to learn the art of ensemble performance. Most important of all, it is wonderful musical fun!

There now appears to be a great deal of interest and activity in the performance of Baroque music. However, in spite of a burgeoning interest in Renaissance and Medieval music in universities, colleges, and metropolitan centers, singers elsewhere miss a golden opportunity by not taking the initiative in pre-Baroque programming. This period represents an untapped song recital resource not only in the volume of materials available, but also in its easy adaptability to more attractive programming. Since choices of pre-Baroque instruments are extremely flexible, the very search for a decision compels the singer to experiment, to be inventive, to use his ingenuity and musicianship. When old instruments are not available,[1] he must experiment with modern instruments in an attempt to match colors or to find new textural combinations that reflect his musical responses to this repertoire.

Young voices are particularly well-suited, vocally, to the music of this period. The ranges are narrow. Transpositions are possible. There is, of course, a strong temptation to use the vibrato-less tone approved of by many musicologists specializing in this period. On the other hand, given the Baroque period's instrumental ideals for sound, a change of vocal color is almost inevitable. Be sure to consult your voice teacher, who may object to a tone with less vibrato. The chest voice, required for Spanish and Basque repertoire, should also be subject to the approval of your voice teacher. In any case, vocal colors for this type of music are legion.

A plethora of student instrumentalists interested in such repertoire is waiting to assist in programs using these materials. Of the surfeit of compositions from these periods, what survived is, at the very least, of great interest, and, at best, truly worthwhile musically.

Craig Timberlake, the noted singer/educator, reminds us that ensemble music in general provides us with a real and pertinent value at the academic level, where students have occasion to perform along with other students. Activity in music-making among students most surely accelerates the learning process. Perhaps of even greater value to the student is the collaboration of student and teacher, or the fortuitous opportunity to perform with a visiting artist on campus. Such matters as coordinating dynamics, matching vibrato and vowels, improving phrasing and style, are heightened through rewarding teamwork. Remember that, since Baroque practice dictates that middle A shall be tuned at 415 cycles per second rather than 440, the pitch of accompanied pieces will generally be one-half step lower than modern concert pitch. One word of caution: Robert Donington refers to singers being "sadly taxed by virtuoso Baroque parts."[2] Make sure you are up to the challenge.

1. Certain universities, such as Indiana University, have extensive collections of old instruments available to students.
2. *The Performer's Guide to Baroque Music* (New York: C. Scribner's Sons, 1974).

Performance Problems of Early Music

Let us now speak of the difficult task of formulating a credo for performers of early music, where the bulk of ensemble repertoire lies (with the possible exception of twentieth-century music). We must be greatly encouraged by the constantly growing understanding of the spirit of early music as well as the great body of factual information now available. Yet all this interest leads frequently to a belief—often puritanical in its zeal—that reticence and authenticity go hand in hand. One forgets the robustness of early music. In this repertoire there are less *notations* of expression, but not less *expression*. Rather, flexibility is the challenge of early music interpretation. Of course, one must make suitable choices—imaginative, practical, and musicianly.

It is hard for those of us who are not scholars, however anxious we are to contribute to and abide by musicological standards, not to be intimidated by the musicologists. Yet, strictest standards cannot be applied either to ornamentation or realizations, because improvisation, as an art, cannot move with strictest correctness. No music, except possibly electronic music, can be performed without cross-pollination between performers and composers. Baroque music above all relies on the performer's creativity, requiring a high degree of blending between the two. Because the Baroque style allows the performer to be wholly responsible for the expression, we do expose our discernment, awareness of style, and stylistic leanings when we perform it.

The most rational approach to many aspects of early music interpretation is to know the peripheries of the style and then do the obvious thing; this is most likely what performers did at the time. If a stylistically untutored singer attempts to perform this early repertoire he will inflict wrong interpretations upon it. A singer equipped with the training that will allow him to put knowledge out of his mind exactly as he has always done with the music known since childhood will produce the right expression.

A modern model for dealing with early music might be described as a combination of musicianship and musicology—not just the instinctive assurance of the professional musician, and not the objective learning of the professional scholar. This music demands substantial experience plus a working musicological background. Therefore, the young student will be obliged to rely upon the knowledge of his teachers.

In the Baroque, there are no definitive interpretations, even from the same performers, only individual interpretations within the confines of style. Perhaps, when searching for the guiding philosophy, it is wise to ask how, approximately, this passage might have been interpreted on a typical occasion of the era by an adept performer from the period. Always remember C. P. E. Bach's dictum: "A musician cannot move others without himself being moved."

The repertoire list in the appendix (Voice with Instruments) makes no attempt to be a comprehensive list; it is intended simply to excite the singer's imagination to the wealth and breadth of materials available. In addition, we suggest one magnificent source for these materials: "Solo Vocal Chamber Music with Instrumental Accompaniment," by J.S. Haruda, published on demand in 1960 by University Microfilms (Ann Arbor, Michigan). This is a doctoral thesis from the State University of Iowa. Also, there is the invaluable cross-referenced catalogue of all the Bach cantatas, *Handbook of Johann Sebastian Bach's Cantatas*, by Werner Neumann, published by Associated Music Publishers in 1947, recently reprinted by Breitkopf and Härtel, Leipzig.

VOICE WITH OTHER VOICES

Doubtless there will come a time in your singing career when the pleasures of collaboration with another singer will entice you. Our advice is: succumb immediately! Using your voice with another voice or two is truly enjoyable; ensemble between voices, as compared to voice with instruments, presents new skills to be explored.

Common decisions on matters of interpretation must be made; various aspects of vocal balance must be worked out; problems issuing from visual or plastic requirements of the new dual situation must be solved. On the other hand, the joys of collaboration are very real and the literature is compelling and vast. A singer who tastes of this literature cannot help but experience a musical and artistic growth. Most especially a young singer will find duets and trios, not to mention larger ensembles, an admirable way of trying his wings before an audience with somewhat less personal responsibility.

In the appendix we have given a list of suggested duets, trios, quartets, and some compositions for several voices which sing separately. In this compilation you will find primarily duetti da camera with some additions from more obscure operatic literature. The duets, trios, and quartets fall generally into three categories: (1) those in which the vocal parts voice one thought, either in harmony or with canonical devices as in "Ich wollt', mein Lieb'" by Mendelssohn; (2) those in which the characters are specifically named or designated by gender or are in some way identifiably different from each other, as in "Er und Sie" by Schumann or "Die Nonne und der Ritter" by Brahms; (3) those in which , though gender is not clarified and characters are not named, and though they do not voice a common thought, it is somehow clear that there are two personalities open for your interpretation. An example would be Rossini's "Duetto di due gatti," which calls only for Cat number 1 and Cat number 2, clearly defined by the music to be two different personalities. The delineation of the characters is totally open to interpretation, limited only by the combination of artists who perform it—two men, two women, or one man and one woman.

You will observe that the bulk of camera duets are drawn from the eighteenth-century composers and the Romantic German composers. For this reason, achieving program balance when attempting an entire recital of duets is somewhat of a feat. All of the musical and vocal advantages accruing to the singer of vocal chamber music with instrumental accompaniment as described in the beginning of this chapter hold true for the performance of vocal ensemble works, with the added dimension of matching vibrato and tone to those of another vocal instrument. Furthermore, the addition of a multi-voiced cycle would highlight a vocal ensemble program in that it possesses all the interesting attributes of a solo-voiced cycle. The following is a list of composers who have written more than a nominal amount of duet literature. If you are pressed for time, start with them.

Heinrich Albert	Johannes Brahms
Johann Sebastian Bach	Johann Christian Bach
Ludwig van Beethoven	François Couperin
Luigi Carissimi	Peter Cornelius
Anton Dvořák	Marco da Gagliano
Charles Gounod	George Friedrich Handel
Zoltán Kodály	Claudio Monteverdi
Felix Mendelssohn	Henry Purcell
Giacomo Rossini	Anton Rubenstein
Max Reger	Robert Schumann
Heinrich Schütz	

There are, of course, many cantatas of J. S. Bach within which are beautiful duets for various voices. Some of these are published separately and are listed in the appendix (Voice with Other Voices). Others can be found only in the cantata itself. Consult the aforementioned *Handbook of Johann Sebastian Bach's Cantatas* by Werner Neumann.

A further suggestion: many, if not most, compositions intended for two-, three-, and four-part choruses can be sung as solo voice duets, trios, and quartets. We have included some examples in the appendix (Voice with Other Voices). By looking through the various octavo editions, investigate for yourself this rich source of vocal ensembles.

13 The Song Cycle

AN ATTEMPT AT DEFINITION

The art song is one of the smallest musical forms. It averages five pages in print, three and one-half minutes in performance. These two facts are the most practical reasons for the practice of grouping songs together. In a larger form they are ensured importance beyond their compass.

In contemplating a chapter on song cycles we were struck by an unforeseen need for clarification: when is a song cycle not a cycle? The search led us through no less than six dictionaries, several music history books, three magazine articles, and a doctoral dissertation, and yielded a bewildering oversupply of definitions that ranged from very strict to very free. The following even dozen song cycle definitions represent but a small portion of those culled from the above sources:

1. A song cycle is a "series of lyric poems, belonging together on account of their content and character" (*Musikalisches Conversations-Lexicon*).

2. A song cycle is a "thorough musical treatment" of a complete lyric cycle (lyric here means poetic), "combining into one song book" songs that pertain to one poetic subject or songs set to texts written by one poet (*Die Liedercomponisten*).

3. A song cycle should, by recurrence or transformation of recognizable tonal patterns be "designed to form a musical entity" (*Harvard Dictionary of Music*).

4. A song cycle is a series or string of art songs, preferably for solo voice and piano accompaniment, each song being a complete musical unit and capable of being lifted out of its cyclical context (Luise Eitel Peake).

5. A song cycle is a "meaningful selection" of poems from a lyric cycle for composition as a song cycle (*Das deutsche Lied zwischen Schubert und Schumann*).

6. A song cycle is the "critical chaining" of songs with otherwise unrelated texts (*Das deutsche Lied zwischen Schubert und Schumann*).

7. "A song cycle is a circle or series of songs relating to the same subject and forming one piece of music. . . in which the motive of the first reappears in the last and closes the circle" (*Grove's Dictionary of Music and Musicians*).

8. The number of songs in a song cycle can range anywhere from three to thirty or more provided they are "capable of being sung consecutively" (*Oxford Companion to Music*).

9. A song cycle "should have a common theme or story" (*Cyclopedia of Music and Musicians*).

10. Song texts are "of related thought and character" in a song cycle (*Harvard Dictionary of Music*).

11. "A song cycle is a group of poems by either a single poet or several poets that are set to music. The texts of the poems are usually closely related. The text generally has an overall theme (idea) in some cases fairly specific (*Die schöne Müllerin*) and in others very general (*Dichterliebe*)" (*Harper's Musical Dictionary*).

12. A song cycle is an art form in which songs are laid out to suggest infinite time or space, thus establishing an ideological center (Luise Eitel Peake).

After many intriguing and informative hours of contemplating the issue, we came to the conclusion that a cycle is a cycle if the composer says it is!

A HISTORICAL SURVEY

If your mind now boggles at this confusing array of indefinite definitions, it is quite understandable. You might also wonder, as we did, why there has been so little research done on this major musical form, why most books treat it briefly if at all, and why most discussions treat individual cycles, not the cycle form but only its style and structure. Luise Eitel Peake, whose two definitions appear above,[1] has written a fine doctoral dissertation on this subject ("A Preliminary Inquiry into the Beginnings of the Romantic Song Cycle"). She, too, was confounded by the overlappings and contradictions found in the accepted song cycle definitions that had accumulated throughout the years.

Her first step was to reject Beethoven's cycle *An die ferne Geliebte* as the generally accepted "original" song cycle. She challenged the assumption that the genre of poetry to which Beethoven's songs were set sprang up abruptly out of nowhere, fashioned perfectly for the "new" song-cycle form. Believing that amateur poets like Jeittele and Müller (author of the poems *Die schöne Müllerin*) could not suddenly have created a new style for vocal music, she explored ever earlier periods, looking for likely precursors.

As you read the following descriptions of the song cycle ancestry derived by Ms. Peake from her research, you will understand why the boundary lines in most definitions are so blurred, even though the idea of unity—musical or literary—appears to be the one common desideratum among them all.

1. Adam de la Halle's early work, *Jeu de Robin et Marion* (ca. 1285), is described variously by Gilbert Reaney[2] as a "pastoral comedy" or "early comic opera" and by Luise Peake as a "trouvère song cycle."

2. Sixteenth- and seventeenth-century England, Italy, and France produced lute song cycles, madrigal cycles, and wreaths and garlands of songs dedicated to ladies of quality.

3. Instrumental dance music of the sixteenth century (a slow dance in duple time followed by a fast dance in triple time) was transformed into the vocal double song—a miniature cycle?—the second song a parody[3] of the first.

4. In the seventeenth century the double song is found in three variations: (a) as a semi-dramatic dialogue, (b) as a pastoral scene, and (c) as an echo song, with two singers alternating solos until the final

---

1. Definition 12 offered by Ms. Peake is the one she prefers.
2. Dennis Stevens, *History of Song* (New York: W.W. Norton, 1962), p. 30.
3. Our misleading modern concept of the parody (synonyms include: satire, ludicrous imitation, burlesque, caricature, farce) is remote from the original meaning—"the creative process in which a melody gives rise to a lyric poem." Examples of familiar parodies are (1) "My Country 'Tis of Thee," "God Save the Queen," and the "Egmont" Overture, all written to the same tune; (2) Columbia University's official song written to go with the tune of a Protestant hymn; and (3) most of Goethe's lyric poems. A parody in the 1800s meant the shaping of the lyric poems to the musical forms of specific tunes sought out by the poet. In Goethe's reference to his parodies as being written to "some of the most wretched German tunes" can be seen the genesis of our modern erroneous image of a parody.

duet. Eventually it was expanded to include three or more songs, instrumental ritornelli, and final choruses, thus resembling what we would now call a cantata. These forms enjoyed great popularity in the eighteenth century as well.[4]

5. Allegorical song series of the seventeenth century were intended to accompany ballet. This type of allegorical ballet was succeeded by the English masque of the eighteenth century. Late in the century, song cycles of allegorical-pastoral nature were often staged in England.

6. The Italian solo cantata of the early seventeenth century resembles the extended double song in its setting of dramatic or pastoral narrative poems with arias and recitatives for one, two, or three voices. The difference lies mostly in the recitative. Frequent use of two contrasted arias also reminds us of the double song. Furthermore, with all these forms there is a certain resemblance to the masque.

7. Heinrich Albert, as a result of the influence of the Italian solo cantatas, wrote cyclical song forms about 1715. By 1750 the Italian form was very popular in Germany. German secular cantatas of the late seventeenth and early eighteenth centuries contained songs, not arias, and frequently no recitatives as well. There were also cycles of solo cantatas.

8. In the late eighteenth century two forms appeared: the scena, containing arias and recitatives; the more song-like form, the Lied-cantata also came on the scene.[5]

9. Songs of eighteenth-century Germany were not written or published separately. They came before the public in collections, united by their title, by the dedication, or by the order of the songs. They were arranged in the sense of the narrative, or by their literary affinity, or alphabetically. At the end of the century these large collections were sometimes grouped for use in church, school or home, or for specific social groups.

10. The intelligent and artistic circles of eighteenth- and nineteenth-century Germany produced the Liederkreis game.

> Liederkreis referred originally to a group of people who met of an evening to divert themselves with this game of poetry and song. In poetic form they constructed stories with familiar characters and objects. These poems were arranged in pairs on either side of a familiar center song intended to be guessed from clues offered by the pairs of poems.

4. A more modern use of double song is Hugo Wolf's setting of Goethe's "Die Spröde/Die Bekehrte."
5. An example is J.C.F. Bach's "Die Amerikänerin" (1776).

Appropriately costumed, the Liederkreis members posed picturesque groupings while singing the songs. These songs were eventually published in collections bearing the name Liederkreis in the title.

Liederkranz referred to a Liederkreis in which flowers were highlighted.

Liederzyclus referred to a circle of songs with neither flowers nor puzzles.

Liederspiel indicated a party event with songs which might or might not be staged, with or without scenery and costumes.

Professional musicians and poets began to appropriate the game for themselves; the result was more art form, less entertainment.

11. At the same time, Zumsteg, whom Schubert admired, wrote extended narrative ballads. The transitional form between solo cantata and song cycle was called the Kantatenlied.

12. Around 1800 Goethe and his fellow poets were writing a large number of patriotic and spiritual poems specifically intended to go with tunes, even as pop composers do now. Song is music that thrives on the repetitions which poetry avoids. For this reason, poets began to stretch out their material from one poem into many, so that they would be more adaptable to music. The material of one poem, parodied,[6] sufficed for a whole series of songs.

13. Composers began to arrange texts for musical results, not literary continuity. In this manner Beethoven set six Gellert poems; C. P. E. Bach set fifty-four.

14. Another type of collection or cycle was a set of occasional songs for dramas, epic poems, even novels, in which the order was not musical, but literary.

15. About 1815 a new, more adaptable song style developed for which made-to-order poetry acted as a libretto. Cycles began to be regarded as imaginary circles with theoretical centers. Not until 1820, however, had so much happened in literature and music that a poet—Heine—could knowingly construct a song cycle libretto, *Tragödie*. It was based on a folk song that occupied the second position in a three-poem libretto, parodies on either side. In effect, the first was the build-up; the second the tragic poem; the third the restful conclusion.

16. The word *Liederkreis* appears thus on the title page of Beethoven's work in 1816: *An die ferne Geliebte*, ein Liederkreis von Al. Jeitteles. Beethoven used Jeitteles's lyric cycle (a poetic form) as an opera composer uses a libretto. Both Beethoven and Schubert thought of *Liederkreis* as a literary form set to music. Even though

6. See note 3, above.

An die ferne Geliebte is now generally conceded to be the typical, if not the first, song cycle, at the time some maintained that it was not a cycle, but one long song (in spite of the fact that the motif of song number one reoccurs in the last song) for this reason: it changes tempo and material but has no pause. So much do song-cycle related forms overlap that, upon analysis, *An die ferne Geliebte* might also be characterized as a cantata with no recitatives.

This raises the question of whether a cycle is one song separated into sections or separate songs with separate titles. (Notice that once more we feel the inadequacy of the compositional guidelines referred to earlier.) The large proportion of Romantic song cycles seem to be a compilation of songs rather than the sectioning of a larger vocal work into divisions. Another question arises: should the form be regarded as musical or literary? If we measure our answer by the general convictions of most people, then we must conclude that music, not poetry, is the form. At its very simplest, although the lines of demarcation between related forms are patently extremely loose, a cycle consists of songs or song segments combined into one artistic whole, whatever techniques are used.

If one concedes that Beethoven's cycle was the first to exemplify the ideal, then it is a fair premise in the continuing debate that the definition that is fleshed out by *An die ferne Geliebte* came *after* the fact, not before it. The absence of a good definition led to a revolving circuit in which composers and editors tried to live up to whatever definition they felt was valid.[7]

The prototype described in the *Grove's Dictionary* definition is best illustrated by Schumann's *Frauenliebe und -leben* or Debussy's *Fêtes Galantes*. This type of cycle is the ideal served by Jules Massenet (the first French composer to write true song cycles) in *Poèmes du Souvenir*, the model for his succeeding five cycles.

Possibly, all the other definitions could be crystallized into inclusive guidelines stipulating one or more of the following requirements: a common theme, all poems by the same poet, each song with a life of its own as well as an integral life, a returning motive at the end of the cycle. The largest group of cycles falls within these boundaries.

Poème d'un Jour, a song cycle by Gabriel Fauré, may be considered a representative example. It has a common theme among the songs, but lacks a musical return at the close. Other cycles with a strong literary cohesion but lacking a plot, sometimes called "lyric" cycles are *Das Marienleben* by Hindemith, *Chansons de Bilitis* by Debussy, *Vier ernste Gesänge* by Brahms, *Kindertotenlieder* by Mahler, and *Songs and*

---

7. Beethoven's opus 48, *Sechs Lieder von Gellert*, were arranged in "proper" order by someone else; his publisher, not Beethoven, bestowed the six titles on the song sections of *An die ferne Geliebte*. Hindemith, worried about song 5 of *Das Marienleben* rewrote a second version so that it would have cyclic unity.

Dances of Death by Moussorgsky.[8] One interesting example of a cycle based upon a musical idea rather than a literary theme is Castelnuovo-Tedesco's *1830*. It utilizes three Bach preludes from the *Well-tempered Clavichord* over which the voice part, using Alfred de Musset's poetry, is suspended.

As for the general overall theme we may list, in addition to the *Dichterliebe* by Schumann, *Die Winterreise* and *Schwanengesang* by Schubert,[9] and *Nuits d'Eté* by Berlioz. In these examples a grouping of barely related songs are held together and merit the term cycle because the title assigned it suggests a most general theme idea.

It becomes evident that the Romantic composers chose poems to make their own librettos.[10] It is rare to find a complete lyric (literary) cycle set as a song cycle. Aaron Copland, in his preface to *Twelve Poems of Emily Dickinson* says:

> The poems centre about no single theme but they treat of subject matter particularly close to Miss Dickinson, nature, death, life, eternity. Only two of the songs are related thematically, the seventh and the twelfth. Nevertheless the composer hopes that, in seeking a musical counterpart for the unique personality of the poet, he has given the songs, taken together, the aspect of a song cycle.

One senses from these words Mr. Copland's struggle with the very heart of the matter.

Before the Romantic song cycle came to its fruition, cycle composers needed a poem which equaled a musical form. The habit of using poetry written by wives, friends, and talented amateurs further limited the range of musical possibilities. Composers began to use major poets, and as serious poetry loosened its forms, so did the cycle begin to be more complex and to extend its formal boundaries.

A vast spectrum of poetic subjects and musical styles and techniques marks the twentieth-century cycle. At the turn of the century a great interest in Oriental ideas was evinced; translations of Oriental poetry were used by composers in almost all the western countries. American composers especially wrote many cycles based on ethnic themes—however naively from our point of view—such as Indian, Black, and Creole. After World War II another wave of interest in Asian and Eastern arts marked a return to Haiku and the earlier poetic form, Tanka, as subjects for cycles using the newer compositional techniques.

8. The subject of death was distasteful before 1800, but an obsession to the Romantic composer.

9. Compiled and titled by the publisher, not Schubert.

10. Schumann chose from forty-eight Heine poems for his Opus 24 and twenty-six poems from diverse poets for his Opus 25, *Myrthen.*

Composers began to use prose as well as poetry. Single extended literary works were divided and given different musical treatments. Later on in the twentieth century, composers tended to use works by either very old or very modern writers. Cycles were written for voice, piano, and another instrument, for voice with one instrument, not the piano, and for more than one voice. Cycles that were intended to be acted out were actually accompanied by directions. All of these forms are still available and in use.

Having described the evolution of the song cycle since very early times and having circumnavigated the confusing and shadowy area inhabited by the major characteristics of song cycles, we come full circle to the single mandatory precept—that unity is the central necessity for a cycle. It can be achieved by musical means, among which are cyclic key schemes, repetitive rhythmic devices, onomatopoetic ideas, or by a unified literary theme. Therefore, when the composer does not state that his work is a cycle,[11] but you suspect that it is, the best indications are: a title, the presence of a single poet's work, or a unity of thematic material expressed by many poets—and possibly all three. So, a cycle is a cycle if the composer says it is, and sometimes even when he doesn't!

THE CYCLE IN PERFORMANCE

In some respects the cycle is somewhat simpler to perform than a mixed group of songs. The musical style is that of a single composer, and the singer may linger in its atmosphere for a longer time. Throughout the cycle he remains one person, whether he be a specific person who develops through life's different ages (*Frauenliebe und -leben*), a general type of person such as the poet in the *Dichterliebe* who expresses himself in various attitudes, or as narrator who relates a story (*Fêtes Galantes*). The who, where, when, and why of the protagonist is clearly understood by the audience at the outset of the cycle. In this way the one-voiced cycle is similar to the operatic role. Its interpretation offers more theatrical potential. Certainly the double song, multi-voiced cycles, and Liederspiel present myriad dramatic opportunities. Then, too, it is to your advantage that the order of the songs within a cycle is preset and need not be arranged to achieve variety.

However, these very same benefits to the singer do present problems in such matters as the investigation of psychological development of the

11. Ned Rorem titles his *War Scenes* a "Suite of Songs."

character and the sustaining of one idea over a long span of time. Also, it must be remembered that the momentary but welcome respite furnished the singer by applause is missing in cycle performance.

PROGRAMMING

The decision to program a cycle as opposed to a mixed group has one inherent benefit: variety is assured by the very existence of a cohesive and neatly bound group of songs based on one subject. There is no question but that the addition of a cycle also provides some measure of sophistication.

Let us suggest to the singer who feels not quite up to the performance of a major cycle that he acquaint himself with the many shorter ones. We also suggest he use his own ingenuity in putting together what might be called a "home-made" cycle—some five or six songs chosen from a major cycle that hold together well and offer some continuity of thought, such as selected songs from Schubert's *Die Winterreise* or *Die schöne Müllerin*, and *Das Marienleben* of Hindemith. Another plan is to invent a theme of your own, then find songs of several different composers which fit effectively into that theme.

As an example of the vast possibilities of the home-made cycle, the following long list is offered. From this list of songs and cycles (from which you can draw single songs) that have in common thoughts by and about children, you can put together your own cycle. This list might also prove fruitful to a singer seeking light, charming encores.

"A Piper" (John Duke)
"Just Spring" (John Duke)
"If I Was Only You, My Dad" (Erno Balogh)
"La Grenouille Américaine" (Eric Satie)
"Jack-in-the-Box" (Daniel Wolf)
"Miaou" (Heitor Villa Lobos)
"Brigid's Song" (David Diamond)
"Sonatina" (Celius Dougherty)
"Och, Moder, ich will en Ding han" (Johannes Brahms)
"When I Bring to You Colored Toys" (John Alden Carpenter)
"The Sleep that Flits on Baby's Eyes" (John Alden Carpenter)
"De Ronda" (Joaquín Rodrigo)

"The Greatest Man" (Charles Ives)

"Common Bill" (arr. Ernst Bacon)

God Makes Ducks (Henry Mollicone)

Trois Histoires pour Enfants (Igor Stravinsky)

Berceuses du Chat (Igor Stravinsky)

Chantes Fables (Soulima Stravinsky)

Nursery (Modest Moussorgsky)

Charm of Lullabies (Benjamin Britten)

Cinq Chansons de Lise Hirtz (Georges Auric)

Five Songs of Crazy Jane (Peter Aston)

Tit for Tat (Benjamin Britten)

Friday Afternoons (Benjamin Britten)

Trois Enfantines (Arnold Bax)

Four Child Songs (Roger Quilter)

Three Children's Songs (Sergei Prokofiev)

Ludions (Eric Satie)

Trois Chansons de la Petite Sirène (Arthur Honegger)

Three French Nursery Songs (Alan Rawsthorne)

Children's Rhymes (Karol Szymanowski)

Chansons Enfantines (Gabriel Grovlez)

Animals and Insects (Louis Gruenberg)

Ungereimtes (Boris Blacher)

Improving Songs for Anxious Children (John Alden Carpenter)

Four Animal Songs (Emanuel Chabrier)

The Children (Theodore Chanler)

Chinese Mother Goose Rhymes (Bainbridge Crist)

Trois Chansons de la Jungle (Roger Delage)

Ogden Nash's Musical Zoo (Vernon Duke)

Childhood Fables for Grownups (2 vols.) (Irving Fine)

Canciones Infantiles (Garcia Abril)

Nonsense Songs by Edward Lear (Dudley Glass)

Songs to Children's Poems (Ray Green)

Seven Children's Songs (Edvard Grieg)

Mother Goose Songs (Charles Haubiel)

New Songs of Old Mother Goose (John Koch)

Drei Fabeln (Vycpálek Kricka)

Les Chansons de ma Mère d'Oie (Tristan Klingsor)

Vocal literature abounds with song cycles in all styles and in all languages. Musicians tend to view the song cycle as possessing certain requisite attributes—lengthiness, solemnity, and gravity. The repertoire list of song cycles found in the appendix attempts to reveal a perhaps hitherto unknown breadth of alternative features—brevity, lightheartedness, and wit.

GUIDELINES FOR PRACTICE

1. Using works by American composers, put together in a home-made cycle three or four contemporary songs which have a religious theme.

2. Form your own Goethe cycle, using his poems set by many composers.

3. With Ophelia as a subject, design a cycle from such composers as Berlioz and Strauss.

4. Invent a theme of your own and construct a home-made cycle.

5. Devise a home-made cycle called "The Nightingale's Song" in which you use songs by Russian, German, French, and Spanish composers, some songs accompanied by flute.

6. Put together a cycle composed of "Mad Music" by Purcell.

14 Folk Music and Popular Music

In the opinion of this writer it seems most advisable to treat folk songs primarily as music and not as some quaint examples of folklore. In other words, unless the singer can wholeheartedly accept the text and the music of a folk song as such, and unless this text and its musical expression can produce within him an emotional reaction sufficiently strong to warrant a performance, it would be better not to try to perform such songs.

Sergius Kagen[1]

THE INFLUENCE ON SERIOUS COMPOSITION

Mr. Kagen correctly elevates the folk song to a somewhat higher level of regard than is often accorded it. Some of us tend to forget, even after studying our informative musicology texts, just how often and in what subtle ways folk music in general has influenced the greatest composers in many of their most sublime compositions.

1. *Music for the Voice* (Bloomington: Indiana University Press, 1968), p. 636.

The wave of nationalism that followed German Romantic domination over European music brought about an extensive use of folk melody in composed works. (It is interesting to note that medieval and Renaissance composers used folk melodies in their compositions.)[2] The simple regularity and symmetry of folk music and dance forms show up in the structure of classic music, which abounds with such patterns.

In *National Music*, by Ralph Vaughan Williams (London, 1934), the English composer expressed the belief that all truly great music is derived from the folk traditions of a composer's native soil. Manuel de Falla stated that folk music is the path to an international concert style. Igor Stravinsky borrrowed phrases liberally from folk music and transformed them with his own particular formula of writing. Indeed Stravinsky's music has been criticized as lacking in original melody because of his abundant use of folk tunes. To which he responded that "great composers do not imitate; they steal."

Beginning with Claude Debussy, whose interest was sparked by the Javanese gamelan, composers of the recent past used non-Western folk styles in their compositions: Santoliquido (Persian and Arabian), Tcherepnin and Griffes (Chinese), Holst (Hindu), to mention but a few. In the last twenty years, nonWestern music has commanded a growing interest among contemporary composers.

Arnold Schoenberg, however, in his philosophical book *Style and Idea*[3], asserts that folk music is not adaptable to larger works of music. The requirements of larger forms and the simple construction of folk tunes, he says, can never be blended into one work. He reminds us that Johannes Brahms used actual folk melodies only in his small pieces and that the folk tunes themselves are not to be found in the German composer's larger works—only the "flavor and perfume" of folk music is there. Even so, the influence is present, though subtle.

Schoenberg's exact argument is that folk melodies cannot be expanded into a full musical development. In this sense, he may be right. On the other hand, a folk tune can be, and indeed has been, used effectively in large works while at the same time retaining its essential simplicity with little or no development. The issue is debatable. Be this as it may, folk music exults in the smaller form of song whence it grew, and it is within this realm that we are concerned with it.

The discovery and systematic rescue of folk music is of comparatively recent date, but its influence has already made itself felt to some purpose. In the future such influence may even be extended. Furthermore, our present trend toward folk music in the popular field is to many

2. For example, Palestrina used the folk tune "L'Homme Armé" in one of his Masses.
3. *Style and Idea* (New York: Philosophical Library, 1950).

people a source of hope after what they regard as the excesses of the rock era.

PROGRAMMING

Folk music may be classified in five categories:

1. the true folk song (or what is generally regarded as the true folk song) with a harmonized accompaniment as near to the original as possible
2. the unaccompanied folk song
3. a concert arrangement with more pianistic elaboration by either a major or an unrecognized composer
4. a folk melody with new words added, or folk verses with newly composed music
5. an art song in folk style

The true folk song described in category 1 is seldom chosen for inclusion in recitals. The reasons are apparent. Yet many very beautiful folk melodies are left lying on library shelves waiting to be sung. Here is an excellent opportunity for an enterprising singer/accompanist team to create its own arrangements and elaborations, thereby involving and extending their artistic imaginations. They will subsequently be rewarded with a satisfying credit on their program pointing out that the realizations are original.

With the labyrinthine evolution of folk melodies in any land, an original poem may have been set to more than one melody, just as any popular tune may easily have been used for more than one poem. In most music libraries one can discover collections providing thorough discussions or excellent footnotes that clarify the origin and the history of any song in question.

As to performance of true folk songs described under category 1 above, Sergius Kagen, bearing in mind that natural folk music is in a sense faultless since it originally springs from an instantaneous flash of inspiration, suggests:

1. utmost simplicity
2. understatement rather than so-called dramatic projection
3. clear, unaffected diction, not marred by any attempt to imitate a dialect
4. clear delivery of the melodic line

5. caution regarding the trap of imitating the mannerisms of an untrained singer

Most folk songs are simple and balanced in structure with strong melodic curving phrases. While studying the song for breathing places, care should be taken to prevent the breaking of phrases whenever possible so that the continuity and flow of both the text and the music may remain intact.

Songs in strophic form offer fine opportunities for the inventive accompanist described earlier. Unless, of course, the song has already been arranged, the accompanist may feel free to elaborate and invent ideas which highlight the verses' content; e.g., in the case of Spanish music, he might well invent more florid accompaniments in the style of Spain's national instrument, the guitar. Discretion and taste are mandatory. The only form of accompaniment that strikes a discordant note is one in which a harmonic scheme entirely at variance with the spirit of the words and melody is used.

Unaccompanied folk singing (category 2) is in all likelihood the most improvisatory form of performance imaginable. It is an unlearned and singular talent possessed by few, and it is wholly instinctive. Here the singer breaks all the rules of music while maintaining a rhythm and conviction totally his own. A singer possessing this talent will never fail to captivate his audience. Lacking the talent, he will most assuredly bore them to distraction. Be cautioned not to plan more than one such song per program!

Examples of concert arrangements described as category 3 are found frequently on recital programs. To name some of the finest: Benjamin Britten's six volumes of English folk songs, Aaron Copland's two sets of old American folk songs, Marie-Joseph Cantaloube's *Chants d'Auvergne* (four volumes), and Béla Bartók's superb *Village Scenes*, the Hungarian composer's unparalleled accomplishment for the voice.

Bartók's self-confessed aim was to place traditional folk songs within the complex yet apt twentieth-century environment, not distorting but enhancing their individual character. Of such compositions Bartók has written:

> Many people think it is a comparatively easy task to write a composition round folk tunes. A lesser achievement at least than a composition on "original" themes.
>
> This way of thinking is completely erroneous. To handle folk melodies is one of the most difficult tasks; equally difficult if not more so than to write a major original composition. If we keep in mind that borrowing a melody means being bound by its individual peculiarity we shall understand one part of the difficulty. Another is created by the

special character of a folk melody. We must penetrate into it, feel it, and bring it out in sharp contours by the appropriate setting. The composition round a folk melody must be done in a "propitious hour" or—as is generally said—it must be a work of inspiration just as much as any other composition.[4]

We offer a listing of composers who have arranged folk melodies in concert form:

Ernst Bacon	Louis Gruenberg
Béla Bartók	Joseph Haydn
Arnold Bax	Gustave Holst
Ludwig van Beethoven	Johann Nepomuk Hummel
Luciano Berio	Charles Ives
Paul Bowles	Zoltán Kodály
Johannes Brahms	Felix Mendelssohn
Max Bruch	Joachim Nín
Harry Burleigh	Ignaz Pleyel
William Byrd	Henry Purcell
Samuel Coleridge Taylor	Ottorino Respighi
Manuel de Falla	Elie Siegmeister
Celius Dougherty	Igor Stravinsky
John Edmunds	Jan Pieterszoon Sweelinck
George Gershwin	Virgil Thomson
Louis Moreau Gottschalk	Ralph Vaughan Williams
Percy Grainger	Carl Maria von Weber

Upon analysis of the five groups of folk song permutations described above, it becomes apparent that songs corresponding to category 4 are hybrid forms, and that any examples from category 5 are folk songs only in mood or atmosphere.

The hybrids mentioned in category 4 are of two kinds. Examples of folk melody with new words can be found in many of the Herbert Hughes's Irish song arrangements. Poets of the Romantic era such as Robert Burns, Thomas Moore, and Sir Walter Scott wrote beautiful verses to enhance popular tunes of the day. Poetry, possibly less than great, fitted to pure folk music and urban street music can be found in the early forms of Spanish lyric theater, in particular the *tonadilla escenica*. The tonadilla was a form of popular theatrical entertainment that combined singing, dancing, and acting, usually lasting fifteen or twenty minutes, and performed between acts of a play. The subjects were usually local, current, and often bawdy, bringing onto the stage such person-

4. From an essay by Bartók ("On the Significance of Folk Music") written in 1931 published in *Béla Bartók Essays*, ed. Benjamin Suchoff (New York: St. Martin's Press, 1976), p. 345.

ages as gypsies, army officers, ladies of ill-repute, etc. The life span of a typical tonadilla was about two weeks to a month. The tonadilla escenica affords the very best example of a successful fusion of (1) pure folk music of rural origin, (2) essentially popular urban street music, and (3) conventional instrumental and vocal technique.

Two superb examples of new music added to folk verse are Hugo Wolf's songs from the Italian and Spanish collections and Gustav Mahler's songs from *Des Knaben Wunderhorn*. Wolf's settings of the enchanting *rispetti* and *velutti* by Italian poets (mostly anonymous) have been translated by Paul Heyse into German. They have considerably more of an art song than a folk song quality. Achim von Arnim and Clemens Brentano in 1805 published *Des Knaben Wunderhorn*, the most important collection of German folk verse. Mahler's songs set to these verses have more folk quality than do Wolf's.

With the exception of the guitar, availability of most national instruments—the balalaika, the lute, the mandolin, the bagpipes, the Scandinavian cantele (an ancient zither)—or, for that matter, their respective players, is scant. Were they plentiful, their participation in a recital program would add great interest and variety. There is, however, no reason why standard instruments such as the flute, clarinet, viola, or cello cannot be utilized as accompanying instruments with or without the piano. Here too is another opportunity for the adventuresome accompanist.

In a strange and beautiful way, well-sung folk music touches the hearts and minds of most audiences. Having heard the heart-warming songs of Spain sung by Victoria de los Angeles, the exquisite Welsh melodies sung by Thomas L. Thomas, the moving spirituals of Marian Anderson, and the very beautiful *Deutsche Volkslieder* of Brahms sung by Elisabeth Schwarzkopf and Dietrich Fischer-Dieskau, no one is likely to forget them.

Because of the more limited vocal range and overall simplicity of folk songs, the wise vocal teacher might advise them for young singers preparing their first recitals. Then, too, if a young singer's ethnic background gifts him with a good command of a foreign language and/or an allied stylistic intuition, it certainly behooves him to take advantage of folk song repertoire.[5]

The audience and its attitudes must ever exert a strong influence upon our programming and performing decisions. The essential quality of folk music is, of course, nationalistic while that of the art song is universal. It is for this reason that those singers of a particular ethnic background appear to be, in the minds of the general audience, best suited to the performance of that particular repertoire. As our planet

---

5. Whatever your ethnic background, it is advisable to consult source books which offer detailed information about folklore and legend relating to your song(s). See p. 280 for a list of suitable titles.

daily becomes more and more "one world" the time may come when folk songs can be sung by all people equally effectively. As of now, the German sings best of his background, the Frenchman and the Russian of theirs, the Black man of his, and the Oriental of his.

THE TWENTIETH CENTURY

In twentieth-century America, popular music took the place of folk music.

> It would seem permissible to place all popular songs in the general category of folk music, for that is where they clearly belong. They have the same habit of being passed on by word of mouth, the same dependence upon simplicity of melody, the same leaning toward monotony of rhythm, the same balance of responsibility between text and time.[6]

Just as folk music has in the past made its impression strongly felt upon such serious music, popular music has followed suit. Jazz (ca. 1925), along with its predecessors, ragtime (ca. 1890) and the blues (ca. 1900), have influenced much serious music since their respective births in America. Charles Ives incorporated many popular music elements into his compositions. Ravel's Violin Sonata has a blues movement, and in his Piano Concerto for Left Hand jazz timbres, phrases, and rhythms abound. There is a fine example of jazz writing in Ned Rorem's "Psalm 148" from his *Cycle of Holy Songs*. Poulenc and members of Les Six worked on the fusion of popular and classical elements during the 1920s in Paris, using music hall melodies, circus tunes, jazz in a mix with a chic Stravinsky-derived overlay. Both ragtime and jazz play a part in Darius Milhaud's *Chansons de Négresse* as in his "Cocktail aux Clarinettes." Gunther Schuller, influenced by the music of Duke Ellington, experimented with classical and jazz styles to produce what he labeled "third-stream" music. With the gradual assimilation of jazz into serious music, performers as well as composers no longer had to choose one style to the total exclusion of the other. Proponents of music's technological future insist that pop and rock will one day be consolidated with the techniques of "classical" music in a manner agreeable to both sides.[7]

6. Sigmund Spaeth, *A History of Popular Music in America* (New York: Random House, 1948), p. 11.
7. Jean Pierre Rampal the flutist, who began his career in serious music, has recently added jazz to his immense discography. The condescending attitude of serious musicians toward Benny Goodman, who was among the first to straddle jazz *and* serious music, no

Among Blacks in America, jazz and religion represented an escape from oppression and anguish. Even outside of America spiritual autonomy and the privilege of free speech is identified with Black people striving for equality. Although jazz itself has now become traditional and conventional, its quality of improvisation has worked tremendous influence on twentieth-century music, perhaps not with the atonalists but certainly with all other kinds of new music, particularly aleatory compositions.

Lest we snobbishly discount popular music, with its simple, sometimes childlike, appeal, let us remember that Mozart wrote minuets, which were the light dance music of his day. Brahms made extensive use of the clodhopper rhythms and bucolic tunes of the Ländler dance form. Debussy wrote a cake walk (Children's Corner) and Hindemith wrote ragtime piano pieces (Dance Suite). Nonsense refrains, the "dooby-dooby-dos" of the 1950s, for instance, and the "yeah, yeahs" of the 1960s and 1970s, are not attributable to popular music alone. Elizabethan madrigals abound in "Hey, nonny, nonny!" Surely there is both worthy and inferior popular music as there is worthy and inferior serious music.

Each spring, heralding the arrival of "pop" and "prom" concerts, there comes a spate of articles debating the relative merits of "light" and "serious" music. Long a champion of third-stream music, Gunther Schuller on May 14, 1978, discussed at length in the Sunday New York Times the aspects of what he calls "establishment stigmatization." The elite group of major artistic institutions have decreed the boundaries which rigidly separate serious, light, and pop categories of music, he says. This effectively produces a group of regular concertgoers who must turn away from lighter fare, denying themselves the enjoyment of a broader spectrum of musical styles, and another group who attend only "prom" concerts (although, Mr. Schuller says, they would go to "serious" concerts if a more varied fare were presented). Mr. Schuller believes that light and serious music do not differ in quality, but in complexity of development. In his notes for the 1978 New York Philharmonic Prom Concerts Mr. Schuller states: "It can be shown that the popular can be serious, that the serious can be popular, and that both terms are irrelevant in the face of real quality and musical genius. I know of no category or style of music which doesn't have generous examples of superb quality and—not surprisingly—many examples of average or exceedingly impoverished work. Thus, in all forms of music one can find the good coexisting with the bad."

Popular composers like Irving Berlin, Cole Porter, George Gershwin, Jerome Kern, and Richard Rogers used jazz and the popular idiom

---

longer greets performers like Jean Pierre Rampal when he does the same. The lines of demarcation have now dissolved, particularly because of the influence of contemporary music.

to bestow upon us the only true American theatrical genre, musical comedy, replacing the once popular Viennese operetta style of Victor Herbert, Sigmund Romberg, and Rudolf Friml.[8]

By definition, popular music is music that is heard often. Television, juke boxes, movies, and restaurant background music (also banks, bus stations, and other public gathering places) all provide us with a constant stream of it—a fact in itself not a deterrent to its inclusion in a recital. However, any popular songs we hear today are strongly associated with the personality of a particular popular singer, who seeks to create a style of performance that is unique unto himself rather than a reflection of the composer's intent. For the pop singer today, the right arrangement, more than the song itself, helps to insure success for him. His vocal style is blueprinted on the song he sings. This blueprint usually involves the use of a vocal technique very different from the technique of a legitimate singer.

Some pop singers adopt a rough and asthmatic sound to indicate passion or lust. Country western seems to demand an authentic regional accent that is placed in or near the nose. The heavy amplified sound of hard rock describes the anger of social revolution and personal torment through the hoarse cries of the singer. How the future may alter the present vocal status quo in popular music will be an interesting speculation.

> "Popular style," in fact, is a combination of the performer's personal idiosyncracies, the public's expectations, and the total style's general rules of timbre, ornamentation, dynamics, vibrato, tempo, pronunciation and other elements."[9]

For the recital singer to attempt to compete with an established stylized version of a song, so quickly taken to the heart of the American popular song lover, is to court disaster. There is, however, one part of popular music that might fit into the formal recital—the song that, by reason of its mood or musical construction, is enhanced by the legitimate voice. Such songs as "Lonely Town" from Weill's *Street Scene*, "Rosabella" from *Most Happy Fella*, "My Lord and Master" from *The King and I*, or "Soliloquy" from *Carousel* are deserving of our respect.

With regard to the popular singer whose vocal standards admittedly are not ours, let us also admit that the dramatic and interpretive standards of the very best ones should possibly be ours. Have you ever known a good popular singer not to completely involve himself in the song he is about to sing? "As she set herself before each piece, Miss DeGaetani

8. Generally considered a master composer of total serialism, Milton Babbitt actually started his career working in Tin Pan Alley publishing firms and at that time gained his encyclopedic knowledge of Broadway musicals.
9. John Vinton, ed., *Dictionary of Contemporary Music* (New York: E. P. Dutton, 1974).

gathered the audience as well as drawing us already at least halfway into the expressive universe of that particular song before even a note had sounded." The *New Yorker* review of the brilliant mezzo-soprano Jan DeGaetani tells of an interpretive ability we take for granted in a popular singer, but too often find lacking in a legitimate singer.

Today's best popular music, valid and unrivaled in its specialized performance, has its own recital outlet in the media of supper clubs, television, the movies, and personal appearances. The supper club artist today merits the full apparatus of critical review from both newspapers and television newscasts. Because of its kinship with folk music, popular music has earned the right to be accepted by a larger public. In what manner the musical elite may pass judgment upon it is another matter. Popular music—today's folk art—continues to wield its influence. Perhaps it is not too fanciful to imagine the recital of the future as a combination of the best qualities of the popular performer—his audience charisma and traditional ability to "sell the song"—and the legitimate recitalist—his cultured musical and vocal style along with his vast and varied repertoire of the world's song literature.

Suggested Readings in Folk Music and popular Music for the Recital Singer and Accompanist:

Standard Dictionary of Folklore, Mythology, and Legend, Maria Leach, ed.; Funk and Wagnall.
A Treasury of Southern Folklore, B. A. Botkin, ed.; Crown Publishers, Inc.
America in Legend, Richard M. Dorson; Pantheon Books.
The Book of Negro Folklore, Langston Hughes and Arna Bontemps; Dodd, Mead and Co.
Folklore on the American Land, Duncan Emrich; Little, Brown and Co.
Folksongs in Settings by Master Composers, Herbert Haufrecht; Funk and Wagnall.
A History of Popular Music in America, Sigmund Spaeth; Random House.

15 The Future of the Song Recital

When I started my first tours twenty years ago, the
audiences were made up almost entirely of old people.
Today, at least half of them are young.

Dietrich Fischer-Dieskau[1]

THE NEED FOR CHANGE

Dietrich Fischer-Dieskau's statement is heart-
warming. It is good to learn that audiences for serious music in general
are made up of a high proportion of young people. It does come to mind,
however, that Fischer-Dieskau's audiences are not altogether typical.
His fame and discography now precede him, whereas twenty years ago
the people came to hear him at least partly because of their love for song
literature. After Fischer-Dieskau—what? Will the recital form expire
altogether when the German baritone and a handful of other fine European singers are no longer with us? Will their places be taken by a new
group of European stars, leaving the recital fundamentally as it is
today—a highly sophisticated, specialized, and essentially private art
form, dominated by an exaggerated reverence for the European artist?
Need we regard the recital as this and only this?

1. Quoted in Peter Heyworth, "Too Much an Artist to Be a Star," *New York Times*,
   January 17, 1971.

As stated in the introduction, those of us who care must clarify the picture, see the problems involved, revise our thinking, and reevaluate some of our beliefs if we wish to stimulate a reanimation of the old form, or indeed fabricate a new form.

His audiences understood very well what the seventeenth- or eighteenth-century composer was doing. The musical conventions within which he composed were strict, and his audience knew exactly what to anticipate. The nineteenth-century audience expected (until around the turn of the century) to encounter songs in a salon setting, and to find at a public concert operatic arias—perhaps a song or two, maybe a duet with an assisting artist, accompanied by an orchestra. By the early twentieth century, song recitals had gone public. Although it is doubtful whether they understood more than its snob appeal, even the large portion of the musical public (who now enjoy television most) attended solo recitals during the 1930s and the 1940s. After World War II drastic changes, stemming from the electronics revolution, were felt. Television, movies, and the long-playing record replaced serious live music as a cultural medium for entertainment. Older people still went to hear recitalists, but younger people (except for the very knowledgeable elite), conditioned by the informality and group forces of rock and twentieth-century avant-garde music, found one lone singer doing the same old repertoire in a very formal situation (let us be frank) boring and anachronistic.

No matter what the makeup of the audience, we believe it is not too simplistic to say that their common desire is to be entertained. Opera is obvious entertainment. The symphony orchestra with its wondrous maze of tonal color and variety has within its makeup a natural entertainment value, whatever the discernment of the listener. The declining solo recital, which is a miniature medium, must triple its capacity to entertain. To quote Paul Sperry, the fine concert tenor, "To me the performer has a responsibility to the public as well as the music. For a performer steadfastly to refuse to be entertaining is to deny half of his responsibility."[2]

It must be acknowledged that the use of such a criterion immediately raises the hackles of many serious musicians. Perhaps if we used the word "enjoyment," such feelings could be soothed. In any case, whatever the terms in which the idea is couched, the audience wishes to enjoy its sojourn in the hall—in diverse ways and at various musical levels to be sure. The enthusiast, whose musical background and appreciation is superior, will particularly enjoy new and unusual programming drawn from past or avant-garde sources. The connoisseur, who tends to go with prevailing tastes and fashions in music, will enjoy hearing the up-to-date, the newest, the freshly discovered, the resurrected-after-long-years-of-

2. John Gruen, "The Tenor from the Harvard Business School," *New York Times*, February 8, 1976.

neglect, and the innovative currently being celebrated in the press. The majority will enjoy an evocative and moving experience (which demands superb interpretations) and titillating programming with much variety. When we have proven to the typical audience member that a recital can be an entertainment, he will soon be his own man, emancipated from enjoying only what he is told to enjoy, and most important, he will return again! This is what it means to "build an audience."

Bruce G. Lunkley, president of the National Association of Teachers of Singing from 1976 to 1978, has said:

> The programming of a solo recital for a general audience seems to have become a lost art. Too many programs are basically historical and linguistic with little thought given to an audience which is usually made up of aficionados, amateur singers, some musically competent and a few musically elite. The artist has to plan a program that can be co-experienced with all of these people and that will give him or her an opportunity to use the voice well with varied colors, dynamics, ranges, and in ways that will capture the imaginations and emotions of those who have come to hear. Surely that means more songs in English, more appealing and immediate songs, some humor, some drama, some tears, perhaps. It means repertoire that is diverse but comprehensible by *both* artist and audience. Each song is an event—a fragrance to be inhaled by the audience, savored, and remembered.

Apropos the mass audience, Beverly Sills's much-quoted advice to " 'poison' the minds of the children at an early age" seems a good rallying cry for those who wish to reanimate the recital from the ground up, as it were. Paul Sperry also tells us to look to the very young when trying to reconstruct an audience for song literature. Make children aware of songs; let them sing and act songs in school. The child of the town baker who plays second flute in the local orchestra is easily led to an appreciation of orchestral music as she comes regularly to hear Daddy (and the orchestra) play. Two examples of states in which no efforts are spared to rear their children in a musical environment are North Carolina and Connecticut. Some schools with good music instruction have even broadened their programs to teach electronic music on an elementary level, preparing students for a world we adults will never live to see.

However, figures garnered by the ongoing project entitled "The National Assessment of Educational Progress" are very disturbing since the results indicate that much of the country's elementary school music is being taught imperfectly, if at all. The number of nonresponses to the project's request for information seemed to indicate that there were many schools offering no musical instruction whatsoever. Of those who responded, only 23% of upper grade schools (a smaller percentage for lower grades) had music taught by specialists; 38% said that music was taught by a combination of specialists and classroom teachers; 30% used only the classroom teachers, who are often musically illiterate. In an article about the National Assessment published in the *College Music Symposium* (Fall, 1977) Alan Buechner agrees with Jacques Barzun: we cannot know who will decide to enrich his life with music or the other arts. This does not however excuse the school from providing a general education in the arts which would prepare the individual child to decide for himself.

Although intellectual activity (of which the arts is one type) is and will remain elitist, Americans have long been prone to regard superior activity of the intellect with disfavor, since it must be earmarked as "undemocratic." Thus the popular disparaging references to "elitist" musical organizations, "elitist" music, "elitist" programs. It is precisely this fear of elitism that condones the spending of government funds on projects such as street dancing or basket weaving. Meanwhile, amidst all this hubbub over philosophy of art, American children are herded once a year to a patronizingly designated "young people's" concert or are taken on an annual trip to a museum that houses an appropriately labeled "children's" exhibit. What America needs are long-range, attractive, and, most of all, consistent programs for the young if they are to grow up with a sympathy and feeling for the arts. To this end, money could effectively be spent on an extended program for children, subsidizing free (or very low-priced) tickets to appropriate song recital programs and other serious music.

Music lovers tend to become wary of talk about infusing entertainment and innovation into the recital form. How shall we preserve our high performance standards? they ask. To which we respond with a question: Are we so sure that our standards are high? Perhaps they are more rigid than elevated.

Before renovations of the recital form are discussed, it should not prove too controversial to say that higher standards in the present recital form would be in order. We refer not so much to vocal standards—although more versatility would be welcome—as musicianship, acting, and programming skills in reverse order of need. The musicianship of the American singer is improving constantly; we believe it has been proportionately higher than that of Europeans since the end of World War II. During the last decade, however, an ever larger audience has learned to appreciate the skills and standards demanded of solistic playing in chamber groups. The contemporary ballet also is no longer an art of soloists but of individual dancers in well-directed cooperative groups. Twentieth-century American singers, too, must not limit themselves to perpetuating the past. They must not be afraid of what they may be losing, but equip themselves rather to be present within what is currently happening or about to happen in music. Limited musical skills limit the singer to a specialized repertoire of sorts.

As to standards of dramatic performance in recital, they are for the most part woefully inadequate. Especially is evocative interpretation called for from those singers who are not gifted by nature with a phenomenal vocal instrument. The absence of interpretive ability is consistently blamed on the lack of the gift of dramatic "flair," as if only God could dispense the capacity for communication. The first step in revitalizing the drama of the recital is to stop relying on flair and insist upon real acting training. The standards upheld by the art of the living actor have in no way been as avidly sought by the recital singer as those vocal and musical standards to which he is for the most part dedicated.

Distilled from the many points discussed above are two incontrovertible basics necessary to a fine recital: the ability to sing music beautifully and the ability to impart the meaning of words effectively. To quote Mr. Sperry: "I strongly feel that when properly done, a voice recital is an evening of storytelling in the hands of a good storyteller."[3]

Recital programming is by far the most eminent candidate for improvement. A great deal can be done by original, skillful, inventive programming to erase the image of the recital as a snobbish occasion, frightfully stilted, with monotonous programming, sometimes even poorly interpreted.

One of the most pernicious contributions to the earlier decline of the recital took place during the heyday of organized community concerts. Big concert bureau managers deliberately restricted programs of American artists to the very lowest level of repertoire they could get away with, employing with a vengeance the "give 'em what they want" excuse. On the other hand, they sent out European artists. Some were fine recitalists who, having the reputation and thus the clout to withstand the extreme pressures put on them by the managements, sang extremely specialized, demanding programs that the knowing audience expected of them. The others were opera stars, by no means at home in the recital tradition, who therefore sang recitals composed of operatic arias interspersed with a few song groups, such as someone's four old favorites. Whenever managerial artistic philosophy was challenged, visions of a life of penury, caused by *not* giving them what they wanted, were persistently conjured up.

The need for artists as well as anyone else to earn a living need not be gainsaid. Countless fine American recitalists certainly had to bow to the financial facts of life. Sometimes their careers were truncated. Sometimes they survived, if only by acquiescing ignominiously to the infamous "package" system. Local committees were told that their only chance of having the internationally renowned Madame W in their concert series was to purchase the less worthy American singers X, Y, and Z. With one

3. Ibid.

stroke of this brush Americans were tarred by their own management as inferior artists who required such tactics in order to secure engagements. The great American inferiority complex that in those days held the mass audience in thrall to the "superior" European artist was sustained, and the decisions about recital programs were kept firmly in management hands.

The degree of commercialism to which these managers were absolutely dedicated prompts our statement that they bear a large part of the blame for the state of affairs during the 1950s and 1960s. A pertinent simile is to liken the situation to strip mining, which continually takes—as much as the traffic will bear—with no intention of returning anything to the land. These nonspecialized programs of American artists, even though smugly and determinedly "lowbrow," did not keep the audiences from being bored; they destroyed the young, new audience in embryo, so to speak; they perpetuated the great American myth that culture must be dull and colorless; they grievously harmed even the American recitalist and the recital itself. After the advent of television, patently disastrous for their commercial position in cultural entertainment, they made little effort to restructure the image or content of their concert series, except under duress.

To be more specific, most of the large management organizations who controlled the recital art in the past held their programming to a dogmatic formula: familiar classics, two groups in a foreign language (preferably not German) and an American group. This format included several famous operatic arias. As a result, programs similar to the following one were sent out to the untutored public in the 1930s and 1940s.

I.	Star vicino	Rosa
	Phillis hath such charming graces	Old English
	Ah, forse è lui (La Traviata)	Verdi
II.	Aria from Dinora	Meyerbeer
III.	Im Waldeinsamkeit	Brahms
	O, quand je dors	Liszt
	Serenade	Leoncavallo
	Pastorelle delle Alpi	Rossini
	INTERMISSION	
IV.	Piano group	
V.	Mad Scene (Lucia di Lammermoor)	Donizetti
VI.	Norwegian Echo	(arr. Thrane)
	Dream Song	Warford
	Midsummer	Worth
	Se saran rose	Arditi

Cursory inspection of the above program testifies to very poor programming by any standards, and a noticeable attitude of condescension in "playing down to the public." Programs changed very little until the late 1940s and early 1950s when singers began to tighten their programs somewhat into minimally better coherence and unity, relegating famous operatic arias to special sections of their own.

I.	Ombra mai fù (*Xerses*)	Handel
	Danza, danza, fanciulla	Durante
	Vittoria, vittoria	Carissimi
II.	O cease thy singing, maiden fair	Rachmaninov
	Miranda	Hageman
	The rose enslaves the Nightingale	Rimsky-Korsakov
	Serenade	Carpenter
III.	Two arias:	
	E lucevan le stelle (*Tosca*)	Puccini
	M'apparì (*Martha*)	Von Flotow
	INTERMISSION	
IV.	Piano group	
V.	Aubade (*Le Roi d'Ys*)	Lalo
	Sombrero	Chaminade
	Le Miroir	Ferrari
	Chanson Norvégienne	Fourdrain
VI.	Ballynure Ballad	(Irish trad.)
	Loch Lomond	(Scottish trad.)
	O, what a beautiful city	Spiritual
	Witness	Spiritual

In the 1960s, due to the insistence of individual singers who demanded their artistic rights, a small change came about. Groups were unified better and were not totally composed of the most hackneyed songs. Complete Hugo Wolf groups were (however infrequently) becoming acceptable (!) as were some modern (if limited to neo-Romantic) songs. However, by the 1960s the recital business had started its decline. Infuriated and disillusioned audiences resented the condescending attitude; the general poverty of programming commanded neither respect nor interest from the better educated mass audience (thanks to the long-playing record in part). Innovations in the recital form and improvements in presentation techniques simply did not come in time. In its vulnerable condition, the song recital was no match for television.

Today, too late, we do find some excellent programs sent out by management, such as the following program of the brilliant recitalist Phyllis Curtin.

I. Twelve Poems of Emily Dickinson   Copland
           INTERMISSION

II. From *Sneden's Landing* Variations   Thomson
      Courtship of the Mongly Bongly Bo

III. Three poems of Paul Goodman   Rorem
      Youth, day, old age and night
      See how they love me
      The Serpent

Final data to be entered in the saga of "big business" concerts: in the 1970s it has become financially necessary for certain managements, formerly devoted to serious music, to send out pop and rock artists.

INNOVATIONS

Recognition of today's scant interest in song recital does not mean surrender. We believe that in the long run, given better recital skills on the part of the singer (with a big emphasis on acting) and careful programming, interest can again be stimulated—and not only from sophisticated enthusiasts. Given the time, perhaps by some kind of sponsorship, we can continue to make some new converts; we can forge a new audience who can be led to enjoy unfamiliar music, to appreciate the art of recital.

Programming skills can be divided into two types: new ideas for whole programs and the detailed implementation of those ideas in song-to-song and group-to-group decisions.[4]

Using larger forces, e.g., vocal chamber ensemble compositions, for part of the program; adding another singer, or singers, for all or part; planning programs around a theme; making a big effort to program a lot of songs in the English language or translated into English; deliberately broadening the scope of the repertoire to include some less than "masterpieces" of song—all of these principles applied properly can arouse the interest of a mixed audience, providing of course that the singing, acting, and musical tools of the singer are up to snuff.

Theme recitals are well-accepted and lend themselves easily to good publicity—in itself a major issue to be coped with successfully. One type of theme can easily be found in the work of a poet set by many composers. A balance between unity and variety is inherent in such a plan.

---

4. Eminent voice teacher Daniel Ferro reminds us that recital themes and innovations should be carefully geared to individual talents.

Grieg, Honegger, Satie (and many more, probably) set Hans Christian Anderson's words.

Charles Griffes and John Alden Carpenter both set Oscar Wilde.

Bartók, Schubert, Castelnuovo-Tedesco, Wolf, Schumann, Dallapiccola, and Rimsky-Korsakov all set Heinrich Heine.

And so on. Most intriguing is the discovery of an unexpected name in such a list. Knowing that Rimsky-Korsakov and Dallapiccola set Heine poetry is, for instance, useful to the program or the group built around this idea. (See Chapter 11.) Who in addition to Barber, Krenek, Badings, and Martino set James Joyce? Who besides Chausson set Maeterlinck? Who in addition to Grieg set Ibsen? Worth examining in this light for workable possibilities are Robert Frost, Hölderlin, and Malarmé.

Cathy Berberian, who consistently draws a large audience because of her programming and her artistry, has for years done a fin-de-siècle program in costume with a partial set. She reports that she has a recital called "Folklore and the Composer," with works in twenty languages by twenty-three composers, including Szymanowski, Beethoven, and Milhaud. Two other ideas she has already implemented are her "Secondhand Songs" program, composed of songs that were not always in that form, and a recital of works by women composers, soon to be published. A program with more than one singer is well-suited to themes such as The Lied Tradition from Mozart to Weill; German Secular Music of the Late Renaissance (using Renaissance instruments); church seasons such as Advent to Epiphany, or Lent and Good Friday (also with instruments); The Sound of Pictures (bringing to life the "sound" of musical images in paintings, or working in subjects from paintings in local museums).[5]

A fertile musical imagination can find many such ideas for theme recitals, erudite or otherwise. If one toyed with philosphical and musical thoughts such as (1) who were the composers who followed where Stravinsky led; (2) what Stravinsky took from the techniques of other composers such as Rimsky-Korsakov and Schoenberg; (3) collaborations between Stravinsky and other professionals such as Picasso; (4) what artists proceeded in the wake of Picasso; (5) the elements of folk music used by Stravinsky, and so on—who knows what theme for either a group or a recital might ensure.

Eva Gautier is described, by those who were privileged to benefit from her wisdom, as possessor of the greatest collection of song literature. She was able to put her hands on any choice within minutes. She is quoted by the fine American baritone Lawrence Chelsi as saying, "Be brave! Do not separate yourself from the mainstream of American mu-

---

5. These interesting theme programs are offered by the New York Soloists Quartet under Gomer Rees's management.

sic." Although she reached an advanced age in our lifetimes, having made her debut at Queen Victoria's funeral, she was not as old-fashioned as we. Taking her own advice, she included "Alexander's Ragtime Band" in her program at Yale. She bolstered her point by relating how Ravel, too, was so interested in the directions being taken by American music that he once asked her for an introduction to George Gershwin.

Theodore Uppmann, who created the part of Billy Budd in Britten's opera of that name, regularly does a group called "Two Soliloquies"— from *Billy Budd* and from *Carousel*. Alan Titus performed his New York debut recital with an accent on jazz, including compositions by Milhaud, Weill, W.C. Handy, and Joplin. There is pop music and there is good popular music. Some of it deserves to be included in programs. At least it must not be excluded out of hand. Open your mind to the possibility, and then make the decision as to its musical worth.

So few listeners have the background to understand what is done in a song recital that pressing for American and British music and/or English translations of other song literature becomes a forceful method for reviving or creating an interest in song rectial. There are various valid points of view with regard to English translations. Consider them before determining whether to exercise your option. What follows are five principal arguments advanced by what shall be designated the Original-Language-Only proponents each followed immediately by a rebuttal typical of their opponents.

1. Singers' words cannot be understood anyway, so why lose the beauty of the original setting?

> Not always true. But even if true, most people answer, "If I am not going to understand the words, then I would rather not understand them in my own language."

2. The English language, being unmusical, is vastly inferior to other languages for singing. Its paucity of vowels, especially pure ones, and its overabundance of consonants render it unmelodious and difficult to sing.

> To demolish this argument one need look no further than the wealth of successful music originally written in English—Elizabethan songs, Handel's *Messiah* and other oratorios, Gilbert and Sullivan works, contemporary English and American compositions, Broadway musical comedy. We have been overmodest in England and America about singing in our own language. Every other nation takes for granted that things will be sung in the language of their country. Any language can be eloquent and musical to those who understand it. Even the sibilants and gutturals in Greek and German do not repulse those who speak the language.

3. Because they sound clumsy, wooden, labored, or commonplace, many English translations destroy the mood created by the music.

Yes, some are less than elegant or moving. But this does not mean that there should be no translations, only that there should be better ones. Some publishers are gradually replacing the old translations with new ones. Composers themselves certainly never—to our knowledge—opted for leaving their works in the original language, if, on the occasions of performance, there existed an opportunity for them to be translated into the language of the country.[6] When the audience knows the language or the song well, a translation is not necessary, but an unsophisticated audience must understand it or it loses interest.[7]

4. Most English translations are inadequate at the outset. To dovetail the prosody and phrasing of the composer's vocal line in a glove-like fit with a literal and correct translation is virtually impossible.

It is difficult, but not impossible, to translate poems so well that the original meaning is disclosed without injury to the music. How literal it can be is another question. Sometimes an idiomatic expression of the general meaning, while safeguarding the musical line as conscientiously as possible, is more important.

For example, one might choose in a recitative to modify the music (let us say, two sixteenths for one eighth) for the sake of the text, but in an aria or song the line and subtleties of the music are too important to the composer to justify rhythmic or musical changes. In a good translation the close relationship between text and music can be preserved.

5. The specific words and/or syllables that the composer had in mind when he wrote his music are destroyed by substituting English words.

Sometimes this is true. When true, you must weigh the gains against the loss to the audience members who would not have understood the text in the original language. (Only when the audience can listen in the original language is there no loss.) The subtle association of the original word with the original music is less crucial than connection between the text meaning and its music. Very often the musical happenings only make sense in the light of the inner life of the text. Therefore, enjoyment and understanding frequently hinge upon

6. Menotti saw personally to the French translation of his works when they traveled to Paris. Schoenberg requested that *Pierrot Lunaire* be done in the language of the country even though he was, by his own admission, gratified at his ability to be inspired by just the first few lines of poetry.

7. Mozart wrote in Italian when his work was intended for courts where foreign languages were *de rigueur*, but wrote in German when the composition was intended for the regular German-speaking public.

knowledge of the text. To an English-speaking audience more is gained than is lost by telling the tale in English.

It quickly becomes apparent that the task of providing an expert translation—whether or not one accepts the premise of its advisability—is a formidable one. Richard Dyer-Bennet, who in 1974 made a complete English translation of *Die schöne Müllerin*, gives his own guidelines: (1) if not singable above all else, then all other factors are meaningless; (2) it must sound as though the music had been fitted to it (that is, the new poetic images must be equivalent to the originals and the prosodical arrangment of stresses and accents must match the original music); (3) the rhyme-scheme of the original poetry must be kept because it gives shape to the phrases; and (4) liberties must be taken with the literal meaning when the first three requirements cannot otherwise be met. Mr. Dyer-Bennet counts as successful a translation that is "singable, reasonably accurate, and modestly poetic." One must agree.

Most objections to singing in English come from those cultivated individuals whose love for the original words will not countenance an inferior poetic substitution. Those who come to hear Schubert Lieder, for instance, come to hear them in German because they know the literature and the language. Because we, too, are members of a specialized audience, we would prefer to hear Lieder in German. But as teachers and musicians who wish the song recital to prosper, we hesitate to close the door on any potentially helpful possibility. Singing Schubert in English might reach those who would not otherwise come at all and might eventually wean them to original language listening. It is interesting to remember that England and America are the only countries to believe that songs must be done in the original language.

When the broad subject of innovations is opened for discussion, the first suggestion is generally to transform, adapt, or alter in some way the song recital form itself. Many musicians have tampered with the form lately, and many are considering doing so. It is quite possible that this may prove necessary.

Lukas Foss's original idea has been successfully adapted to a marathon program for more than one singer (One comes and goes as one wishes, pays only for the part one stays to hear). Changing the name from "song recital," which according to Cathy Berberian scares some people off, to "an evening of song" or "a Baroque matinee" or the like, has been suggested. Abandoning the fixed and unconditional principle that only one singer and one accompanist are permitted is promisingly healthy. The tactic of programming singer plus chamber group, singer plus another singer in duet or joint recitals is already so prevalent as to be almost taken for granted.

Many singers and educators are excited by the idea of vocal lecture-recitals. Noncommercial televison can play an important role. It is very interesting to hear artists speaking seriously about their performance and their program especially when musical authority is combined with an outgoing nature and a spirited wit. Cathy Berberian has an idea for a vocal lecture-recital on this subject: the historical use of the voice. The format of lecture-recital would lend itself very well to theme ideas.

Including dance or poetry on a recital—Renaissance vocal music side-by-side with Renaissance dance, or poetry readings together with poetry set to music and sung—are extremely attractive programming ideas. A program was presented in New York by poets reading potential song texts and libretti from their works (with a special invitation to composers), followed by a short program of chamber music.

Companion programs open up many possibilities. Envisage the poetry of Garcia Lorca set to music and performed in a recital the day before the opening of a play by Garcia Lorca in the same locale, or music of oriental inspiration sung and played in a recital during a two-week exhibition of oriental brocades at the local museum. Most of us are quite aware of Charles Ives's predilection for overlaying familiar tunes, in fragments and in toto, on his original themes. Why not put together companion programs linking his music with art—one lecture-recital discussing and demonstrating how in Ives's songs these tunes emerge from the surrounding motives, varied continually by melodic and harmonic means; one art lecture-cum-slides pointing out similarities between these Ivesian techniques and those used by the artists who managed to produce, in their many paintings of one particular scene, qualities of individuality with each repetition (Cézanne being one such painter).

Here is a less conventional example. After surveying the following list of related artistic activities one could find many ideas for a special "Blank Art" weekend festival of companion programs (using whatever forces are locally available) into which your program could fit.

The Ramones rock ensemble plays rock with no more than two or three chords, consisting of the same short phrase repeated over and over at a constant dynamic level.

Michael Snow makes experimental films in which a single image is seen on the screen for ten or twenty minutes.

Robert Wilson directs tableaux vivants that are totally without movement.

LaMonte Young composes music such as one piece in which a 60-cycle hum is supposed to be prolonged eternally.

Trish Brown choreographs "accumulation dances" that consist of short gestures endlessly strung together in a chain.

Minimalists like Barnett Newman, Jules Olitski, and Kenneth Noland, are producing art that others call non-art.

K.C. and the Sunshine Band's recordings are made of repetitive background punctuated by repeated catch-phrases.

Richard Hell has written a rock anthem called "The Blank Generation."

Intra-art programs can be put together from such sources.

Vocal composers can also help bring about a brighter future for the song recital. Debussy, Busoni, Scriabin, Prokofiev, Ives, Bartók, Britten, Poulenc, and Hindemith were some of the last to compose large bodies of music for soloists. When chided by singers who ask for more good songs in English, vocal composers of today often reply that it does not pay to write songs these days. We remind these composers that there is one form of vocal music that has been exploited relatively little. It is what is called, for lack of a better term, the "scena." It is essentially a concert piece for voice, rather lengthy, in which the protagonist develops thoroughly a full psychological and dramatic situation. Verdi's "L'Esule" (1839), although almost a cantata, illustrates the form. Spontini and Niedermeyer were among the first French composers to exceed the limits of the "romance," although they still titled it so, by giving it a richer, orchestra-like accompaniment, making it resemble a "scène." The scene, so popular in France until 1845, was a free structure whose accompaniment imitated the orchestra while the vocal part included recitative and aria. Longer scenes might today be called dramatic cantatas. Berlioz, with his "scène lyrique," "Cleopâtre," has given us one beautiful example, in spite of the fact that its adaptability to the piano is doubtful. Although not elaborate scenes, one might place in this category certain extended ballads and concert arias by Schubert and Loewe and Beethoven's "Der Wachtelschlag."

Poulenc, following in the former French tradition of the "scène," composed at the end of his life a magnificent example of the genre, "La Dame de Monte Carlo." Samuel Barber, no doubt recognizing the principle, as did Poulenc, that the lyric scene is a more difficult problem when written for the piano, composed his "Andromache to her Son" for soprano and orchestra. Both Sir Arthur Bliss, with his scena "The Enchantress" (Theocritus text), and Ernst Krenek, in his Opus 57, "Monolog der Stella" (Goethe text), were intrigued with this form. Stockhausen wrote "Spiral" for one singer and short wave; Joseph Horovitz has written a scena for mezzo called "Lady Macbeth"; Nicola Le Fann's scena "Il Cantico dei Cantici II" is for unaccompanied female voice.

In any event, here certainly is a market for composers and the possibilities are endless. Why not a scena for more than one voice, such as Jack Beeson's "Piazza Piece" for tenor and soprano with piano?

Rebikov's "Vocal Scenes for Voice and Piano" are actually intended to be performed with simple scenery plus an extra actor who speaks or is mute. The singer interested in bringing the full artillery of his acting ability to the recital stage may find within this type of vocal composition all he could wish for.

Innovations with lighting offer other possibilities. Rimsky-Korsakov and Scriabin created charts of colors associated with special keys; Scriabin's "Prometheus" was scored to include a keyboard of light, throwing colors on a screen; a color score accompanied Schoenberg's short allegorical music drama *Die glückliche Hand*; and Nono and Berio experimented with multi-media works. Works of this type or new ones for voice and light-symphonies could be written and programmed. Or, more simple to implement, why not different lights for each group of songs?

A prime objective for many musicians is to break down the excessive formality of the recital. "Performance of Ives' vocal music is still too much influenced by song recital formalities."[8] In one performance of Ives's "The Last Gamboleer" scored for violins, piccolo, and kazoo, placed as the last number on the recital, the entire instrumental ensemble was led off stage in Pied Piper fashion by the singer (doubling at the kazoo), to the utter delight of the erudite audience.

A bare stage, a big black piano, one singer, and one pianist all alone for ninety minutes can be glorious when the voice, skills, music and interpretation are world-famous. But changing the dress between halves— not really a corrupt practice—might help a performer not quite so spectacularly endowed. At least the audience, jaded by many hundred thousand dollar television extravaganzas, will see a new picture for the second half. Every ounce of glamor that does not destroy the dignity of the music should be welcome, since it heightens the excitement of the recital.

Another effective way to break down formality is to talk more from the stage. Many musicians suggest that translating orally makes two contributions: it adds informality while giving the all-important translations in the most palatable way. Prejudice against speaking from the platform about the music is hard to overcome in sophisticated musical centers, but how can its efficacy and interesting aspects be denied? Let us only be sure that the performer has the necessary skills and uses them in good taste.

In the electronic era why should the use of multimedia effects be suspect on recitals? Use of contemporary music, such as voice with tape or prepared piano, could add great variety to ordinary programs. Cathy Berberian says that she always takes care to program an easy-to-take group on either side of a new or particularly difficult work—thus insuring a just hearing for the composition by avoiding the tensions and de-

8. Peter Yates, *Twentieth Century Music* (New York: Minerva Press, 1968), p. 265.

fense mechanisms that could accumulate in an audience if preceding works were also difficult. Mixed-media compositions with live and recorded music, actors, singers, projected slides, motion pictures, lights, or all of the above are open to various interpretations. This gives creativeness to the audience; sometimes they are invited to interreact with the performers. What an excitement one composition of this sort could engender by giving the recital its own "happening."

The whole art of publicizing recital events must be rethought. Once the program can offer an unusual event, it must be handled to best advantage in the press. Composers of new pieces ought to be persuaded to be present and talk about the work; the promise of their presence must be exploited in the media. A dignified announcement is not enough to wipe out recital's image as tedious or uneventful. Happily, in the media one now sees the beginnings of creative advertising in which the newest camera techniques and the newest advertising styles are exploited in order to give effective public notice of solo musical events. Some methods formerly reserved for rock musicians are being adopted by serious artists. With Mostly Mozart T-shirts highly visible in Lincoln Center Plaza how long will it be before we see a Hermann Prey poster or a Janet Baker bumper sticker?

Happily we do witness here and there signs of imagination and some fine experimentation among American singers. Craig Timberlake, when chairman of the Music Department at Columbia Teachers' College, during his singing of Sauguet's three unaccompanied songs for bass, showed great originality in his use of an overhead projector displaying the actual music as he sang. What a wonderful way to extend enjoyment of a difficult contemporary composition at first hearing! A well-known concert baritone used slide projections of the appropriate French art masterpieces while singing Poulenc's *Le Travail du Peintre*. An opera singer who was not particularly gifted as a song recitalist built a fascinating program by performing five famous operatic scenes, discussing them before singing, while at the same time applying the suitable makeup in front of the engrossed audience. Elaine Bonazzi, the brilliant singing actress, suggests that in doing experiments of this type the singer should make a point of using a qualified stage director.

To innovate, it may be necessary to bend the nineteenth-century tradition somewhat. We believe that the worthwhile goal of reviving interest in song recital should be served by any means—superior skills and good taste being the only immutable barriers to be observed. Any visual reinforcement that heightens the excitement should be permissible.

A good way to make a beginning, it has been suggested, would be to return to the setting where evenings of song took root—the salon. The many persuasive arguments for returning to the salon have their origins in the facts of late twentieth-century life. As exemplified by the Schu-

bertiads, song evenings flourished in very good health so long as they re-
mained in smallish places. At the time of this writing, financial statements prove that only a handful of world-famous artists can fill a hall of
the size necessary to make a reasonable profit for those concerned. Since
smaller is really better and larger is not feasible, why not find a way to
bring up a new audience in the proper small setting? Nostalgia for the
earlier decades of the twentieth century is everywhere evident in the entertainment world. Grass-roots support for the arts is in a developing
state in America. Could not the song recital in some way catch on to the
general upswing found locally in support for the performing arts? To
begin without a lot of money would not be an insurmountable task. The
scenario might go like this: A very experienced singer who has retired
from active professional life to teach in a metropolitan center eventually
moves to a small town in a neighboring state. There he builds up a studio
of promising students. Some years later, two youngish pianists, fleeing
big-city life, come to this town to live. After the pleasures of bucolic life
lose their impact, thoughts return to the joys of music. All three deplore
the stupefying lack of local cultural entertainment. Soon they improvise
a far from rigid schedule of musical evenings among their three houses—
sometimes joint, sometimes solo performances. Sooner or later some
local musicians from neighboring towns are invited to attend the musicales. Inevitably they are included in the programming, as are the more
polished students of the various teachers. Children of the performers and
the invited guests are encouraged to attend. Refreshments are served.
Programming is very carefully screened for utmost variety, so as not to
scare off neophytes in the art of listening to live serious music. Those
who speak well are asked to speak about the compositions. A composer
living nearby is invited to perform his works and discuss them. Soon the
houses prove too small to accommodate those who wish to be present
and the programs are moved to the local library. With the larger room,
young recitalists beginning to make a reputation are brought in as guest
artists.

The end of the story is not an end. The original three professional
musicians, having pointed the way, live to see the well-attended concerts
become a regular feature of community life in the five companion towns,
sparking an interest in solo recital and live music again. Residents are
given active pleasure in the music as well as a new-found reverence for
their own local arts. Families sharing music in the home, amateur musicians striving to raise their standards and their skills, children becoming
aware of music naturally because parents are performing, community
pride in fellow citizens as artists, breaking down the typical American
notion that only imported virtuosos are worth hearing, learning to value
local artists who stay in town as much as those who leave, pursuing an
understanding of the music of our century with avant-garde composi-

tional techniques explained by the composer himself, discovering that pleasure in music increases by sharing in it—is it possible that all these benefits might come to the community that embraces the old-fashioned virtues of evening musicales?

Lest we appear to look at our scenario with glasses far too rosy, let us remind each other that in small towns scattered all over this nation there are village music men and women who follow their unsung mission with boundless devotion and personal modesty. One such person is John Burnett, conductor of the Danbury (Connecticut) Community Orchestra. "He is a legend; he feels that the whole community should be permeated with music and that everyone is inherently musical; he has given a helping hand to every young talent who came through Fairfield County in the last three decades; even the milkman comes to sing songs at his house,"[9] comments one of his musical colleagues. Igor Kipnis, the harpsichordist, is one of Mr. Burnett's young talents who went on to make a professional career of distinction. The maestro himself insists that *his* students adore Vivaldi, Handel, and Bach, and would be bored stiff with the "hearts and flowers stuff" that most junior orchestras play. Most teachers and directors make a mistake when they underestimate youngsters and beginners, he says.

The Orchestra of Our Time, formerly a chamber orchestra based in Philadelphia from 1964 on, moved in July of 1978 to the South Bronx, an unlikely choice it would seem. Joel Thome, its founder and director, explained the move as stemming from a philosophical approach he had developed over the years about "the relationship of the orchestra to our times. I feel that it must be involved in community activity. We have been doing this already. In addition to college and university residencies, where contemporary music was the concern, we have had community residencies as far distant as Jackson, Michigan, and Huntsville, Alabama. In Philadelphia we have done work in prisons, helping inmates to come together to rehearse and perform.

"The image of the South Bronx needs to be turned around. All one hears about is its negative aspect. But there is an incredible spirit in the people; there's a tremendous musical impulse there, a great deal that arises culturally."[10] Although Mr. Burnett's and Mr. Thome's special interests are orchestral literature, just imagine what *one* such dynamo whose field was vocal music could do for song recital if he turned his formidable energies to it.

As one surveys the financial situation facing all the arts, the salient fact of the third quarter of the twentieth century is that the arts are more popular than ever but sponsored with proportionately fewer private dollars all the time. It is generally believed that federal and corporation dol-

9. Robert Sherman, "A Real-Life Music Man," *The New York Times*, August 7, 1977.
10. "The South Bronx," *The New York Times*, July 9, 1978.

lars are the only answer to lessening private support. This is largely true for schools also. The National Endowment for the Arts (NEA) is buying art as any other commodity, but handicrafts and ethnic programs are included in the funding available, thus cutting back the effective support for the arts. In addition, the NEA has a new matching grant policy. Since the local groups must now hire fund raisers, their expenses are higher, and the administrators spend their time primarily making sure that art is a paying business. Corporations give the largest part of their money to television where it is considered advertising. In per capita contributions to the arts as of 1977, the United States still holds its position at the bottom of the list of all major countries. These grim facts pertain even to the very popular arts, such as theater and the visual arts, but most of all to the solo recital, which in the United States surely has the very last priority of all cultural entertainment.

Now that financial problems of the arts are more pressing, philosophical discussions linked with government spending are sure to center on whether standards can be maintained despite wide dissemination of cultural activity on a grassroots level. In cultural circles, fears of "elitism" alternate with fears of "populism"—just when the arts are under pressure to attract an audience sufficiently affluent to be capable of contributing to funds matched by government and foundations. We do not believe that a policy of disseminating culture to reach the widest number is going to corrupt high culture, nor will it prevent creativity of the highest order from flourishing. Dance, an art form once stereotyped as elitist, is now enjoying unprecedented popularity, with its values untainted thereby. "Culture is popular through whom it reaches, not through its very nature," said André Malraux while he was France's Minister of Culture. No sector of society has an exclusive hold on good or bad art. The real point is not whether Gershwin is superior to Mozart. The point is that gardening and yoga should not be confused with culture. The official mind has of late confused leisure activities, and how to manage leisure time, with the problems of culture.[11] "One is merely the means to the other," says Malraux.

We believe that the song recital can, as did ballet and modern dance, build for itself a new audience and (assuming a mandatory improvement in recital standards, with a heavy emphasis on varied programming) educate it in the art. Ballet accomplished this feat while under a sponsorship that afforded the necessary time to build its new audience and to educate them by high quality performance, varied programming, and a complete lack of snobbery to appreciate the art.

While few will challenge the claim that, through the NEA, the

11. In 1973 a study commissioned by the American Council for the Arts in Education concluded that more Americans were interested in the arts because they engaged in "amateur and hobby-oriented activities."

government is giving more money to the arts than ever before, many would take exception to the way both government and foundation money is dispersed. Rather than using these funds to subsidize further study for young singers, we would like to suggest an underwriting of concert tours for young, well-trained singers in towns where there are no present provisions for such events.[12] This could help bring about a grass-roots revival of song recital culture, while at the same time giving pleasure to audiences otherwise unaware or deprived of the art, and giving to the young singers room for growing and experience itself. Canada, a model worthy of emulation in this respect, has long subsidized its artists in the best way—creating and funding opportunities for them to sing publicly.

Universities and colleges, once the bastions of musical conservatism, began in the 1960s to welcome younger avant-garde composers. They were subsidized and gifted with a very important commodity—a built-in audience. Periodically they made forays out of academic seclusion to give the world infusions of the "new." Thus did universities make an immense contribution to twentieth-century music.

If, as Nicolas Nabokov[13] says, "one of the two great events of the twentieth century is American music taking off," why cannot a new American recital form, unhampered by tradition, be devised? The university is the logical place to find an inventor, plus the knowledgeable, loving hands to nurture it. The audiences are there (most solo recitals take place in universities and colleges); the forces are there (artists-in-residence, student soloists, visiting artists, accompanists, instrumentalists, good teachers in all disciplines); the resources are there (rehearsal rooms, libraries, auditoriums of proper size, good pianos, ancient instruments); and the new composers are there!

Concert managers generally concede that the stronghold of American recital art today lies not with a general public that buys tickets to the big city concert hall but rather in university and college communities, the major purchasers and presenters of music today. Recitals are usually required for voice students. Recitals by faculty and visiting artists are many. Furthermore, students more than ever before have power to exert their influence. It is our opinion that the future of the recital can be rooted here, where the climate and opportunity exist.

There can be no question that the pre-television days of extensive recital tours have passed. The university is now the only place, economically feasible, in which to restudy and revive the recital form. All means for dramatically extending recital repertoire are available in academe. Ample opportunity exists for training the singer-student, not only in the

---

12. Some states' councils for the arts do contribute some partial funding in this direction.
13. Author of the introduction to Virgil Thomson's *American Music since 1910* (New York: Holt, Rinehart, and Winston, 1971).

obvious skills but also in background knowledge and peripheral disciplines. Implied is the scheduling of courses on the recital art with its attendant components, acting techniques, accompanying ensemble, etc. When taught by competent teachers who have had practical experience, as is done in many universities today, such courses accomplish a great deal. At universities, song recital is often the only form open to vocal students wishing to work on aspects of public performance.

Professor Lunkley, quoted above, adds these à propos thoughts:

> We, as teachers of singing, should try to help our students, their families and interested friends, understand the style and appropriateness of the solo recital as an intimate event as opposed to the constant flow of visual circuses with which they are confronted on television. We need to help people understand and experience the excitement and satisfaction of the smaller event. Our efforts to support local concert presentations, particularly solo recitals, should never cease. We need to place these events before our students, and assist them to attend. Our own recitals and those of our students must be planned in such a way that they prove to be very special musical moments for those attending. We must accept the responsibility for helping our students see the diverse possibilities of song program planning and encourage them to find repertoire that is challenging, appropriate and stimulating for their audiences.

In summation, let us look to the college campus as the place to stress new performance forms for recital, to encourage skills in chamber music and small ensemble groups, to study the ramifications of programming and its impact upon the audiences, to create new art forms, to promulgate the cause of new music, to concentrate the scholarship of the musicologists upon the art of performance, to prepare performers in the art of involving audiences of all ages by talking to them on and off the platform, to promote a cross-fertilization of artists.[14]

The United States is just beginning to have a music history and a lot of it is being written in the universities. We have a new generation of teachers who are not afraid to teach the vocalism of contemporary music. (Their functions for the first time include instilling an understanding of *live* performance.) Since World War II a large proportion of first-rate composers and teachers have been domiciled in the United States. The New Music, the new forms, the new performers, the new audiences thirsty for avant-garde music are largely located in the university and college communities. These "captive" audiences can be shown (only with the highest standards for performance skills, however) how the great art

14. We are beholden to Jerrold Ross of New York University for much of this summation, which articulates brilliantly our views on the subject, from his article: "The Performing Arts on Campus," *College Music Symposium* vol. 17 no. 2, Fall, 1977. p. 77–82.

of the recital ought to be, and they in turn may generate an enthusiasm that is infectious.

We are now old enough as a nation; we have here everything we need to make a new structure for the American song recital. Marcella Sembrich did her part to change things, and she did it single-handedly. The old form, which is, alas, close to moribund, was served well by its expert practitioners—Pears, Fischer-Dieskau, Tourel, Souzay, Schwarzkopf, Frijsch, Anderson. Why not a new formula now? Not only are composers creating new musical techniques, but performance forms themselves have undergone mutation. This is a time, as in the sixteenth century, when tradition is being assessed; much of it is being rejected. Short of breaking completely with tradition, perhaps the song recital can at least accommodate the facts of the twentieth-century life. We hope that in five or ten years some of the critical and pessimistic statements of this book will prove to be obsolete, for that would indicate that a renaissance of the song recital had indeed been accomplished.

Appendix

GUIDE TO USE

Composers' names appear in alphabetical order and, in the case of early composers, are followed by their dates. Under each name the compositions are listed in alphabetical order of the titles. To the degree that the information is available, you will find:

on line 1:   the title of the composition

the opus number, catalogue number, or volume number

the name of the poet(s) or text source

the number of songs

the language(s) of the text

the comparative difficulty of the composition

the duration of the composition

the type of composition

on line 2:   the voice(s) category

the accompanying instrument(s)

on line 3:   the editor(s)

the publisher(s)

the publisher's agent(s)

Generally speaking, where proper information is available, and unless contradicted by an indication in parentheses, the language of the title (line 1) is the language of the text. Titles are alphabetized as they appear on concert programs. The articles a, an, the (in all languages) are placed in their proper order; they are not relegated to the end, separated by a comma (e.g., *The Nursery* under T; "Die Stadt" under D). Numbers, when they appear as the first word of a title, are alphabetized in the language of the title (e.g., *3 Lieder* under D (rei); *6 Canciones* under S(eis); *5 Mélodies* under C (inq); *4 Songs* under F(our).

A slash between indications of voice categories or accompanying instruments (line 2) means that either the first or the second is suitable; (e.g., S/T indicates *either* Soprano or Tenor; fl/S rec indicates that *either* flute *or* Soprano recorder is suitable). A semi-colon between indications of voice categories means that *both* the first *and* the second ranges are available; (e.g., high, pf; low, pf means that the composition comes in *both* voice ranges). When the two voice categories are written without punctuation a vocal ensemble is indicated; (e.g., SA means a Soprano-Alto duet; highmedlow indicates a trio for high, medium and low voices). The words *any voice* generally describe the vocal requirement for a contemporary composition where any voice that *can* sing it *may* sing it. The indication *all voices* means that all voices can sing it in the key printed or, failing that, that it can easily be transposed to suit each individual voice.

When accompanying instruments are followed by parentheses enclosing other instruments, this indicates that one instrumentalist plays *both* or *all* instruments listed (e.g., fl (picc, A fl) means that the flutist also plays a piccolo and an Alto flute during the composition).

A limited amount of cross-referencing has been done. Those vocal chamber music or vocal ensemble compositions that are cyclic or contain multiple individual components (with the exception of cantatas) have been cross-filed under both Song Cycles and Voice with Instruments, or under both Song Cycles and Voice with Other Voices. Compositions for vocal ensemble that have instrumental accompaniment have been cross-filed under both Voice with Other Voices and Voice with Instruments.

If difficulty in locating any listed work for voice with other voices is encountered at the retail music store level, check the *octavo* editions of that publisher. Most compositions intended for 2-, 3-, and 4-part choruses can be sung as solo vocal duets, trios, and quartets. Do not, in other words, assume that a composition for vocal ensemble is out of print until you have checked the octavo edition.

The publisher's name (line 3) is in capital letters followed by the agent's name in parentheses. Infrequently, the publisher in question has an agent or parent company which, in turn, has an agent. In such cases, the intermediary agent is omitted from the repertoire lists (although his name appears on the Publishers List). Thus, only the final American agent is indicated when listing each composition.

The legend OFC (Obtainable from the Composer) is used in the listing of unpublished works that are nevertheless obtainable from the composer, whom the reader may contact about obtaining materials, with the help of the address found under OFC in the Publishers List. AMC on line 3 of the listing refers to the American Music Center in New York. It indicates that the composition, even though unpublished or out of print, is in their library. Contact them for further information. The address is found in the Publishers List, which starts on p. 544. Other out of print compositions are marked NYP LIBE, indicating that they are in the New York Lincoln Center Library for the Performing Arts; they may well be found in libraries elsewhere. The legend LIBE C refers to the Library of Congress in Washington where all copyrighted works by American composers, published or unpublished, in or out of print, are filed.

At the end of each repertoire list (Song Cycles, Sets, and Collections, Voice with Instruments, Voice with Other Voices) will be found a corresponding, representative selection of volumes from various publishers. Each of these anthologies contains works by many composers. Those collections that are selected from the oeuvre of one composer will be found under his name in the alphabetical list proper (e.g., a collection of Schubert duets will be found under Schubert, Franz; a duet anthology by various German composers will be located at the end of the Voice with Other Voices list).

This volume does not purport to be a catalogue of published vocal works. Rather, we offer the repertoire lists as a general aid to programming. We have been compelled for reasons of limited space to keep the information spare and lacking in detail. Our aim, in the case of anthologies unified by subject rather than by one composer, is simply to call the reader's attention to the existence of such volumes and to suggest their general contents. For further details we recommend the large volume *Vocal Music in Print*, edited by Nardone and published by Musicdata, Inc., and the fully annotated, superb two-volume set *Repertoire for the Voice*, edited by Espina and published by Scarecrow Press, as well as the old standby, Sergius Kagen's *Music for the Voice*, published by Indiana University Press. Consult also the master catalogues at your retail music store, where all composers contained within such volumes should be noted. Do not neglect your library, where you have the added advantage of finding the older, sometimes out of print anthologies.

LIST OF ABBREVIATIONS

A:	Agent:	**Bar**	baritone voice	**B tmb**	bass trombone
A	alto voice	**B**	bass	**bvl**	bass viol
acap	a cappella	**B-Bar**	bass-baritone		
accord	accordian	**bcl**	bass clarinet	**Cat**	Catalan
anon.	anonymous	**bfl**	bass flute	**cbsn**	contrabassoon
arr.	arranged by	**Braz**	Brazilian	**cel**	celeste
A sax	alto saxophone	**bsn**	bassoon	**cem**	cembalo

chamb	chamber	hpscd	harpsichord	qnt	quintet
Chin	Chinese	Hung	Hungarian	qt	quartet
cl	clarinet				
Col S	coloratura soprano	instr	instrument(s)	rec	recorder
		It	Italian	Russ	Russian
combo	combination	Jap	Japanese	S	soprano voice
cont	continuo			sac	sacred
Contr	contralto	kybd	keyboard	sax	saxophone
cym	cymbal	Lat	Latin	sep	separate(ly)
Czech	Czechoslovakian	low	low voice	Slav	Slavic
				Sp	Spanish
Dan	Danish	mand	mandoline	stgs	strings
diff	difficult	med	medium voice	stqt	string quartet
dm	drum	med dif	medium difficult	Supp	Supplement(s)
Dram S	dramatic soprano	med easy	medium easy	Swed	Swedish
		Mez	mezzo soprano	syn	synthesizer
dul	dulcimer	min	minute		
				T	tenor voice
ed.	editor, edited	narr	narrator	tamb	tambourine
elec	electronic	Nor	Norwegian	timp	timpani
Eng	English			tmb	trombone
enghn	english horn	ob	oboe	tpt	trumpet
eq	equal	obblig	obbligato	trans.	translated by
		OFC	Obtainable from Composer	treb	treble
Finn	Finnish			tri	triangle
fl	flute	Op.	Opus		
Flem	Flemish	opt	optional	var	various
Fr	French	orch	orchestra	vc(s)	voice(s)
		org	organ	vibra	vibraphone
Ger	German	orig	original	vla	viola
glock	glockenspiel			vln	violin
grp	group	perc	percussion	vol	Volume
gtr	guitar	pf	piano		
		pic	piccolo	ww	woodwind(s)
har	harmonized	Pol	Polish		
Heb	Hebrew	Port	Portuguese	Xmas	Christmas
high	high voice	pub	published	xylo	xylophone
hn	French horn				

REPERTOIRE LISTS

Voice with Instruments

ABBADO, MARCELLO:
  Cantata
    Female vc, 6 instr
        ZERBONI (A: Boosey)
  Ciapo
    Female vc, 9 instr
        ZERBONI (A: Boosey)
  15 Poesie T'ang

    Mez, fl, ob, cello, pf
        ZERBONI (A: Boosey)

ABSIL, JEAN:
  5 Mélodies
    Mez (1); Mez/Bar (2); T (1); S/T (1), stqt/pf
        CBDM (A: Elkan H)

ADAM, ADOLPHE-CHARLES:
Ah, vous dirai-je, maman (Mozart)
Bravura Variations
    high, (fl, pf)/(fl, 2 ob, 2 cl, 2 bsn, 2
    hn, stgs)
        ed. Schmidt RIES (A: Peters)

AHRENS, JOSEPH:
Angelus Silesius Liederbush (diff)
    S, org
        WILLY MULLER (A: Peters)
Regnum Dei (Lat) (med diff)
    Bar, fl, ob, enghn, hn, cl, bsn, kybd
        WILLY MULLER (A: Peters)

AHRENS, SIEGLINDE:
3 Songs on Latin Psalm Texts (diff)
    B, org
        WILLY MULLER (A: Peters)

AITKEN, HUGH:
Cantata #1 (Elizabethan poets) (diff)
    T, ob, vln, vla, cello
        OXFORD
Cantata #2 (Rilke) (diff)
    T, fl (pic), ob, vla, cello, bvl
        OXFORD
Cantata #3 (Barnstone) (med diff)
    T, ob, vla
        OXFORD
Cantata #4 (Machado) (med diff)
    S, fl, ob, cello, bvl
        OXFORD
Fables
    STTB, fl, 2 ob, bsn, stg qnt
        ELKAN V (A: Presser)

ALBERT, HEINRICH:
Ausgewählte Arien
    var (1-2) vcs, cont
        CONCORDIA
Der Mensch hat nichts so eigen (Dach)
(from THE GERMAN SOLO SONG)
    med, cont
        ARNO
11 Lieder (easy)
    high, cem, lute
        BARENREITER (A: Magna)
12 Duets for Two Equal and Mixed
Voices
    2 eq vcs, cont
        ed. Noack
        BARENREITER (A: Magna)

ALEXANDER, JOSEF:
Songs for Eve Vol 1, 2
    S, harp, vln, cello, enghn
        GENERAL (A: Schirmer)

ALGAZI, LEON:
4 Mélodies judéo-espagnoles
    med, pf/harp, (opt fl, cello)
        SALABERT

AMATO, BRUNO:
Two Together
    S, tuba
        SEESAW

AMBROSI, ALEARCO:
Voices
    S, narr, fl, ob, cl, bsn, vibra, org,
    cem, vln, vla, cello, bvl
        SONZOGNO (A: Belwin)

AMES, WILLIAM:
Among the Gods
    S, cl, stqt
        ACA

AMLIN, MARTIN:
Black Riders
    A, pf, cello, harp, vibra
        SEESAW
Requiem
    A, pf, perc
        SEESAW

AMRAM, DAVID:
3 Songs for America (8 min) (diff)
    B, (fl, ob/enghn, cl/bcl, hn, bsn, 5
    stgs)/pf
        PETERS

ANDERS, E.:
Flötenlieder für Sopran, Flöte, und
Klavier Op. 109
    S, fl, pf
        ZIMMER (A: Peters)

ANDERSON, BETH:
An Argument (easy)
    bvl, tuba
        ACA
He Says He's Got
    Mex, gtr
        ACA
Music for Myself (diff)
    Mez, vibra
        ACA
Paranoia
    Mez, 2 fl/pf
        ACA
She Wrote
    Female vc, 2 vln, elec tape
        ACA
Tulip Clause (diff)
    T, A fl, bcl, cl, T sax, cello, org, bvl,
    timp, elec tape
        ACA
Woman Rite
    Mez, elec org
        ACA

ANDERSON, T. J.:
Beyond Silence (Hanson) (15 min)
    T, cl, tmb, vla, cello, pf
        ACA

ANDERSON, T. J.: (cont'd.)

Block Songs (Lomack)
high, Children's toys (pitch pipe,
jack-in-the-box, musical busy box)
ACA
Variations on a theme by M. B. Tolson
(cantata)
S, vln, cello, A sax, tpt, tmb, pf
ACA

ANDRIESSEN, HENDRIK:

Cantique Spirituel
S, pf/org
ALSBACH (A: Peters)
Cantique Spirituel
S/T, stgs
DONEMUS (A: Peters)
Crucem Tuam (sacred)
A, stgs
DONEMUS (A: Peters)
Fiat Domine (sacred)
Mez, stgs
DONEMUS (A: Peters)
Miroir de Peine
S, stgs
DONEMUS (A: Peters)
O Sacrum Convivium
S, org
DONEMUS (A: Peters)
3 Romantic Songs
Mez, fl, ob, pf
DONEMUS (A: Peters)
3 Sonnets Spirituels
high, org
DONEMUS (A: Peters)

ANDRIESSEN, JURIAAN:

To Wet a Widow's Eye
AT, cl, perc, gamba
DONEMUS (A: Peters)

ANDRIESSEN, WILLEM:

3 Liederen
Med, 2 fl, 2 ob, 2 cl, 2 bsn, 4 hn, 2
tpt, timp, stgs (also pf)
DONEMUS (A: Peters)

ANERIO, GIOVANNI FRANCESCO:
(1567-1630)

3 geistliche Konzerte (Lat)
Bar, cont
ed. Ewerhart BIELER

ANGELINI, LOUIS:

Songs of Nod
low, fl/ob
AMC

ANTONIOU, THEODOR:

Chorochronos III
Bar, elec tape, pf, perc
BARENREITER (A: Magna)

Epilogue (Homer's ODYSSEY)
Mez, speaker, ob, hn, gtr, bvl, pf,
perc
BARENREITER (A: Magna)
Moirologhia for Jani Christou (Tolia)
Bar, (pf, fl, cl, gtr, 2 perc)/pf
BARENREITER (A: Magna)

ANTUNES, JORGE:

Microformobiles II
Bar, 5 instr
ZERBONI (A: Boosey)

APIVOR, DENIS:

6 Canciones de Federico García Lorca
Op. 8 a
med-high, gtr
BERBEN (A: Presser)

APONTE-LEDÉE, RAFAEL:

La Ventana Abierta
AAA, fl, cl, tpt, pf, 2 perc, vln,
cello, bvl
SEESAW

APOSTEL, HANS ERICH:

5 Songs for Medium Voice Op. 22
med, fl, cl, bsn
UNIVERSAL (A: E-A)

ARCADELT, JACQUES:

8 Madrigals
ATTB/4 instr
ed. Thomas LPME (A: Galaxy)

ARGENTO, DOMINICK:

Letters from Composers (real letters:
Chopin, Mozart, Schubert, Bach,
Debussy, Puccini, Schumann)
high, gtr
BOOSEY
To Be Sung upon the Water (Words-
worth)
high, pf, cl (opt bcl)
BOOSEY

ARIOSTI, ATTILIO: (1666-1740)

La Rosa (cantata) (ItGer)
high, 2 vln, cont
ed. Weiss DEUTSCHER (A: Broude)
L'Olmo (cantata) (ItGer)
high, 2 vln, cont
ed. Weiss DEUTSCHER (A: Broude)
Vuol ch'io parta
S, fl, ob, cl, bsn, harp
CARISCH (A: Boosey)

ARNE, THOMAS: (1710-1778)

A Wood Nymph (EngGer)
S, S rec/fl, kybd (opt 2 vln, cello)
ed. Salkeld SCHOTT (A: E-A)
Delia (cantata)
high, stgs, cont
SCHIRMER

The Morning
    S, S rec/fl, (opt stgs), kybd
            ed. Salkeld SCHOTT (A: E-A)
Under the Greenwood Tree
    S/T, S rec/fl, pf/hpscd (opt 2 vln,
    cello)
            ed. Bergmann SCHOTT (A: E-A)

ARNOLD, MALCOLM:
    5 William Blake Songs
        A, stgs
                                    EMI

ARRIGO, GIROLAMO:
    Episodi
        S, 4 fl (1 player)
                HEUGEL (A: Presser)

ASCONE, VINCENTE:
    Montes de mi Quequay
        med, pf qnt
                        SOUTHERN PEER

ASTON, PETER:
    My Dancing Day
        ST, fl, cl, 2 vln, vla, cello
                    NOVELLO (A: Belwin)

ATOR, JAMES:
    Haikansona
        Mez/A, ob, A sax, cello
                                SEESAW

ATTAIGNANT, PIERRE: (1552)
    Tant que vivrai
        med, gtr
            ed. Pujol ESCHIG (A: Associated)

AUBERT, LOUIS FRANÇOIS-MARIE:
    L'Heure Captive (Dommange)
        Bar, vln, pf
                    DURAND (A: Presser)

AVNI, TZVI:
    Collage
        med-high, fl, perc, elec tape
                                BOOSEY

AVSHALOMOV, JACOB:
    Little Clay Cart (ancient Hindu)
        med-high, fl, cl, perc, vln, cello,
        banjo/gtr
                                    ACA
    Two Old Birds (Hoskins)
        S, cl, pf
                                    ACA

AZPIAZU, JOSÉ DE:
    5 Canciones Populares Españolas (Sp)
        med-high, gtr
                        UME (A:Associated)
    La Flor de la Canela
        med-high, gtr
                    RICORDI (A: Schirmer)

Zorongo Gitano (Sp)
    med-high, gtr
                RICORDI (A: Schirmer)

BABBITT, MILTON:
    A Solo Requiem (Shakespeare, Hopkins
    Meredith, Stamm, Dryden)
        S, 2 pf
                                PETERS
    Composition for Tenor and 6 In-
    struments
        T, fl, ob, vln, vla, cello, hpscd
                        ASSOCIATED
                (A: Schirmer/Associated)
    Philomel (Hollander) (20 min)
        S, recorded S, elec tape
                        ASSOCIATED
                (A: Schirmer/Associated)
    Phonemena
        S, elec tape/pf
                                PETERS
    2 Sonnets
        Bar, cl, vla, cello
                                PETERS
    Vision and Prayer (Thomas) (15 min)
        S, synthesizer
                        ASSOCIATED
                (A: Schirmer/Associated)

BACH, C.P.E.: (1714–1788)
    Fecit Potentiam (MAGNIFICAT)
        Bar/B, 3 tpt, stgs
                BREITKOPF L (A: Broude)
    Ich töre öffnet euch (AUFERSTEHUNG
    UND HIMMELFAHRT) (sacred)
        Bar/B, 2 ob, 2 hn, 2 tpt, stgs
                BREITKOPF L (A: Broude)
    Phyllis und Thirsis (cantata)
        ST, 2 fl, cont
                                GERIG
        (A: Belwin); BREITKOPF L (A: Broude)

BACH, ERIK:
    Lamentation (Eng)
        S, perc, gtr
                                EGTVED

BACH, JOHANN CHRISTIAN: (1735–1782)
    Concert and Opera Arias (12)
        high, pf, opt fl/ob/vln
                    ed. Landshoff PETERS

BACH, JOHANN CHRISTIAN:
    4 Scotch Songs
        1: med, vln, vla, cello, ob, pf
        2: med, 2 vln, 2 fl, bsn
        3: med, 2 vln, 2 fl, bsn
        4: med, 2 vln, 2 fl, bsn
                        arr. Bach; ed.Fiske
                        SCHOTT (A: E-A)

BACH, JOHANN CHRISTIAN: (cont'd.)
Recitative and Aria of Arsinda (LA
CLEMENZA DI SCIPIONE) (It)
S, fl, ob, 2 hn, cem, vln, cello, stgs
PETERS
2 weltliche Arien
T, 2 fl, stgs, cem
ed. Walter
BREITKOPF L (A: Broude)

BACH, JOHANN CHRISTOPH: (1642-1703)
Ach, dass ich Wassers g'nug hätte
(cantata)
Mez/A, org, 5 stgs
BREITKOPF L (A: Broude)
Ach, dass ich Wassers g'nug hätte
(cantata)
A, org, stgs
ed. Schneider
BREITKOPF W (A: Associated)
Siehe wie fein und lieblich ist es
(sacred cantata)
TTB, stgs, org
BREITKOPF L (A: Broude)
Wie bist Du denn, o Gott, in Zorn
gebrannt (cantata)
Bar/B, bsn, stgs, cem
BREITKOPF L (A: Broude)

BACH, JOHANN MICHAEL: (1648-1694)
Auf, lasst uns den Herrn loben (sacred
cantata)
Mez/A, org, stgs
BREITKOPF L (A: Broude)

BACH, JOHANN NICOLAUS: (1669-1753)
Der jenaische Wein- und Bierrufer
TTB, stgs, cem
BREITKOPF L (A: Broude)

BACH, JOHANN SEBASTIAN:
Ach, Gott, wie manches Herzelied
(Cantana 58)
SB, cem, stgs, ob d'amore
BREITKOPF W (A: Associated)
Amore Traditore
B, hpsch
SCHOTT
Arias from Cantatas (4)
A, org
ed. Pidoux
BARENREITER (A: Magna)
Arias from Cantatas (Vol 1, 2, 3)
S, instr
KALMUS (A: Belwin)
Arias for Alto Vol 1, 2, 3
A, obblig instr, pf/org
ed. Mandyczewski
BREITKOPF L (A: Broude);
KALMUS

Arias for Bass
B, obblig instr, pf/org
ed. Mandyczewski
BREITKOPF L (A: Broude);
KALMUS
Arias for Soprano (Vol 1-4)
S, obblig instr, pf/org
ed. Mandyczewski
BREITKOPF L (A: Broude)
Arias for Tenor (Vol 1-3)
T, obblig instr, pf/org
ed. Mandyczewski
BREITKOPF L (A: Broude);
KALMUS
Before Thy Cradle
highlow, pf
arr. Gordon
SKIDMORE (A: Shapiro)
Bekennen will ich seinen Namen
A, 2 vln, org (opt cello, bvl)
ed. Landshoff PETERS
Bereite sich, Zion
A, vln, cont
BARENREITER (A: Magna)
Beside Thy Manger Here I Stand
med, cont
CONCORDIA
By Waters of Babylon
med, org, vln; med, org, fl; med,
org, ob
ed. Lovelace BELWIN
Comfort, Comfort ye my People
med, stgs, cont
CONCORDIA
Der Herr denket an uns (EngGer) (Can-
tata 196)
TBar, pf/org
PETERS
Duet from Cantata 49
SB, ob, org, stgs
BREITKOPF W (A: Associated)
Duets for Soprano and Alto with Ob-
bligato Instruments (Vol 1-3)
SA, obblig instr, pf/org
ed. Mandyczewski
BREITKOPF L (A: Broude);
BREITKOPF W (A: Associated)
Doch Jesus will der Frommen Schild
(#46)
A, 2 treb rec, ob da caccia/ enghn/
vla
SCHOTT (A: E-A)
Durchlaucht'ster Leopold
SB, 2 fl, bsn, stgs, cem
BREITKOPF L (A: Broude)
Esurientes (MAGNIFICAT)
contr, 2 treb rec/2 fl, kybd
ed. Dürr SCHOTT (A: E-A)

Geist und Seele wird verwirret (cantata)
Mez/A, 2 ob, enghn, bsn, stgs, org,
cem
BREITKOPF L (A: Broude)
Gott, man lobet dich in der Stille
(GerEng)
A, cem, stgs, 2 ob d'amore
BREITKOPF W (A: Associated)
I Follow with Gladness
S, pf, opt fl/vln
PATERSON (A: Fischer C)
Ich bin in mir vergnügt (cantata 204)
S, fl, 2 ob, stgs, cont
KALMUS (A: Belwin)
Ich geh' und suche mit Verlangen (cantata 49)
SB, enghn, cello, stgs, org/cem
BREITKOPF L (A: Broude)
Ich geh' und suche mit Verlangen (cantata 49)
SB, ob, org, stgs
BREITKOPF W (A: Associated)
Ich habe genug (cantata 82) (GerEng)
Bar/B, ob, stgs, cem
BREITKOPF L (A: Broude)
Ich habe genug (cantata 82) (GerEng)
B, ob, cont, stgs
BREITKOPF W (A: Associated)
Ich habe genug (cantata 82) (GerEng)
S, fl, org, stgs
ed. Hellmann
BREITKOPF W (A: Associated)
Ich weiss, das mein Erlöser lebt (cantata 160) (Easter) (GerEng)
T, vln, bsn, cont
BREITKOPF W (A: Associated)
Jauchzet Gott in allen Landen (cantata 51)
S, tpt, stgs, cont
HANSSLER (A: Peters)
Jauchzet Gott in allen Landen (cantata 51)
S, tpt, stgs, cem
BREITKOPF L (A: Broude)
Jauchzet Gott in allen Landen (cantata 51)
S, tmb, stgs, cont
BREITKOPF W (A: Associated)
Jesu, dir sei Preis gesungen (from cantata 142)
A, 2 A rec, cont
NAGELS (A: Magna)
Jesu, dir sei Preis gesungen (from cantata 142)
S, 2 S rec, cont
HANSSLER (A: Peters)

Jesu, lass dich finden, lass doch meine
Sünden (GerFr)
A, cem, stgs, 2 ob d'amore
BREITKOPF W (A: associated)
Jesu, praise (cantata 142) (GerEng)
Mez/Contr, 2 treb rec/2 fl, pf
ed. Bergmann SCHOTT (A: E-A)
Jesus nimmt die Sünder an (cantata 113)
T, fl, cont
ed. Baron OXFORD
Jesus, unser Trost und Leben
S, 2 S rec, cont
HANSSLER (A: Peters)
Lord Jesus Christ, Thou Prince of Peace
med, fl, cont
CONCORDIA
Mein Herze schwimmt ins Blut (cantata 199)
S, ob, bsn, cem, stgs
BREITKOPF W (A: Associated)
Mein Herze schwimmt ins Blut (cantata 199)
S, 2 ob, bsn, stgs, cem
BREITKOPF L (A: Broude)
Meine Seele rühmt und preist (cantata 189)
T, fl, ob, cont, 3 stgs
BREITKOPF W (A: Associated)
Mer Hahn en neue Oberkeet (Cantata 212)
SB, fl, hn, stgs, cem
BREITKOPF W (A: Broude)
Non sa che sia dolore (cantata 209) (Ger)
S, fl, stgs, cont
KALMUS (A: Belwin)
Non sa che sia dolore (cantata 209) (ItGer)
S, fl, stgs, cem
BREITKOPF L (A: Broude)
Non sa che sia dolore (cantata 209) (Ger)
S, fl, cont, stgs
BREITKOPF W (A: Associated)
O du angenehmer Schatz
A, 2 fl, bsn, cont
HANSSLER (A: Peters)
O holder Tag, erwünschte Zeit (cantata 210) (Marriage) (GerFr)
S, fl, ob, stgs, cem
BREITKOPF L (A: Broude)
O holder Tag, erwünschte Zeit (cantata 210) (Marriage) (Ger)
S, fl, ob, hn, stgs, cont
KALMUS (A: Belwin)
O Sacred Head Now Wounded (ST. MATTHEW PASSION)
med, fl, cont
CONCORDIA

BACH, JOHANN SEBASTIAN: (cont'd.)
On My Shepherd I Rely
    S, pf, opt vln
            PATERSON (A: Fischer C)
Piccolo Magnificat
    S, fl, org, vln, vla, cont
            ed. Paccagnella SANTIS
Recitatives and Arias from Cantatas
(21) Vol 1
    high, cont
            ed. Pidoux
            BARENREITER (A: Magna)
Quodlibet (Der Backtrog)
    SAT, cello, cont
            BREITKOPF L (A: Broude)
Recitatives and Arias from Cantatas
(23) Vol 2
    low, cont
            ed. Pidoux
            BARENREITER (A: Magna)
Schafe können sicher weiden
    S, 2 rec, cont
            BARENREITER (A: Magna)
Schweigt stille, plaudert nicht (Cantata
211) (Coffee Cantata)
    STB, fl, stgs, cem
            BREITKOPF L (A: Broude);
            BREITKOPF W (A: Associated);
            KALMUS
Seufzer Thränen, Kummer, Not (med
diff)
    S, ob/vln, cont
            ed. Keller
            BARENREITER (A: Magna)
Sheep May Safely Graze (GerEng)
    S, 2 treb rec/2 fl, pf
            ed. Hunt SCHOTT (A: E-A)
Stone Above all Others Treasured
(GerEng) (cantata 152)
    S, treb rec/fl, vla d'amore/vln, pf
            ed. Hunt SCHOTT (A: E-A)
The Lord Bless You (Marriage) (GerEng)
    high, cont; low, cont
            CONCORDIA
The Only Son from Heaven
    med, stgs, ob, cont
            CONCORDIA
Tritt auf die Glaubensbahn (Xmas)
(GerEng) (Cantata 152)
    SB, fl, ob, stgs, cem
            BREITKOPF L (A: Broude)
Tritt auf die Glaubensbahn (Xmas)
(GerEng) (Cantata 152)
    SB, rec, ob, cem stgs
            BREITKOPF W (A: Associated)
12 Sacred Duets from Cantatas Vol 1,
2, 3, 4
    SA, instr, kybd
            PETERS

Unschuld Kleinod reiner Seelen
    S, fl, ob, vln, vla
            ed. Smend
            BARENREITER (A: Magna)
Vergnügte Pleissen-stadt (GerEng) (Can-
tata 216)
    SA, 2 fl, ob, vla, cem
            LIENAU (A: Peters)
Vergnügte Pleissen-stadt (GerEng) (Can-
tata 216)
    SA, 2 fl, ob, pf, stgs
            ed. Schumann
            BREITKOPF W (A: Associated)
Vergnügte Ruh', beliebte Seelenlust
(cantata 170)
    A, org, cont, stgs, ob d'amore
            BREITKOPF W (A: Associated)
Vergnügte Ruh', beliebte Seelenlust
(cantata 170)
    Mez/A, (stgs, org, cem)/(fl, ob, cem)
            BREITKOPF L (A: Broude)
Virga Jesse floruit (Magnificat) (diff)
    SB, cont
            BARENREITER (A: Magna)
Vor Deinen Thron
    vc ad lib, descant rec, treb rec, B
rec
            ed. Sherman SCHOTT (A: E-A)
Was Gott tut, das ist wohlgetan (Ger)
    T, opt fl, pf
            BOOSEY
Weichet nur, betrübte Schatten (can-
tata 202) (Marriage)
    S, ob, bsn, stgs, cem
            BREITKOPF L (A: Broude);
            BREITKOPF W (A: Associated)
Weichet nur, betrübte Schatten (can-
tata 202) (Marriage)
    S, ob, stgs, cont
            KALMUS (A: Belwin)
Widerstehe doch der Sünde (cantata
54) (GerEng)
    S, stgs, cem
            BREITKOPF L (A: Broude)
Widerstehe doch der Sünde (cantata
54)
    A, cont, stgs
            BREITKOPF W (A: Associated)
Wir eilen mit schwachen
    SA, pf
            ed. Ochs
            BREITKOPF L (A: Broude)
With Joyful Heart I Praise my Saviour
(Eng)
    A, kybd, 2 vln, (opt cello, bvl)/(opt 2
vln, cello)
            ed. Landshoff PETERS

With Loudest Rejoicing
SA, cont
                         CONCORDIA
Wohl euch, ihr auserwählten Seelen
(GerEng)
A, 2 fl, cem stgs
          BREITKOPF W (A: Associated)
Yet Jesus will the Righteous Keep (can-
tata 46) (GerEng)
A, 2 treb/2 fl, ob da caccia/enghn/
vla/vln
          ed. Champion SCHOTT (A: E-A)

BACHELET, ALFRED:
Chère Nuit
S, opt vln, pf (2 keys)
                    LEDUC (A: Presser)

BADINGS, HENK:
Armageddon
S, wind symphony, elec tape
                              PETERS
4 Cradle Songs (Dutch)
low, stgs
               DONEMUS (A: Peters)
3 Old Dutch Songs
Bar/A, fl, harp
               DONEMUS (A: Peters)
3 Sacred Songs from Old English Texts
(Eng)
A, ob, org
               DONEMUS (A: Peters)

BAIRD, TADDEUSZ:
5 Songs (PolGer)
Mez, 16 instr
                 CHESTER (A: Magna)
4 Songs (PolGer)
Mez, chamb grp
                 CHESTER (A: Magna)

BALASSA, SANDOR:
Antinomia (Hung)
S, cl, cello
               BUDAPEST (A: Boosey)

BALAZS, FREDERIC:
Sonnets after Elizabeth Barrett
Browning
high, 4 stgs; high, fl, ob, cl, bsn,
harp, stgs
                              ACA

BALES, RICHARD:
Beneath a Weeping Willow's Shade (F.
Hopkinson)
Bar, fl, cl, ob, bsn, 2 hn, perc, harp,
stgs
          arr. Bales SOUTHERN PEER

Ozymandias
S, fl, 2 cl, ob, bsn, 2 hn, stgs
                         SOUTHERN PEER

BANCQUART, ALAIN:
Proche
B, cello/vla
                      JOBERT (A: Presser)

BANKS, DON:
Tirade
med, pf, harp, perc
                         SCHOTT (A: E-A)

BANTOCK, GRANVILLE:
3 Idylls from Greek Anthology
A, fl, opt cello
                      CRAMER (A: Brodt)

BARBE, HELMUT:
Requiem 1965
S, fl, ob, bsn, vla, cello, bvl
               HANSSLER (A: Peters)

BARBER, SAMUEL:
A Hand of Bridge Op. 35 (Menotti)
SATB, chamb orch/pf
                              SCHIRMER
Dover Beach Op. 3
Bar/med, stqt/pf
                              SCHIRMER

BARRAQUE, JEAN:
Chant après chant (Barraqué; Broch)
S, 6 perc, pf
                              BRUZZI
Séquence (Nietzsche)
S, 3 perc, vibra, cel, pf, harp, vln,
cello
                              BRUZZI

BARTLET, JOHN: (ca. 1606–?)
A Book of Ayres
medmed-high (1-2) vcs, pf/lute
          ed. Fellowes STAINER (A: Galaxy)

BASSANI, GIOVANNI: (1657-1716)
Cantata a una voce
high, pf
          realized Malipiero NYP LIBE
Nascere, nascere, dive puellule (Lat)
A, cont
          ed. Ewerhart BIELER

BASSETT, LESLIE:
Time and Beyond
Bar, cl, cello, pf
                              PETERS

BAUR, JURG:
Herz stirb oder singe (4)
high, fl, stgs
               LITOLFF (A: Peters)

BAUTISTA, JULIÁN:
4 Cantos Callegos
Contr, fl, ob, cl, vla, cello, harp
SOUTHERN PEER

BAVICCHI, JOHN:
To the Lighthouse
S, hn, pf
SEESAW
Trio #3
A, vln, cello
SEESAW

BEALE, JAMES:
Lamentations Op. 35 (sacred)
S, fl, pf
ACA
Proverbs Op. 28 (sacred)
Bar, enghn, vibra, pf/cello
ACA
3 Songs Op. 33
S, vln, vla
ACA

BECK, CONRAD:
Die Sonnenfinsternis (cantata)
A, fl, cl, hspcd, stgs
SCHOTT (A: E-A)
3 Herbstgesänge (Rilke)
high, org/pf
SCHOTTS (A: E-A)
Herbstfeuer (6)
A, chamb grp
SCHOTT (A: E-A)
Kammerkantate nach Sonetten der
Louise Labé
S, fl, pf, stgs
SCHOTTS (A: E-A)

BECKER, G.:
Moirolgi
high female vc, 2 cl, bcl, harp
ZIMMER (A: Peters)

BECKER, GUNTHER:
Rigolo
high, fl, cl, vln, cello, pf, treb instr
GERIG (A: Belwin)

BECKER, JOHN:
Psalms of Love
med, org
ACA

BECKER-FOSS, JURGEN:
4 geistliche Konzerte
A, vln/2 vln/S rec, org
HANSSLER (A: Peters)

BECKWITH, JOHN:
4 Songs (Jonson) (VOLPONE)
Bar, gtr
BERANDOL

BEDFORD, DAVID:
Music for Albion Moonlight
S, fl, cl, pf, vln, cello, harmonica
UNIVERSAL (A: E-A)
That White and Radiant Legend
S, narr, 8 instr
UNIVERSAL (A: E-A)
The Tentacles of the Dark Nebula
T, 3 vln, 2 vla, 2 celli, bvl
UNIVERSAL (A: E-A)

BEEKHUIS, HANNA:
Dormeuse
3 female vcs, fl, cello, harp
DONEMUS (A: Peters)
Les Deux Flûtes
Mez, 2 fl, pf
DONEMUS (A: Peters)
Nocturne
SABar, pf
DONEMUS (A: Peters)
Reflets du Japon (Fr)
A, vla
DONEMUS (A: Peters)
3 Church Lieder
med-high, pf, cello
DONEMUS (A: Peters)
3 Lieder from Gezelle
S, pf, cello
DONEMUS (A: Peters)

BEESON, JACK:
A Creole Mystery (Hearn)
med, stqt
BOOSEY
The Day's No Rounder than its Angles
are (Viereck)
med, stqt
BOOSEY

BEETHOVEN, LUDWIG VAN:
Come to Me (sacred)
high, org, harp/pf; low, org, harp/pf
SCHIRMER
Complete Works (reprint of Breitkopf
Edition)
var instr and vocal combos
UNIV MUS ED
English, Italian, Scottish Songs
med (1-2) vcs, vln, cello, pf
KALMUS (A: Belwin)
5 Arien
T (1), S (2), B (2), chamb grp
BREITKOPF W (A: Associated)
Gesänge mit Orchester Vol 2
var vcs, chamb instr
BREITKOPF W (A: Associated)

Neue Volksliederheft
var vcs, pf, vln, cello
ed. Schünemann
BREITKOPF L (A: Broude)
No, non turbati (scene and aria)
Op. 92
S, stgs/pf
BARENREITER (A: Magna)
O welch ein Leben! Ein ganzes Meer
(from 5 ARIEN)
T, 2 ob, 2 bsn, 2 hn, stgs
BREITKOPF W (A:Associated)
PART SONGS (See Voice with Other
Voices)
6 Irish Songs
med, vln, cello, pf
ed. Bennett MERCURY (A: Presser)
6 Scottish Songs
med, vln, cello, pf
ed. Bennett MERCURY (A: Presser)
12 Scottish Songs Op. 227
1-3 vcs, pf, vln, cello (TB (2); STB
(3); SAB (1))
PETERS
20 Irish Songs (with 25 Irish Songs)
med (1-2) vcs. vln, cello, pf
KALMUS (A: Belwin)
25 Irish Songs (with 20 Irish Songs)
med (1-2) vcs, vln, cello, pf
KALMUS (A: Belwin)
25 Scottish and Irish Songs Op. 108
med (1-2) vcs, vln, cello, pf
BARENREITER (A: Magna);
KALMUS (A: Belwin)
26 Welsh Songs Op. 226
med (1-2) vcs, vln, cello, pf
KALMUS (A: Belwin)
23 Folksongs (Tyrol, Swiss, Swedish,
Spanish, others)
med, pf, vln, cello
ed. Schünemann
BREITKOPF L (A: Broude)

BEHREND, SIEGFRIED:
Bergerettes (Fr folk) (18th century)
med, gtr
SIKORSKI (A: Associated)
Impressionen einer spanischen Reise
(Suite #6)
med-high, gtr
SIKORSKI (A: Associated); LIBE C
Jiddische Hochzeit (Marriage) (Ger)
high, gtr
HANSEN F (A: Magna)
Lasst mich leben (cycle)
med-high, gtr
SIKORSKI (A: Associated)

Songs by M. de Cervantes and others
for Guitar and Voice
med, gtr
SCHAUER (A: Associated)
Suite on Polish Folk Melodies (Pol)
med, gtr
BOTE (A: Associated)
Weihnachtsgeschichte (Christmas)
any vc, perc, gtr
ZIMMER (A: Peters)

BELL, CARLA HUSTON:
Suite for a Greek Festival
var vcs, finger cym, S rec, A rec,
vln, vla, cello
AMC

BELLINI, VINCENZO:
Dolente Immagine di Fille Mia
S, fl
ed. Segovia SCHOTT (A: E-A)
Gratius Agimus
S, fl, cl, 2 hn, stgs
BRUZZI

BENEVOLI, ORAZIO: (1605–1672)
Ego autem pro te, Domine (Lat)
S/T, cont
ed. Ewerhart BIELER

BENGUEREL, XAVIER:
Ballade von der singenden Frau in der
Nacht (diff)
SSA, 4 vln, vla, cello, bvl
BARENREITER (A: Magna)
Paraules de cada dia (PortGer) (3) (diff)
Mez, 3 fl, 2 cl, perc, harp, pf, cel,
vibra
MODERN

BENHAMOU, MAURICE:
Mizmor-chir
S, fl, hn, tpt, tmb, vln, vla, cello,
bvl, vibra
JOBERT (A: Presser)

BENNETT, RICHARD RODNEY:
Crazy Jane
S, cl, cello, pf
UNIVERSAL (A: E-A)
Jazz Pastoral
any vc, jazz orch
UNIVERSAL (A: E-A)
London Pastorale
T, chamb grp
BELWIN
The Approaches of Sleep
SATB, 10 instr
BELWIN
Tom O'Bedlan's Song
T, cello
BELWIN

BENSON, WARREN:
Shadow Wood (Williams) (5)
S, ww
MCA (A: Belwin)

BENTON, DANIEL:
Dirge
S, vln, fl, A fl, tpt, 4 perc, cello,
bsn, bass tmb
SEESAW
Love Song
S/A, fl, harp
SEESAW
Lux Aeterna
Contr, bvl, org
SEESAW
2 Shakespeare Songs
S, vln, fl, bcl
SEESAW

BENVENUTI, ARRIGO:
Cantus Gemellus
S, fl
BRUZZI

BERGER, ARTHUR:
3 Poems of Yeats (from WORDS FOR
MUSIC, PERHAPS)
med, fl, A cl, cello
NEW MUS ED (A: Presser)

BERGER, JEAN:
5 Songs (Mary Stuart, Queen of Scots)
med, fl, vla, cello
SHEPPARD (A: Boonin)
4 Sonnets (PortEng)
male/med, pf/4 stgs
SCHIRMER
6 Rondeaux
med, vla
SHEPPARD (A: E-A)
3 Canciones (Sp)
med, pf, vla, cello
SHEPPARD (A: Boonin)

BERIO, LUCIANO:
Agnus
SS, 3 cl
UNIVERSAL (A: Schirmer)
Chamber Music (Joyce)
med, cl, cello, harp
ZERBONI (A: Boosey)
Circles (cummings)
female vc, harp, 2 perc
UNIVERSAL (A: Schirmer)
El Mar la Mar
S/Mez, fl, 2 cl, accor, harp, bvl
UNIVERSAL (A: Schirmer)
Folk Songs
Mez, fl, pic, cl, bsn, vla, harp, bvl
UNIVERSAL (A: Schirmer)

O King
Mez, fl, cl, vln, cello, pf
UNIVERSAL (A: Schirmer)
Melodrama from OPERA
T, fl, cl, perc, pf, elec org, vln,
cello, bvl
UNIVERSAL (A: Schirmer)

BERKELEY, LENNOX:
4 Poems Op. 27 (St. Teresa d'Avila)
Contr, stgs
CHESTER (A: Magna)
Songs of the Half Light Op. 65 (5) (de
la Mare)
high, gtr
CHESTER (A: Magna)
Stabat Mater (Lat)
SSATBarB, chamb grp
CHESTER (A: Magna)

BERLINSKI, HERMAN:
Psalm 23
high, fl
PRESSER

BERLIOZ, HECTOR:
Complete Songs of Berlioz Vol 1-10
var (1-2) vcs, pf (SBar; TB; SMez;
SContr; highhigh; 2 eq vcs)
KALMUS (A: Belwin)
Hector Berlioz Works Vol 1-20
var instr and vocal combos
ed. Malherbe; Weingartner
UNIV MUS ED
Le Jeune Patre Breton Op. 13 #4
S/T, hn, pf
BREITKOPF L (A: Broude)
Les Nuits d'Eté Op.7
S/T, 2 fl, ob, 2 cl, 2 bsn, 3 hn, harp,
stgs
BREITKOPF W (A: Associated)

BERMUDO, FRAY JUAN: (ca. 1510–ca. 1555)
Mira Nero de Tarpeya
med, gtr
ed. Azpiazu UME (A: Associated)

BERNABEI, ERCOLE: (ca. 1620–1687)
Heu me Miseram et Infelicem (sacred)
S/T, cont
ed. Ewerhart BIELER
In Hymnis et Canticis
S/T, cont
ed. Ewerhart BIELER

BERNHARD, CHRISTOPH: (1627–1692)
Aus der Tiefen ruf ich, Herr, zu dir
(cantata) (med diff)
S, 2 vln, cont
ed. Grusnick
BARENREITER (A: Magna)